THE EMPTY CRADLE

ALSO BY PHILLIP LONGMAN

Born to Pay

The Return of Thrift

THE
EMPTY
CRADLE

*How Falling Birthrates
Threaten World Prosperity
And What To Do About It*

PHILLIP LONGMAN

BASIC
B
BOOKS

NEW
AMERICA
BOOKS

A New America Book, Published by Basic Books,
A Member of the Perseus Books Group
New York

Books published by Basic Books are available at special discounts for
bulk purchases in the United States by corporations, institutions, and
other organizations. For more information, please contact the Special
Markets Department at the Perseus Books Group, 11 Cambridge Center,
Cambridge MA 02142, or call (617) 252-5298, (800) 255-1514 or
e-mail special.markets@perseusbooks.com.

Designed by Trish Wilkinson
Set in 11.5-point Goudy by the Perseus Books Group

Library of Congress Cataloging-in-Publication Data

Longman, Phillip.
    The empty cradle : how falling birthrates threaten world prosperity
and what to do about it / Phillip Longman.
        p.   cm.
    Includes index.
    ISBN 0-465-05050-6 (alk. paper)
    1. Demographic transition. 2. Age distribution (Demography). 3.
Population.   4. Fertility, Human. 5. Economic development. 6.
Demographic transition—United States. 7. Demographic
transition—Developed countries. 8. Demographic transition—Developing
countries. I. Title.

HB887.L66 2004
304.6'2—dc22

                                                              2003023840

04 05 06 / 10 9 8 7 6 5 4 3 2 1

To Sandy and Sam

The things that make good headlines attract our attention because they are on the surface of the stream of life, and they distract our attention from the slower, impalpable, imponderable movements that work below the surface and penetrate to the depths. But of course it is really these deeper, slower movements that, in the end, make history, and it is they that stand out huge in retrospect, when the sensational passing events have dwindled, in perspective, to their true proportions.

—Arnold J. Toynbee, *Civilization on Trial*

Contents

Preface

The term "fundamentalism" first came into the American lexicon in 1922, when Harry Emerson Fosdick, a leading liberal theologian, preached on the subject, "Shall the Fundamentalists Win?" At the time, and for many decades later, fundamentalism referred to a specific movement in Protestant theology united in such beliefs as the infallibility of Scripture and Christ's literal return in the Second Coming. Since then, however, the term has taken on a broader meaning, so that today many speak of Catholic fundamentalists and even Islamic fundamentalists. In this book, I use the term to refer to all who rely on literal belief in ancient myth and legend, whether religious or not, to oppose modern liberal and commercial values.

Acknowledgments

I make no pretense of having discovered or developed any new facts or data in this book. If the work has any originality, it is as an interpretive gathering of many disciplines, including history, demography, economics, biology, women's studies, and epidemiology. Though I have been thinking and writing about many of the themes explored in this book for nearly a quarter century, I am hardly the first to spot the worldwide decline in birthrates and the attendant challenge of global population aging. I have merely tried to tease out the deeper, slower movements of history behind these trends, and to show how they may influence the world's future.

I have many to thank for making this interpretive gathering possible, beginning with my colleagues at the New America Foundation. Founder and President Ted Halstead was the first to encourage me to write the book. Fellowship Director Sherle R. Schwenninger has served as a gentle but penetrating editor of the book's early drafts, spotting contradictions and helping with better formulations. Of the many fellows at New America Foundation who offered advice and ideas, I am particularly indebted to Shannon Brownlee for her work on health care, Karen Kornbluh for her guidance on work and family issues, Maya MacGuineas for her expertise on fiscal policy, and Michael Lind for his deep grasp of intellectual and demographic history. I am also indebted to John Mangin for his careful reading of the manuscript, and to Louise Feld for her help as researcher and guide to women's history. I am also grateful to Brian F. Hofland, Director of Aging and Health Programs at The Atlantic Philanthropies (USA) Inc., and his board, for their generous financial support.

Many other friends and colleagues have been instrumental in deepening my understanding of the diverse disciplines and policy realms discussed in the book. Among them are Neil Howe, author of numerous books on the cultural and economic consequences of generational change and population aging, Richard Jackson, director of the Global Aging Initiative at the Center for Strategic and International Studies, and Paul Hewitt, currently deputy director for policy at the Social Security Administration.

I am also indebted to many thinkers I admired from afar who developed important insights—some of which they may now find put to unexpected uses. They include the demographer Nicholas Eberstadt of the American Enterprise Institute, and Jean-Claude Chesnais, an economist and demographer at the National Institute for Demographic Studies in Paris, both of whom have written forcefully about the challenge of global aging. The reader will soon see that I have also borrowed ideas from across the political spectrum, ranging from the feminist economics of Nancy Folbre and Shirley P. Burggraf, to the theories of human capital developed by Julian Simon and Gary Becker. I am particularly indebted to the work of Allan C. Carlson, which, although not widely known, offers deep insights into the history of the family and its relationship to the growth of both big government and big business.

Many editors have had a hand over the years in helping me to develop the themes and ideas that appear this book. I am particularly grateful to James Fallows, Steve Smith, James Impoco, and Tim Noah for helping me to craft the pieces I did for *U.S. News & World Report* on global aging, the cost of children, the bubble economy, and the declining pace of technological progress. These pieces were, as they say in the news business, "too far ahead of the curve," and it took some courage to publish them in a mass-market journal. I am also indebted to Charlie Peters and Paul Glastris of the *Washington Monthly* for their early and sustained support, and to John Berry, who taught me much of what I know about making an argument in print.

I must also express my appreciation for my wife, Sandy, who provided many cultural insights and critical intellectual companionship, while also offering me the moral and emotional encouragement I needed to explore the darker themes that run throughout much of this book. Finally, I would like to bow to my in-laws, Phil and Tina Schrider and their four bright and lovely home-schooled children. Their inspiring example has taught me much about the power of faith in sustaining investment in children, and about the vital potential of family life even in an age that fails to pay its debts to those who form the next generation.

1

The Fundamentalist Moment

Y ou awaken to the news that a traffic jam snarls the morning rush hour. You leave early for your doctor's appointment, but arrive too late to find parking. After waiting two hours for a 15-minute consultation, you wait again to have your prescription filled. You worry about the time away from work because so many people would line up to take your job. Returning home to the evening news, you view throngs of youths throwing stones somewhere in the Middle East and watch a feature on disappearing farmland in the Middle West. As the evening unfolds the third telemarketer of the evening calls: "We need your help to save the rainforest." You set the alarm clock once again; a neighbor's car alarm goes off while another's air conditioner starts to whine.

It is not hard to understand how most of us form the impression that overpopulation is one the world's most pressing problems. The typical American or European may enjoy an unprecedented amount of private space. Compared to our parents most of us live in larger homes occupied by fewer children. We drive ever-larger automobiles, in which we can eat, smoke, listen to digital radio, and interface with the picture phone in splendid isolation. Food is so abundant that obesity has become a leading cause of death.

Still, our day-to-day experiences and the impressions we gather from the media repeatedly suggest that population growth threatens whatever quality of life we enjoy. Sprawling suburban developments worsen traffic, drive up taxes, and diminish our opportunities to enjoy nature. Televised images of Third World famine, war, and environmental degradation prompt the private thought: "Why do these people have so many kids?" Immigrants and other people's children wind up competing for our jobs, our access to health care, our parking spaces, and our favorite fishing holes, hiking paths, or spot at the beach. We can only shake our heads when we read that world population continues to increase by 75 million every year.

Yet as unpleasant as these sensations of overcrowding may be, they are, upon reflection, profoundly important to sustaining our faith in a broad range of political and cultural agendas. Those who are products of the various baby booms that occurred around the globe after World War II are particularly likely to feel oppressed by this sensation of overcrowding and to hold worldviews deeply informed by it.

From their beginning, baby boomers have experienced life as a demographic crunch—Quonset huts for schoolrooms, intense competition for college admission, falling real wages, inflating home prices, and retirement insecurity—caused in large measure by the sheer size of their generation. This generational experience continues to have far-reaching political and cultural implications. It is no coincidence that the first Earth Day, which launched the modern environmental movement in 1970, took place just as the rate of human population growth was reaching an all-time high of 2.06 percent per year.[1] Nor is it surprising that, as this huge generation came of age, social attitudes that had long served to keep birthrates high—prohibitions against abortion, contraception, divorce, and homosexuality, for example, as well as restrictions on women's economic opportunities—began to disappear.

The link between feminism and population control became explicit in 1972 when President Nixon's Commission on Population Growth and the American Future recommended not only government-funded abortions, but also passage of the Equal Rights Amendment as a means of discouraging the fertility of American women.[2] By 1994, the United Nations International Conference on Population and Development made the same link on a global basis: "Advancing gender equality and equity and the empowerment of women," reads one of the conference's adopted principles, "and the elimination of all kinds of violence against women, and ensuring women's ability to control their own fertility, are cornerstones of population and development-related programs."[3]

From the mid-nineteenth century through the 1930s, fears of population decline and "race suicide" among Western elites helped energize campaigns to criminalize abortion and birth control, and to enforce more rigid standards of sexual conduct both within and outside marriage. As one of the leaders of the nineteenth century anti-abortion movement, Edwin M. Hale, put it in his 1867 book, *The Great Crime of the Nineteenth Century*, abortion had to be made illegal because "it lessens the population of a state."[4] By 1873, the federal Comstock Act classified all information about birth control as obscene, and fifty years later, among the arguments lawmakers were still using to justify the statute was a "need for more people."[5] It was also during this period that the word "homosexual" came into the American vocabulary, along with the concept of homosexuality as an identity. Attempts variously to cure or repress people with this identity soon followed, with increasing intensity right through the 1950s.[6]

By the 1960s, however, fears of population decline had given way to mounting concerns about a coming "population bomb," and the culture began to respond accordingly. In the first chapter of *The Feminine Mystique*, Betty Friedan tellingly fretted about the ongoing "population explosion" before comparing the typical, highly fertile American family of that era to a "comfortable concentration camp."[7] Reflecting the changing priorities of a culture that was now struggling to absorb the baby boom generation and that was increasingly alarmed by expert predictions of mass famines, energy shortages, and ecological disaster, the Supreme Court discovered a right to birth control and abortion in the shadows of the Constitution.

Many other belief structures in our society also derive, or are influenced by, a conviction that human population will at least continue to grow. The financing and long-term political viability of social security systems throughout the world, for example, depend on an assumption that each generation of taxpayers will be larger than the one that came before. The American Social Security system, for instance, assumes that the number of workers paying into the system will increase by 30 percent over the next 80 years, and still the system is expected to be running large deficits as early as 2015.[8] In Sweden, just the prospect of population loss has forced the government to make dramatic cuts in the nation's cradle-to-grave welfare state.

In a broader sense, business leaders and champions of capitalism are also invested in the idea that human population will always grow. One reason, as we shall see, is that population growth is a major source of economic growth. More people create more demand for the products capitalists sell, and more supply of the labor capitalists buy. Economists may be able to construct models of how economies *could* grow amidst a shrinking population, but in the real world it has never happened and businessmen know it.

New businesses flock to areas where population is growing, such as the Sun Belt, and avoid or leave areas where population is falling. Across the Great Plains of the United States, for example, where fewer people now live than in the 1920s, thousands of small towns are caught in a vicious cycle of depopulation, as younger workers and local businesses flee in search of economic opportunity, leaving behind shuttered storefronts, empty schools, and understaffed nursing homes. Drought and falling commodity prices may have in this instance set the cycle in motion, but once depopulation begins, new investment soon vanishes. Indeed, capitalism has never flourished except when accompanied by population growth, and it is now languishing in those parts of the world (such as Japan, Europe, and the Great Plains of the United States) where population has become stagnant.

So it turns out that the modern, secular view of the world rests profoundly on the perception that the world will grow ever more crowded. Capitalists may differ from feminists and environmentalists on what they see as the implications of that assumption. But across the spectrum of the Left and Right in secular societies, nearly all prevailing ideologies and agendas would be profoundly challenged by the prospect of human population actually falling.

Capitalists would wonder how they could make profits in a world of scarce labor and shrinking markets. Liberals would be at a loss to show how the welfare state was sustainable. Environmentalists would be robbed of their powerful projections showing human population exceeding the earth's carrying capacity. Feminists could no longer point to the low fertility of educated women as an obvious benefit to humankind.

Were labor supplies again to become as scarce as they were in ancient times, or in the New World two centuries ago, even champions of workers' rights and racial justice might find it difficult to prevail against those who would force people to work against their will. Without population growth providing an ever increasing supply of workers and consumers, economic growth would depend entirely on pushing more people into the work force and getting more out of them each day—a requirement that in previous eras of extreme labor shortage was achieved primarily through brutal work hours, serfdom, debt peonage, indentured servitude, child labor, and slavery.

In a world of falling human population only fundamentalists would draw new strength. For the deep messages of the Bible and the Koran, and of all the world's ancient religions, are relentlessly pro-natal. And so, too, are the fundamentalist ideologies of fascism and racism, with their ambition to breed "supermen" out of ancient bloodlines. All draw on the traditions of a premodern past in which populations were often overwhelmed by death, and group fertility was too important to be left to individual "choice." Population growth underlies our modern concept of freedom.

2

Coffins and Cradles

When asked how long it will take for the world's population to double, nearly half of all Americans say 20 years or less.[1] This is hardly surprising, given the sensations of overcrowding all of us feel in our day-to-day lives and the persistent reports we hear of teeming Third World megacities. Yet looking beneath the surface of events, we can see that world population growth has already slowed dramatically over the last generation and is headed on a course for absolute decline. Indeed, forecasts by the United Nations and others show the world population growth rate could well turn negative during the lifetime of people now in their 40s and 50s, and is very likely to do so before today's children reach retirement age.[2] Long before then, many nations will shrink in absolute size, and the average age of the world's citizens will shoot up dramatically as the elderly in many parts of the world become far more numerous than children.

These predictions come with considerable certainty. The primary reason is the unprecedented fall in fertility rates over the last generation that is now spreading to every corner of the globe. In both hemispheres, in nations rich and poor, in Christian, Taoist, Confucian, Hindu, and especially Islamic countries, one broad social trend holds constant at the beginning of the twenty-first century: As more and more of the world's population moves to crowded urban areas, and as women gain in education and economic opportunity, people are producing fewer and fewer children.

Today, global fertility rates are half what they were in 1972. No industrialized nation still produces enough children to sustain its population over time, or to prevent rapid population aging. Germany could easily lose the equivalent of the current population of East Germany over the next half century. Russia's population is already decreasing by three-quarters of a million a year.[3] Japan's population meanwhile is expected to fall by as much as one-third—a decline equivalent, the demographer Hideo Ibe once noted, to that experienced in medieval Europe during the scourges of the plague.[4]

Yet the steepest drops in fertility, and the most rapid rates of population aging, are now occurring in the developing world, where many nations are now growing old before they get rich. Today, when Americans think of Mexico, for example, they think of televised images of desperate, unemployed youths swimming the Rio Grande or slipping through border fences. However, because Mexican fertility rates have dropped so dramatically, by mid-century Mexico will be a less youthful country than the United States, and its population will be older than Japan's is today. The same is true for much of the rest of Latin America, according to United Nations projections.[5]

The Middle-Aging of the Middle East

Similarly, those televised images of desperate, unemployed youths broadcast from the Middle East create a false impression. Fertility rates are falling faster in the Middle East than anywhere else on earth, and as a result the region's population is aging at an unprecedented rate. It took fifty years for the United States to go from a median age of 30 to today's 35. By contrast, during the first fifty years of the twenty-first

century, Algeria will increase its median age from 21.7 to 40, according to UN projections.[6]

How can this be? Anyone who travels to the Middle East cannot
help but notice the ubiquitous throngs of loitering young people lean-
ing against walls. The phenomenon is so pronounced that there is
even a new North African slang term for these idle youth: "Hittite," a
play off the Arabic word for "wall."[7]

These youths are members of a distinct, and aging, baby boom generation. They are children of the 1980s, whose large numbers derive
not from an increase in fertility rates, but from a dramatic decline in
infant mortality that cannot be replicated in the future. Much like the
American baby boom generation when it was still in its youth, their
large numbers are shaking every institution of their society. But also
like the baby boomers in the United States, they are followed by a
"baby bust" generation. In demographic terms, the Middle East is following the same path as Europe and the United States did in the
1960s and 1970s, only on a more dramatic scale, with the falloff in
birthrates being much steeper, and the resulting aging of population
therefore coming on much faster.

In many corners of the Middle East, falling fertility rates have set off
alarms about national decline. In 1995, Turkish Prime Minister Nec-
mettin Erbakan of the Islamist Refah Party warned, "Our population
which is nearing 65 million is not enough. . . population is the power
by which we shall establish right in the world. These would-be west-
erners (proponents of family planning) are trying to reduce our population. We must have at least four children."[8]

More recently, Recep Tayyip Erdogan, shortly before becoming
Turkey's new prime minister, railed against contraception as "straight
out treason to the state." "Have babies," he told a cheering crowd.
"Allah wants it."[9]

Despite such exhortations, Turkey's fertility rate continues to decline. At 2.32 children per woman, it is now barely sufficient to replace
the population. As a result, Turkey is also among the most rapidly aging

countries on earth, and will have a population structure older than that of the United States by 2050. Iran's fertility rate, meanwhile, has already dropped below replacement levels. By 2025, according to projections by demographer Youssef Courbage, the Middle East as a whole will have a fertility rate of 2.08 children per woman, which is below the amount needed to sustain population growth.[10]

The increasing unwillingness of women in the Middle East to have as many children as their mothers did may in part explain the rise of reactionary fundamentalism in the region. Because of the spread of contraception and female education over the last generation, women of the region increasingly control their fertility. The resulting fall in birthrates allows more and more women to compete directly with men for scarce jobs and political positions, and so the fundamentalists preach (thus far with diminishing success) that Muslim women must stay home and make babies. The old patriarchal order in the Middle East, notes demographer Philippe Fargues,

> rests on two pillars—obedience of the younger to the older and of women to men. Lower fertility rates challenge the first: an only child has no younger sibling to watch over. The second. . . is threatened by changes in society. Girls have better access to education and are marrying later. Through work, they're entering a world of men outside their own family. And there are more single women—something hitherto unknown.[11]

Because of the high fertility rates of the past in the Middle East, a large percentage of the population is now of childbearing age. This means that despite the dramatic decline in the region's average family size, the number of births is still growing. But it is doing so at a greatly slowing pace, with the rate of increase in septuagenarians, octogenarians, and nonagenarians outstripping the rate of increase in children. In thinking about the future of the Middle East, it is important, of course, to reckon with the still expanding population of the region, which puts enormous pressure on water resources and creates many other problems, to say the least. But it is also important to remember that this population is aging rapidly and on a course for absolute decline.

Aging Asia

Similarly, China's low fertility rate, brought on in part by its one-family/one-child policy, has put the country on a course on which by 2020 its labor supply will be shrinking and its median age will be older than that of the United States. By mid-century, China could easily be losing 20–30 percent of its population per generation. Adding to China's demographic meltdown is the spreading use of ultrasound and other techniques for determining the sex of fetuses, which, as in India and many other parts of the world, is leading to much higher abortion rates for females than males. In China, the ratio of male to female births is now 117 to 100, which implies that roughly one out of six males in today's new generation will not succeed in reproducing themselves.[12]

India's fertility rate dropped by roughly a fifth since the first half of the 1990s.[13] Residents of the major southern provinces of Kerala and Tamil Nadu already produce too few children to replace themselves, and this will be true for Indians as a whole by the end of the next decade.[14] Meanwhile, India's sudden drop in fertility means that its population will be aging at three times the rate of the U.S. population over the next half century. By 2050, the median age in India is expected to be 37.9, making its population older than that of the United States today.[15] These projections assume, however, that India does not experience an AIDS pandemic, as now seems increasingly likely. The U.S. National Intelligence Council projects that 25 million Indians could be infected with HIV/AIDS by 2010.[16]

Dwindling Momentum

The global decline in fertility rates, as profound and well established as the trend may be, is hard to spot simply by observing the fabric of ordinary life. Indeed, as I've noted, ordinary life gives most people the opposite impression. That's because, even in areas where birthrates are dramatically below the levels required to avoid population loss even in the near future, the absolute number of people is often still growing.

If this seems counterintuitive, think of a train accelerating up a hill. If the engine stalls, the train will still move forward for a while, but its loss of momentum implies that it will soon be moving backwards, and at ever-greater speed. So it is when fertility rates shift from above to below replacement levels.

The equivalent of the hill is death itself, which is always pushing against any increase in human population. The equivalent of the engine is a fertility rate that consistently produces more births than deaths. When fertility falls below replacement levels, the population continues to increase for a while through sheer force of momentum. But this momentum is a dwindling legacy of a past effort when fertility rates were still above replacement levels.

Specifically, when women born during a period of high fertility (such as the 1950s in the United States) wind up having fewer children than their mothers, population size may well still grow because of the large number of women of childbearing age. But in the next generation, the pool of potential mothers will be smaller than before, and in the generation after that, the pool becomes smaller still. By then the momentum of population growth is lost, or more precisely, is working in the opposite direction with compounding force. Even if a generation comes along in which each woman has more children than her mother did, population decline may by then be inevitable.

Italy provides a good example of both how this phenomenon works and why it goes so largely unnoticed. In industrialized countries, the average woman must bear about 2.1 children over her lifetime to replace the population. The fertility rate of Italy now hovers around 1.2 children per woman, or just 57 percent of the number needed to maintain population size over time.[17] Already the trend has become nearly irreversible. The sharp fall in fertility over recent decades has brought Italian births down from 1 million in the mid-1960s to just over 500,000 in the mid-1990s. The implication, notes demographer Antonio Golini, is that after about 30 years, the pool of potential parents will also fall by half, "and at that point, the population decline will become very intense."[18]

But at least until very recently, the only part of this reality you could observe by walking around the country was a gradually building increase in the number and proportion of old people on streets. Otherwise, with the population still growing by 0.08 percent per year in the late 1990s, the traffic in Rome continued to get worse every year, and the competition for university admission and houses grew more acute.[19] Observing this, Italians, like their counterparts nearly everywhere, could understandably gather the impression that they live in a country that will continue growing ever more crowded.

Yet, the population growth we see all around us, and that so informs our worldviews, is a waning phenomenon. Even in the mighty United States—a nation that in the last two centuries has relied on population growth more than any other to extend its boundaries and project its power—the prospect of rapid population aging is now inevitable, and an absolute fall in population is hardly inconceivable.

3

America's Vanishing Labor Supply

Writing in 1751, Benjamin Franklin exalted in the fecundity of Britain's thirteen American colonies. "There are suppos'd to be now upwards of One Million English Souls in North America, (tho' 'tis thought scarce 80,000 have been brought over Sea)." Franklin was one of the world's earliest demographers, and by his calculations American birthrates (8 children per woman) were double that of Europe and would produce a doubling of the population every 20 years. In another century, he enthusiastically predicted, "the greatest Number of Englishmen will be on this Side of the Water."[1]

Franklin was not far off the mark. Between 1790 and 1830, for example, despite only minimal levels of immigration, the U.S. population grew by 227 percent. And by 1851, the white population of the United States exceeded that of England and Wales by 1.4 million. Today, the fecundity of America's native-born population is long gone. By the early twentieth century, the decline in birthrates among New England's WASP ascendancy was already causing Theodore Roosevelt to mock its pretensions to "Puritan conscience" and to label it as "diseased" and "atrophied."[2] Since then, the phenomenon of falling birthrates has spread to include Americans of all creeds and races.

Today, the United States still has a higher fertility rate than any other industrialized country, but this is only because of its success in attracting large numbers of immigrants who produce comparatively large families. Fertility rates among native-born women are far below what they were in the 1930s, when the privations of the Great Depression forced a sharp decrease in family size. Though the fertility of white women has ticked up slightly in the late 1990s, the last year in which white Americans had enough children to replace themselves was 1971.[3]

Fertility rates among blacks meanwhile are falling faster than among any other racial or ethnic group, with the average African American woman now bearing only 0.1 more children than the average white woman. Because infant mortality is some 137 percent higher among blacks than whites, and life expectancy at all ages is shorter, the black population of the United States is probably not creating enough babies to reproduce itself.[4]

Asian Americans and Pacific Islanders, meanwhile, are reproducing at well below replacement levels. Among major ethnic and racial groups, only Hispanics are reproducing above replacement levels, and that is primarily because of the comparatively high fertility of recent arrivals, who are themselves having decreasing numbers of children.[5] Nationally, the average Hispanic woman of childbearing age produces fewer and fewer children each year, with the rate dropping from 107 per thousand in 1990 to 96 per thousand in 2001—a 10 percent decline.[6]

In 2002, the "crude" birthrate in the United States as a whole—the number of babies born for every 1,000 U.S. residents—reached a record low, having declined by 17 percent since 1990. This trend is primarily due to the aging of the population, which leaves fewer women of reproductive age, and to an increase in the number of women delaying motherhood until their late 30s or early 40s. The total number of children that women now of reproductive age will have over their lifetime can only be known for certain after the fact. But the government's latest estimate of the total fertility rate shows it having fallen by 3 percent since 1990, to just 2.0125 children per woman, which is below the level required to replace the population.[7]

A continued increase in the percentage of women going to college or graduate school, as well as continued social and economic progress for African Americans and Hispanic Americans, could well push this rate down further. According to the National Center for Health Statistics, "A woman's educational level is the best predictor of how many children she will have."[8] Based on an analysis of 1994 birth certificates, NCHS concludes that non-Hispanic white women with college degrees will complete their childbearing with just 1.7 children. College-educated black women produce even fewer children, while college-educated Hispanic women have a below-replacement level fertility rate. The declining fertility rate among Hispanic women in California, which is driven primarily by gains in educational attainment, has put the state on a course on which it could easily see its population of children under age eleven decline by 585,000 between 2000 and 2010.[9]

Newly arriving immigrants also tend to be better educated than in the past, which means that their fertility rates are much lower as well. The large majority of Mexican immigrants these days, for example, have a secondary education. Immigrants arriving from more distant places are likely to have college degrees or higher. For example, the majority of recent immigrants from the Philippines have been to college, while 75 percent from India have a tertiary education.[10]

Because of the low birthrates of recent decades, the number of native-born American workers aged 25 to 54 will not grow in the next two decades.[11] If fertility rates gradually sink to the levels now seen in most other industrialized Nations and the growth of the foreign-born population settles toward 183,000, the U.S. will be losing population by 2042.[12] If U.S. fertility rates converge with those now seen in Japan or Germany, population loss will begin much sooner.

Fifty Floridas

Meanwhile, even if current fertility and immigration rates hold constant, the U.S. population will be aging rapidly. Between 2005 and 2025 the population aged 65 and older will swell by more than 72 percent, according to Census Bureau projections. Even after assuming an 8.4 percent increase in American fertility rates, and continuing robust levels of immigration over the first half of the twenty-first century, the Census Bureau finds that by 2050, one out of every five Americans will be over age 65, making the U.S. population as a whole much older than that of Florida today. The elderly will be more numerous than children, with the population 65 and over outnumbering those 14 and younger by more than 13 million. Over the first half of the twenty-first century, the number of "old old" persons (85 plus) is expected to nearly quadruple—adding the equivalent of an entire New York City of over-eighty-five-year-olds to the population.[13]

The long-term deficits created by population aging in the United States are staggering. The Congressional Budget Office estimates that the combined cost of just two programs—Medicare and Medicaid—will increase from 4.3 percent of the nation's total economic output in 2000 to as much as 11.5 percent in 2030 and to 21 percent in 2050. In other words, before today's five-year-olds turn 65, the cost of these programs alone will be consuming a larger share of the nation's income than *the entire federal government does today*, including the growing cost of interest on the national debt. (See note 16, page 201.)

Nearly every week brings new warnings about the future of old age in America. Government economists have recently calculated, for example, that the U.S. Treasury would have to put aside $44.2 trillion today in order to cover the cost of unfunded pension, health care, and other benefits promised to Americans over the next 75 years. This is more than four times the entire annual output of the U.S. economy. If every American worked for four years and handed over every penny earned to pay down the debt, it still would not go away. Medicare is

the biggest culprit, accounting for more than 80 percent of the short-
fall. Social Security accounts for most of the rest, along with a bundle
of unfunded promises to aging veterans and government employees.
To close this long-term deficit, the economists conclude that "an additional 16.6 percent of annual payrolls would have to be taxed away
forever, beginning today."[14]

But what really would that accomplish? The long-term outlook for
an aging society is not ultimately a question of finance. It's a question
of biology: How many children are born, and for how long after they
grow up do they remain healthy, productive adults?

Because of today's low birthrates, there will be fewer workers available in the future to produce the goods and services consumed by each
retiree. This would be true even if Social Security and Medicare were
fully funded, or even if every American saved up a fat 401(k) balance.
Money is just a claim on other people's labor—a way to persuade them
to do things like serve you food, mow your lawn, or even more to the
point, diagnose your cancer or give you your insulin shot each day.
Without human capital, money is worthless.

The nineteenth century economist Henry George made the point
quite nicely with his example of the "luxurious idler," who imagines
he is living off the legacy of his long-dead father, but who really lives
off the labor of those around him.

> On his table are new-laid eggs, butter churned but a few days before,
> milk which the cow gave this morning, fish which twenty-four
> hours ago were swimming in the sea, meat which the butcher boy
> has just brought in time to be cooked, vegetables fresh from the gar-
> den, and fruit from the orchard—in short, hardly anything that has
> not recently left the hand of the productive laborer. . . What this
> man inherited from his father, and on which he lives, is not actually
> wealth at all, but only the power of commanding wealth as others
> produce it. And it is from the contemporaneous production that his
> subsistence is drawn.[15]

Guns and Canes

Military power also requires contemporaneous production, of both skilled people and materials. Today, the United States thinks of itself as the world's sole remaining superpower, and it is. But as the cost of pensions and health care consume more and more of the nation's wealth, and as growth of the labor force vanishes, it will become more and more difficult for the United States to sustain its current levels of military spending, let alone maintain today's force levels. It may be that national power today is much less dependent than before on the ability to raise large armies. It may be, too, that many of the world's current hot spots will settle down as their populations age. In countries such as Saudi Arabia, Iraq, and Egypt, more than half the population is currently teenage or younger, but by mid-century, more than half will be well into middle age.

Yet the United States will still face threats. Rapid population aging in the developed and developing world may well add to the list of failed states, creating vast new breeding grounds for terrorism and extremism. Already, countries such as Argentina, Brazil, and the former Soviet Union have been deeply destabilized by financial crises largely induced by the unaffordable cost of their pension systems. As we will see in future chapters, China's political and economic system will also be under deep strain due to population aging, as will that of Japan and Korea, while Europe's social cohesion could also be undone by changing demography. Around the world, population aging, in combination with globalization, is causing social safety nets to fray, even as the extended family everywhere declines.

In such a world, the United States may not face any peer competitors in purely military terms, but could well face exceedingly dangerous terrorist threats and pandemics spawned by the chaos of failing states. How will the United States meet these challenges if they emerge? The technologies the United States currently uses to project its power—

laser-guided weapons, stealth aircraft, navigation assisted by the space-based Global Positioning System, nuclear aircraft carriers—are all products of massive and ongoing investments that the United States will not be able to afford if the cost of entitlements continues on its current course. The same point applies regarding the ability of the United States to sustain or increase its levels of foreign aid. If the war on terrorism is indeed a "generational struggle," as National Security Adviser Condoleezza Rice has warned, then the United States will have a very difficult time sustaining its financing.

By 2030, according to the Congressional Budget Office, the three big senior benefit programs (Social Security, Medicare, and Medicaid) plus interest on the national debt may well consume as much as 24 percent of Gross Domestic Product. By 2050, their cost could well rise to 47 percent of GDP, which is more than double what federal revenues are expected to be at the time. Without dramatic cuts in benefits or increases in taxes, all federal spending will eventually go to seniors.[16]

Moreover, even *within* the U.S. military budget, the competition between guns and canes is already becoming extreme. The Pentagon today spends 84 cents on pensions for every dollar it spends on basic pay.[17] Indeed, except when there is a war on, pensions are now one of the Pentagon's largest budget categories. In 2000, the cost of military pensions amounted to twelve times what the military spent on ammunition, nearly five times what the Navy spent on new ships, and more than five times what the Air Force spent on new planes and missiles. Population does not equal power, but no Great Power has managed to maintain its strength while experiencing the degree of population aging the United States faces over the next several decades.

The graying of the federal budget suggests one of many ways in which population aging may become a vicious cycle. As the cost of supporting the elderly has risen, governments have already responded by raising taxes on younger workers, and will be compelled to do so much more in the future. Younger workers, finding that not only does the economy require them to have far higher levels of education than did their parents, but that they must also pay far higher payroll taxes, are less able to afford children, and so have fewer of them, causing a new cycle of population aging. If current projections prove true, the working population of the United States essentially will wind up paying one out of every five dollars it earns just to support retirees, while simultaneously trying to finance more and more years of higher education, as well as paying for a military that sees more and more of its resources devoted to yesteryear's soldiers. Under such a scenario, one can well imagine a collapse in fertility rates similar to that which has occurred in Europe (along with an equivalent loss of military power and world influence) as young people try to protect their diminishing standard of living by having even fewer children.

The Limits of Immigration

Immigration is at best only a partial solution. The United States is able to attract a lot of human capital from abroad that is largely paid for by others. India, to take an extreme example, expends precious resources to maintain world-class universities like the Indian Institute of Technology, which rivals Harvard and Caltech in prestige, only to see two-thirds of each graduating class emigrate abroad, mostly to the United States, where many become CEOs and coveted engineers. However, immigration does less than you might think to ease the challenges of population aging. One reason is that most immigrants arrive not as babies, but with a third or so of their lives already behind them, and then go on to become elderly themselves. In the short term, immigrants can help to increase the ratio of workers to retirees, but in the long term they add much less youth to the population than would newborn children.

Indeed, according to a study by the United Nations Population Division, in order to maintain the current ratio of workers to retirees in the United States over time, it would be necessary to absorb an average of 10.8 million immigrants *annually* through 2050. At that point, the U.S. population would be 1.1 billion, 73 percent of which would be immigrants who had arrived in this country since 1995 or their descendents. Just housing such a flow would require the equivalent of building another New York City every ten months or so.[18] The only way any aging country could close its birth deficit through immigration, notes demographer Jean-Claude Chesnais, would be through "massive immigration of children without their parents," a practice Chesnais properly rejects as reminiscent of the slave trade.[19]

Meanwhile, it is unclear how long the United States can sustain even current rates of immigration. One reason, of course, is the heightened security concerns about terrorism. Another is the prospect of a cultural backlash against immigrants, the chances of which increase as native birthrates decline. In the 1920s, when widespread apprehension about declining native fertility rates found voice in books like Lothrop Stoddard's *The Rising Tide of Color against White World-Supremacy*,[20] the American political system responded by shutting off immigration. Germany, Sweden, and France did the same in the 1970s as the reality of population decline among the native-born started to set in. Aging nations may need immigrants more than ever, but are often fearful of letting them in.

As historian Alan C. Carlson has noted, "among naturally growing modern peoples, immigrants [seem] to be perceived as a healthy addition to successful, expanding social systems. Among a declining people, though, doubts about national identity appear to grow, immigrants become perceived as a threat, and liberality gives way to xenophobia and suppression."[21] The United States reopened its immigration gates in 1965, just as most Americans were starting to conclude that the native-born baby boom would go on forever. If American fertility patterns continue to converge toward those seen in Western Europe today, we certainly have reason to expect a revival of native chauvinism.

The Latin Age Wave

Another constraint on immigration to the United States involves supply. Birthrates, having already fallen well below replacement levels in
Europe and Asia, are now plummeting throughout Latin America as
well, creating the prospect that America's last major source of imported manpower will offer a declining pool of applicants.

Mexico's fertility rate, for example, has already fallen below 2.5
children per woman, and will soon be below replacement levels if current trends continue. The fall in Mexican fertility rates has been so
dramatic that the country is now aging at a far more rapid pace than
the United States and is destined to do so for at least the next two
generations. According to UN projections, the median age of Americans will increase by four and a half years during the first half of the
twenty-first century, reaching 39.7 years by 2050. By contrast, during
the same period Mexico's median age will increase 20 years, leaving
half the population over age 42. Put another way, during the course of
a year, the U.S. population as a whole ages by little more than one
month, while the Mexican population ages by nearly 5 months. Notes
Enrique Quintana, coauthor of a book on Mexico's aging population:
"Picture a scenario in which almost 23 million people are over the age
of 60, most of them have few descendents and many of them scant
savings, no job, no retirement coverage scheme. The results can
hardly be described as anything but catastrophic."[22]

Long before Mexico reaches this point, the supply of Mexicans
available to work in the United States could easily evaporate, as the
example of Puerto Rico shows. When most Americans think of Puerto
Rico, they think of a sunny, overcrowded island that sends millions of
immigrants to the West Side of New York or to Florida. Yet with a fertility rate well below replacement level and a median age of 31.8 years,
Puerto Rico no longer provides a net flow of immigrants to the main-
land, despite an open border and a lower standard of living.[23]

Similarly, most Caribbean nations are either reproducing at below-
replacement levels or tending in that direction. Cuba's fertility rate is

among the lowest in the world. As a result, by 2050 Cuba will have a substantially older population than the United States, with nearly half the population over 49. Other Caribbean countries that will be older than the United States include Guadeloupe, Martinique, Saint Vincent and Grenadines, St. Lucia, and Barbados.[24] Moreover, Argentina, Brazil, Chile, and Uruguay will all have older populations than the United States by mid-century. Indeed, the UN projects that the median age for Latin America and the Caribbean as a whole will be 39.8 by 2050, which is slightly older than its projections for the United States.[25]

The United States also must contend with the reality that it faces increasing competition from Europe in attracting new immigrants from Latin America. Today, Latinos comprise the fastest growing immigrant communities in Italy, Switzerland, Spain, and Britain. Just between 1999 and 2003, the number of legal Ecuadorian immigrants to Spain surged from just 7,000 to 200,000, accompanied by at least that number of illegals.[26]

Competing for Africans

Sub-Saharan Africa still produces many potential immigrants to the United States, as do the Middle East and parts of South Asia. But to attract immigrants from these regions, the United States must again compete with Europe, which is closer geographically and has a more acute need for imported labor. Europe also offers higher wages for unskilled work and more generous social benefits, as well as large, already established populations of immigrants from these areas.[27]

Moreover, it is by no means clear how many potential immigrants these regions will produce in the future. Birthrates are falling in sub-Saharan Africa as well, even as war and disease leave mortality rates extraordinarily high. The fall in fertility has been largest in South Africa, where total births per woman dropped from 6.85 during the early 1950s to 3.29 by the end of the 1990s.[28] As a result of this and the AIDS pandemic, the population of South Africa will fall from 43.4 million in 2000 to 38.7 million in 2015.[29] UN projections for the continent as a whole show fertility declining to 2.4 children per woman by mid-century, which may well be below replacement levels if mortality does not dramatically improve. Today, life expectancy at birth ranges from 32 years in Zambia to just 58 years in South Africa, as compared with 80.5 years in Japan.[30] Recent evidence suggests that women infected with HIV, even if they do not develop AIDS, have lower fertility as a result of miscarriage and sterility brought on by the disease and its associated opportunistic infections.[31] Based on studies in Africa, overall fertility of HIV-positive women is 40 percent lower than that of HIV-negative women.[32] Though the course of the HIV/AIDS epidemic through sub-Saharan Africa remains uncertain, the Central Intelligence Agency projects that AIDS and related diseases could kill as many as a quarter of the region's inhabitants by 2010.[33]

All told, some 59 countries, comprising roughly 44 percent of the world's total population, are currently not producing enough children to avoid population decline, and the phenomenon continues to spread. By 2050, according to the latest United Nations projections, 75 percent of all countries, even in underdeveloped regions, will be reproducing at below-replacement levels.[34] Since in the past the United Nations has consistently underestimated the fall of birthrates and may not have given sufficient weight to the effect of AIDS and other pandemics, many demographers believe the falloff in human population will be even more pronounced.

Indeed, even if human life expectancy continues to improve, current fertility trends will most likely cause human population to peak within the lifetime of today's children and possibly much sooner, after which the number of humans will be headed on a rapidly downward slope. A study by researchers at Austria's highly regarded International Institute for Applied Systems Analysis, published in the prestigious journal *Nature*, finds that there is around a 20 percent chance that world population will peak before 2050, around a 55 percent chance that it will do so by 2075, and around an 85 percent chance that it will be falling by the end of the century. Under the most likely scenarios, the share of the world population over age 60 will increase from 10 to 22 percent, making the world as a whole older than Western Europe or Florida is today.[35] Some share of the human race will of course continue to reproduce themselves, but who will those people be and what will be their motive?

4

The New Human Environment

Demographers once postulated that some sort of biological mechanism must prevent fertility rates from remaining below replacement levels for long. After all, don't we all carry the genes of our Neolithic ancestors, who one way or another managed to produce enough babies to sustain human population? Birthrates might temporarily fall below replacement levels due to war, or plague, or economic upheavals. Demographers speculated as well that as general improvements in living conditions caused fewer infants and children to die, parents would gradually learn that they did not need to produce so many children to create their ideal family size. But demographers never dreamed that whole populations could go on for generation after generation with subreplacement fertility rates. Over time, birthrates would tend toward an equilibrium that would produce at least a stable, if not growing, population—or so demographers just had to believe.

In a broad Darwinian sense, it still may be true that human fertility rates will not remain below replacement levels indefinitely. Human populations with persistently low fertility will eventually fade away. If more fecund tribes or nations replace them, total human population may remain stable over the long term, or even grow. Yet even this scenario is hard to square with the modern reality that, in region after region, across all cultures and religions, and under all forms of government, fertility rates are either already below replacement rates or tending in that direction. Between 1990 and 2000, every major region of the world, including Africa, Asia, Europe, Latin America, and North America, saw total fertility rates declining. Of all the countries in the world with above replacement level fertility, only two saw an estimated rise in the total number of children born per woman, and in both instances, the increase was barely more than zero: Suriname's total fertility rate increased by 0.17 children per woman, and Israel's by 0.01 children. The only other countries that saw their fertility rates rise during the 1990s, according to UN data, were already reproducing at well below replacement levels, and the amount of increase in their fertility was insignificant. France, for example, saw its estimated fertility rate rise from 1.71 children per woman to 1.76, while in Germany the average woman had an estimated 0.03 more children at the end of the decade that at the beginning—a change so slight that it could well amount to no more than statistical background noise.

The trend suggests that something in the human environment has profoundly changed. Anthropologists have shown time and again that in primitive societies, it is the most powerful and influential men who sire the most children. It was therefore also these men and their mates who disproportionately pushed their genes and ideas into the future. By contrast, in today's modern societies, studies show that materially successful men still have more sex, and more sexual partners, than their less fortunate peers, but produce fewer offspring.[1] Why?

As the World Turns

Some biologists now speculate that modern humans have created an environment in which the "fittest," or most successful, individuals are

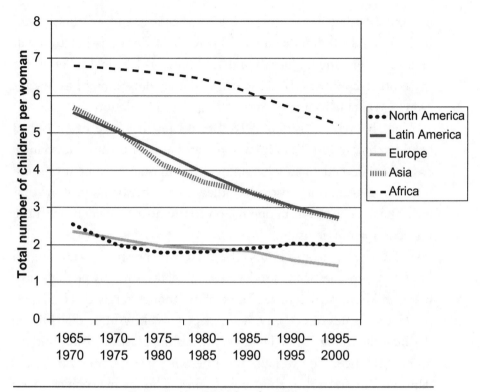

FIGURE 4.1 Fertility by Region

precisely those who have few, if any, children. As more and more of the human race finds itself living under urban conditions in which children no longer provide any economic benefit to their parents, but are rather costly impediments to material success, people who are well adapted to this new environment will tend not to reproduce themselves. And many others who are not so successful will imitate them.

Consider the example of Brazil's birth dearth. The last time most Americans bothered to look, Brazil was a youthful nation whose most pressing social problem appeared to be a growing army of glue-sniffing street urchins. But as Alexandre Kalache of the Pan American Health Organization observes, these street children are aging into street elders, leaving 30 percent of the population marginalized.[2] Today, Brazil is aging 2.1 times faster than the United States, and 3.1 times faster than Holland.[3] By mid-century, 18 percent of Brazil's population will be over 65, making it older than that of present-day Japan.[4] Yet unlike these other countries, Brazil is still underdeveloped, and has few resources available to support its swelling older population.

What happened? Since 1975, Brazil's fertility rate has dropped nearly in half to just 2.27 children per woman.[5] This Catholic country has never adopted a family planning program, so government pressure is not an explanation. Instead, studies of the phenomenon show that births have declined from one region to the next coincident with the introduction of television.[6]

Today, the number of hours a Brazilian woman spends watching *telenovelas*, or domestically produced soap operas, strongly predicts how many children she will have. These soaps, though rarely addressing reproductive issues directly, typically depict wealthy individuals living the high life in big cities. The men are dashing, lustful, power hungry, and unattached. The women are lithesome, manipulative, independent, and in control of their own bodies. The few who have young children delegate their care to nannies.

The *telenovelas*, in other words, reinforce a cultural message that is conveyed as well by many Hollywood films and other North American cultural exports: that people with wealth, people with sophistication, people who are free and self-fulfilled, are people who have at most one or two children, and who do not let their roles as mothers or fathers dominate their exciting lives.

Demographers now put much emphasis on the role of imitation in driving fertility trends, since it is otherwise difficult to explain why fertility is falling so rapidly even in underdeveloped regions. "The great range of conditions under which fertility has begun to fall all over the developing world," notes Alaka Malwade Basu of the Harvard Center for Population and Development Studies, "and the most potent correlates of such decline—education, exposure to the mass media, exposure to the ideologies (rather than the material trappings) of modernization—strongly suggest that the urge to control fertility and to have fewer children than one's parents comes largely from wanting to do what others do."[7]

God and Babies

So where will the children of the future come from? They will come disproportionately from people who are at odds with the modern environment—from people who don't "get" the new rules of the game that make large families an economic and social liability, or who, out of fundamentalist or chauvinistic conviction, reject the game altogether.

Mary Pride, a proud mother, Christian fundamentalist, and home-school advocate has done the math:

> Let's say Christians are 20 percent of the U.S. population. If each Christian family had six children, and the humanists, feminist, and others kept on having an average of one (which is realistic considering how they feel about fruitful heterosexual marriage), then in twenty years there would be sixty of us for every forty of them. In 40 years 90 percent of America would be Christian! This is without outside evangelism. All we'd have to do would be to have children and raise them for Christ.[8]

The question is actually a bit more complicated than that. Some of those children "raised for Christ" might grow up to have other ideas, so some "outside evangelism" might still be necessary. Moreover, those present-day humanists and feminists Pride deplores won't all just die off in 20 years. First they will grow old, and through programs like Social Security and Medicare they will lay claim on Mary Pride's children and their brethren for support in retirement, with perhaps unhappy results.

But this much is sure: The uneducated have far more children than the educated, and the religiously minded generally have bigger families than do secularists. In the United States, for example, fully 47 percent of people who attend church weekly say that the ideal family size is three or more children, as compared to only 27 percent of those who seldom attend church.[9] In Utah, where 69 percent of all residents are registered members of the Church of Latter Day Saints, fertility rates are the highest in the nation.[10] Utah annually produces 90 children for every 1000 women of childbearing age. By comparison, Vermont—the only state to send a socialist to Congress and the first to embrace gay marriage—produces only 49.[11]

The Coming Mutation

Faith is increasingly necessary as a motive to have children. In the modern urban economy, children may provide pride, joy, and companionship, but so do pets, and their cost is much cheaper, particularly if you value your time highly. As we shall see in Chapter 7, the economic burden to parents of raising a typical middle-class child in the United States through age 18 now exceeds one million dollars in direct costs and forgone wages. In today's highly mobile societies, grandmothers and other older family members are unlikely to help with child care. At the same time, the economy requires ever higher endowments of human capital, to the point that a professional woman is unlikely to have completed her education before her prime childbearing years are already behind her.

Yet despite their investment, parents receive an ever-diminishing share of the human capital they help to form in the next generation, thanks to programs like Social Security, which redistribute the next generation's income to parents and nonparents alike. Nor, thanks to the spread of education and the mass media, can parents (except perhaps for homeschoolers like Mary Pride) exert much influence over their children's values, as compared with parents in the past. No wonder, then, that the most educated and most materially successful members of modern societies are those least likely to have children.

If evolutionary biologists spotted such a pattern in any other species—say, a colony of penguins in which, for some reason, those males and females best able to feed themselves exhibited high rates of infertility—what would they make of it? They would pronounce that this colony is either on the road to extinction or on the threshold of a dramatic mutation.[12]

If human population does not wither away in the future, it will be because of a mutation of human culture. On our current course, more and more of the world's population will be produced by people who believe they are (or who in fact are) commanded by a higher power to procreate, or who just lack the foresight to avoid the social and economic cost of creating large families. Such a higher power might be God, speaking through Abraham, Jesus, Mohammad, or some latter day saint. Or it might be a totalitarian state. Either way, for better or for worse, such a trend, if sustained, would drive human culture off its current market-driven, individualistic, modernist course, and gradually create an antimarket culture dominated by fundamentalist values.

Seem far-fetched? Not since the fall of the Roman Empire has the world ever experienced anything on the scale of today's loss of fertility. As sociologist Rodney Stark demonstrates in his well-respected book on the rise of Christianity, at that time Christians had marginally higher birthrates than pagans and practiced less infanticide. They also enjoyed better life expectancy, most likely in part because, in tight-knit early Christian communities, those infected by the various plagues of the era were less likely to be abandoned. The resulting demographic advantage, Stark argues, slowly transformed a marginal Jesus movement into the dominant cultural force of the Western world, as Christian communities gradually out-bred and out-lived their pagan counterparts.[13] Demographic conditions today suggest that a cultural transformation of similar proportions may be in store if secularists increasingly avoid the growing economic cost of raising children, while fundamentalists of all stripes do not.

Unlike in the past, however, today's loss of fertility is not caused by war, famine, plague, or some other passing catastrophe. Indeed, it is in precisely those areas of the world where life is most safe and prosperous that children are scarcest. Thus, there appears to be no law of nature that limits how much human population may shrink in the future so long as modernity spreads. Within several centuries, if worldwide fertility approaches the levels already seen in most of the developed world, this alone could easily create enough negative population momentum to leave fewer people living on the entire planet than live in the United States today.[14] Yet how long can modernity spread if it fails to reproduce itself?

One does not have to assume a world decimated by bioterrorism or nuclear war to see how drastically global culture may shrink and mutate in the twenty-first century. Modernity is not only a major cause of falling fertility, it is a major cause of premature death. In the developing world, for example, death rates for noncommunicable diseases related to Western lifestyle, such as cancers and heart attacks induced by smoking and obesity, are already an even higher source of mortality than infectious diseases such as HIV, malaria, and TB—causing half of all deaths in places such as Mexico, China, and the Middle East.[15] By the year 2020, such diseases of affluence are expected to account for seven out of every ten deaths in lower-income regions. With the spread of global trade and travel, and with the rise of densely populated megacities throughout the developing world, many experts now predict the reemergence of global pandemics on the scale of the plagues of the Middle Ages.[16]

Those who reject modernity thus seem to have an evolutionary advantage, whether they are clean-living Mormons, or Muslims who remain committed to comparatively large families, or members of emerging sects and national movements that combine pro-natalism with antimaterialism. The question we must then embrace is, how can the modern economy, the modern welfare state, and modern principles of equality be sustained in a world in which the threat of population loss becomes ever more apparent?

5

People Power

How long will global fertility rates continue to fall? "Please, for at least as long as I'm around," the man in the street may answer. Isn't the world already overpopulated? Wouldn't there be less pressure on natural resources, more room at the beach, fewer screaming tots on planes, less crime, less traffic, less global warming, less war, if only there were not so many human beings?

Slower world population growth certainly offers many benefits, some of which have already been realized. Many economists believe, for example, that falling birthrates made possible the great economic boom that occurred first in Japan, and then in many other Asian nations beginning in the 1960s. As the relative number of children declined, so did the burden of their dependency, thereby freeing up more resources for investment and adult consumption.[1] In East Asia, the working-age population grew nearly four times faster than its dependent population between 1965 and 1990, freeing up a huge reserve of female labor and other social resources that would otherwise have been committed to raising children.[2]

The general improvement in America's economic performance since the 1970s has also probably been due in part to the era's slowing rate of population growth. Fewer babies meant there were more women available to work for wages. Similarly, the "middle-aging" of America that occurred in the 1990s undoubtedly helped increase the average wage and measured productivity growth, as a rising percentage of the population aged into years in which most individuals are at the peak of their job performance and earning power. The growth in the middle-aged population also probably helped to drive up stock prices and drive down interest rates during that decade, as the share of the U.S. population consisting of middle-aged people saving for retirement dramatically increased.

Yet even if declining fertility rates can bring a "demographic dividend," that dividend eventually has to be repaid. At first there are fewer children to feed, clothe, and educate, leaving more for adults to enjoy. But soon enough, if fertility continues to remain below replacement levels, there are fewer productive workers as well, while there are also more and more dependent elderly, who consume far more resources than children do. Even after considering the cost of education, a typical child in the United States consumes 28 percent less than the typical working-age adult, while elders consume 27 percent more, mostly in health-related expenses.[3] Persons 65 and over receive eleven times more in federal spending per person than do children under age 18.[4] The global fall in fertility, even if it does not continue to deepen and spread, is creating a world for which few individuals, and no nations, are prepared. Simply stated, this is because population growth and the human capital it creates are part of the foundation upon which modern economies, as well as modern welfare states, are built.

Men and Machines

Primitive economies are sustainable without population growth, even if they don't produce much wealth. In 1750, the world's population was about 770 million, reflecting an average growth rate of only slightly above zero over the entire course of human history. Demographer Massimo Livi-Bacci estimates the growth rate of world population from the year 1 A.D. to 1750 was just 0.064 percent per year.[5] In Western Europe during much of this period, reproduction was generally limited by what demographer Ron J. Lesthaeghe calls a tight "nuptiality valve."[6] The Church allowed only those who could marry to have children, and marriage was limited only to those who were fully economically functional. Women without dowries went off to convents. Men without property could not attract a bride.

Accompanying this slow population growth were negligible improvements in living standards. The distinguished economic historian Angus Maddison estimates that the growth rate of the gross domestic product per capita in Europe between 500 and 1500 was zero.[7] Even by 1750, a typical European used roughly the same technology, consumed roughly the same amount of food and energy, and experienced the same short life expectancy (about 25 years) as his or her counterpart 1500 years before.

But then, due mostly to sustained reductions in infant mortality, the population of Western Europe exploded, doubling from 60 million in 1750 to 120 million in 1850. England's population nearly tripled, from 5.8 million to 16.7 million. The Scottish population swelled from 1.3 million to 2.9 million. In the midst of this unprecedented revolution in human population, it became common for even well-educated, sophisticated parents to find themselves presiding over huge families. As historian Paul Johnson notes:

The great financier Sir Robert Wigram had 15 sons and 5 daughters. The Rt. Rev. Henry Bathurst, Bishop of Norwich, was one of 36 children his father had by different wives. Maria Edgeworth was one of her father's 22 children by four wives. . . A study of 50 aristocratic women of that era shows that they tended to marry at age 21 and have an average of eight children, the last at age 39. Working-class women were even more productive, since they were less likely to practice birth control or deny their husbands.[8]

By 1798, the spread of teeming slums in England, along with in-creasing calls to redistribute wealth to the poor, alarmed the political economist Thomas Malthus enough to inspire his famous *Essay on the Principle of Population*. In it, he prophesized that human population growth would geometrically outpace the world's food production, thereby producing mass famine.[9] To this day, Malthusian thinking suf-fuses the environmental movement and casually informs most people's thoughts about the future. But if Malthus was right about the factors that limited human population growth before his time, he was exactly wrong about what the next two centuries would bring. For even as hu-man population has increased more than sixfold since the writing of his essay, the amount each person consumes has increased at a far more rapid pace. On a worldwide basis, per capita consumption in-creased 40 percent faster than population in the nineteenth century, and 34 percent faster in the twentieth century.[10] Instead of widespread famine came a still-expanding system of mass production and mass consumption. Within the United States, population was 3.6 times greater at the end of the twentieth century than at the beginning, but living standards meanwhile are variously estimated to have increased by between 14 and 25 times.[11]

Population and Prosperity

The name historians give to this phenomenon of rising production and consumption is, of course, the "Industrial Revolution." Exactly how and why it occurred is a matter of continuing debate. Certainly, the evolution of strong property rights was a factor, as was the devel-opment of new technologies like the steam engine. Also required was a huge increase in the consumption of natural resources, and in pollu-tion. But population growth was also key, by providing for economies of scale and opportunities for specialization, as well as new incentives to innovate. Today, though they may quarrel about how it all got started or whether it is sustainable, few economic historians would dispute that the Industrial Revolution is an engine that runs on a two-stroke cycle. At one turn of the cycle, rising population creates a spur to the discovery of more efficient means of producing and distributing food, energy, and other scarce goods. At the next turn of the cycle, rising productivity allows the economy to provide for additional increases in population even as each person consumes more and more.[12]

Love this system or hate it, but acknowledge that it is the system that built the modern world. And acknowledge, too, that for better or for worse, population growth is still the prime driver of economic growth. Increase in population causes new houses to be built, new cars to be manufactured, and new law offices to be formed, and it produces the supply of workers needed to meet that demand. Even during the boom years between 1995 and 2000, with their soaring levels of business investment in new technology and surging productivity, fully a third of all the increase in the U.S. gross domestic product came from the sheer growth in the number of workers and the amount of hours they worked.[13]

A nation's gross domestic product is literally the sum of its labor force times the average output per worker. Thus, a decline in the number of workers implies a decline in an economy's growth potential. When the size of the workforce is falling, economic growth occurs, if at all, only through compensating increases in productivity. The European Commission, for example, projects that Europe's potential growth rate over the next fifty years will fall by 40 percent due to the shrinking size of the European work force. Italy expects its working-age population to plunge by 41 percent by 2050, meaning that output per worker will have to increase by at least that amount just to keep Italy's rate of economic growth from falling below zero. With a shrinking labor supply, Europe's future economic growth will depend entirely on getting more out of each remaining worker (many of them unskilled, recently arrived immigrants) even as it has to tax workers at higher and higher rates to pay for old-age pensions and health care.[14]

The United States faces nearly the same challenge. Though the United States has a higher ratio of workers to retirees than does Europe, population aging is just as much of a threat to its standard of living, primarily because of the high cost and inefficiency of its health care system. According to a study conducted by the Federal Reserve Bank of Boston, the projected decline in the size of the U.S. workforce relative to the rest of the population means that the United States will have to increase labor productivity by 40 percent by 2030 just to maintain current living standards. This is perhaps not an impossible task, but one that will probably require tomorrow's aging workforce to labor at least as hard and as long as today's comparatively young workforce, while also being far more receptive to new technology. The calculation also implies that without at least a 40 percent increase in output per worker, American after-tax income will remain stagnant for at least the next generation.[15]

The way business boosters and politicians talk about the economy often obscures the role of population growth in driving the economy. During the boom years of the 1990s, those who celebrated the "new economy," for example, often talked as if sustaining economic growth was simply a matter of engineering smarter computers, or smarter companies. Although rising productivity is indeed a major source of economic growth, growth in the sheer number of workers and consumers is equally if not more important. Indeed, over the last three decades, population growth has accounted for between one half and two-thirds of all economic growth in all industrialized countries.[16]

If one takes a broader measure of national economic output than that of the gross national product—including, for example, the unpaid labor and critical human capital formation provided by parents, as well as by other underpaid caregivers—then the role of technology per se becomes even more diminished as a source of economic growth. As I will explore in greater detail in Chapter 7, an increasing demand for human capital, most of it provided with little or no compensation to its producers, is what most distinguishes the modern economy. What would Microsoft be today if Bill Gates's mother had decided she did not want children, or if countless underpaid schoolteachers had not sacrificed untold hours teaching him and his employees to read, write, and do their multiplication tables?

Moreover, as we will see in Chapter 8, there are strong reasons to doubt whether aging societies can maintain high rates of productivity growth. One reason is financial. Exploding health and pension costs, along with a shrinking tax base, diminish resources available to households, government, and the private sector for investing in the next generation, even as the need for human capital formation increases. Another reason is rooted in the realities of the life cycle. It is not just that most technological breakthroughs and entrepreneurial activity tend to come from people in their 20s and 30s. As one approaches old age, the amount of risk one can prudently afford to take with one's career or savings declines, and so an aging population will likely become increasingly risk averse, favoring Treasury bonds over venture stocks, and steady jobs that promise pensions over speculative startups.

Global Aging and the Global Economy

So it is imperative to ask, Can the engine that created today's affluent societies be made to work without population growth in its cycle? Yes it can, I argue in this book, but it will require thorough reengineering, and not just of the formal economy, but of the family as well.

To name a few of the design challenges: How does industry achieve new economies of scale when the number of consumers is no longer growing, much less perpetually falling? What sustains the value of your house, or your retirement portfolio, when there are ever fewer younger people to whom you might sell your accumulated assets? How can young people afford to raise and educate children if increasingly more of their wages are garnisheed to pay for retirees? How can a government meet its obligations to the swelling ranks of the elderly, much less finance proper stewardship of the environment, when there are fewer and fewer workers to tax? How can nations with rapidly aging or shrinking populations defend themselves militarily against more youthful competitors? How can poor countries attract the capital they need to develop if the rich nations must run huge deficits just to meet the mounting cost of supporting their elderly?

Population aging and decline need not lead to global depression, environmental strain, or war, but they may well. Nations that do not adapt to the new demographic realities of the twenty-first century—primarily by fostering more rewards to parents and other caregivers, investing heavily in the education of the next generation, and pursuing strategies to allow for more productive aging—stand in danger of being consumed by debt, of losing their ability to innovate, and ultimately of losing their identity.

This is true not only for the rapidly aging industrialized countries, but for most developing nations as well, which not only face shrinking or slower-growing export markets, but also are burdened with the unaffordable cost of supporting vastly increased numbers of dependent elders, often without the benefit of even rudimentary public or private pension systems. In Egypt, for example, the size of the elderly population will double compared to the growth in the working-age population by 2050. In China, the ratio of elders to working-age persons will grow nearly fourfold.[17] It took France 114 years for people 65 and above to go from 7 percent of the population to 14 percent. It took the United States 69 years. But it took Japan just 25 years, and it will take Indonesia 22. Notes Joseph Chamie, director of the UN Population Division, "Developing nations don't have the same amount of time to adjust. That shift is creating pressures on governments to respond quickly. Many developing nations don't have the institutions and the financial wherewithal to deal with this." So how will people cope? "They will do what they always did historically," says Chamie. "They will go back to the family."[18]

Properly managed, the vast demographic transition now affecting nearly every corner of the globe could lead to a new era of stability and prosperity, as well as cultural and political maturity, particularly in regions where birthrates are falling and the labor force is still growing. Yet the examples to date of how rapidly aging societies are responding, or failing to respond, to the challenges that await them are hardly encouraging.

6

Fading Nations

In 1907, William Randolph Hearst's *San Francisco Examiner* published a two-part Sunday supplement which warned that "the Yellow Peril is here." Hearst was hardly alone in his prediction that "Japan May Seize the Pacific Coast."[1] Those who did not fear outright invasion feared being out-bred. "We are threatened with an overproduction of Japanese children," warned the *Literary Digest* a few years later. "First come the men, then the picture brides, then the families. If California is to be preserved for the next generation as a 'white man's country' there must be some movement started that will restrict the Japanese birthrate in California."[2]

From the late nineteenth century onward, Asia's rapid population growth has struck fear in American hearts and inspired harsh measures, including denying U.S. citizenship to Chinese immigrants beginning in the 1870s, to contain the "Asian hordes." During this period, Asia's population was not only swelling, but was getting younger, with half of the population of Japan being under age 22 by the time of the attacks on Pearl Harbor.[3]

How different it is today. Fertility rates in Asia have reached such low levels that population loss is inevitable throughout much of the region. Desperate to preserve the nation's identity, the government of Singapore now has its own official matchmaking service, the Social Development Unit, which sponsors American-style speed dating, in which singles have a series of seven-minute encounters in hopes of finding their soul mate.[4] In Japan, where the annual number of births has fallen nearly in half since the 1960s, the government allocated nine billon dollars in 2003 for child-care leave, including a special new program that pays dads who take time off to help raise kids.[5]

"Parasite Singles"

Of all nations on earth, Japan today provides the best object lesson on how difficult it is to maintain prosperity once the supply of youth drops beneath a certain tipping point. From reading the popular business press, you would easily get the impression that the bursting of Japan's "bubble economy" in the late 1980s had nothing to do with demographics. Instead, conventional wisdom offers a standard litany of explanation centered on the supposed defects of Japan's political and financial systems. The country's politicians are in the grip of special interest groups. Its bankers are incompetent, or in bed with cronies and producer cartels. Lavish farm subsidies lead to inefficient use of land and extreme housing shortages. All these factors have certainly played a role in Japan's economic decline, but they don't add up to an explanation. After all, Japan is no more ridden with cronyism and special interest group politics than it was in the prosperous 1970s and 1980s. So what changed?

The answer is the structure of Japan's population, which is now among the oldest on earth. In Japan, as in any country, a growing population of young adults has historically been a major source of expanding production and consumer demand. Members of this age group are typically busy acquiring and furnishing new homes and apartments and buying major appliances, as well as spending money on their children. Any growth in the labor supply comes almost exclusively from members of this age group. Yet between 1980 and 1990, Japan's population aged 25 to 44 declined by 7 percent.[6] Moreover, an unprecedented share of this age group decided to remain single and continue living with their parents, thereby further depressing consumer demand.

Meanwhile, even as Japan's supply of children and young adults was shrinking, its supply of middle-aged people (45–64) was swelling by a massive 42 percent.[7] Middle age is a time of life when people typically have the cost of acquiring a home and raising a family largely behind them, and when they start using more and more of their income to save toward retirement, particularly in a thrifty culture like Japan's. So it happened that the combination of a rapidly growing middle-aged population and shrinking supply of youth caused Japan to experience what Yamada Masahiro of the Tokyo Gakugei University has called the world's first "low birth rate recession."[8]

To be sure, government policies and problems in Japan's banking system also played a role in compounding the effects of falling fertility and population aging. But demography alone is enough to explain why today the country suffers from a massively excessive savings rate, anemic consumer demand, and slow economic growth. Moreover, as we will see in Chapter 9, even Japan's reluctance to reform its financial institutions, and its decline as a fount of new technology, may be intrinsically related to the increasing conservatism and risk aversion that comes with an aging population. As Paul Hewitt, deputy commissioner for policy at the U.S. Social Security Administration, concludes:

> Herein lies a morality tale for the rest of the developed world. Between now and 2020, the European Union and, to a lesser extent, the U.S. will see lifecycle effects strikingly similar to those ravaging Japan. To be sure, rigidities in Japan's capital and labor markets make it a special case. But the technology sector blowout exposes our own growing vulnerability to bubbles.[9]

Whether Japan's low-birth-rate recession becomes a low-birth-rate depression, one cannot know for sure, but it is hardly reassuring to learn that fully a third of the Japanese population will be over 60 within a decade. The growth in Japan's elderly population is so explosive that its finance minister, Masajuro Shiokawa, has proposed, in all seriousness, exporting retirees to the Philippines. "Japan is aging and there are so few people to care for them," Shiokawa lamented in the summer of 2003. "There are so many young people in the Philippines."[10]

The idea is perhaps not as daft as it seems, given Japan's intolerance for immigration, but it is no panacea. Already, the increasing seniority of the Japanese workforce is undermining the country's industrial competitiveness by raising average wages. Between 1980 and 2000, change in the age structure of the population alone added about $741 to the annual cost of retaining a male worker, whose average age is now about 10 years older than in the 1980s.[11] Nearly all economists agree that by the end of this decade, Japan's savings rate will plunge as Japan becomes a society dominated by elders spending down their nest eggs. Meanwhile, the cost of pensions and health care are likely to be so large that Japan will no longer have sufficient capital left to lend or invest abroad, which could well leave debtor countries like the United States highly vulnerable.

Through the mechanisms of the global financial system, a low-birth-rate depression in one major country could easily create a financial contagion that spreads to every nation, regardless of its demographic profile. Forewarnings of such a scenario came in 1998, when Brazil's overburdened pension system contributed to a panic that roiled financial markets around the world, and in 2002, when Germany's burgeoning budget deficits breached the targets set by European Union policymakers and set off a steep decline in European equity prices. Konrad Adenauer, the Federal Republic's first chancellor, once remarked that Germany would always be able to afford generous, unfunded pensions because Germans would always have children. He did not realize, any more than did policymakers in Japan, how dangerous it was to take mothers for granted.[12]

When the Japanese bubble first burst, most Western observers were shocked, and predicted a quick rebound. The country, after all, excelled, and still does, in the quality of its workforce and in its technological prowess. While the energy crisis of the 1970s sent the United States and Europe into recession and prolonged stagnation, Japan continued to thrive, despite having no energy resources of its own. Yet those who thought that Japan's industrial efficiency would lead to boundless prosperity could have avoided their error by looking beneath the surface of Japanese family life.

Young Japanese were beginning to assume new social roles. In the middle of the 1970s, surveys showed that almost 80 percent of respondents, male or female, old or young, agreed with views such as "Women would do better to marry," or "Men should work, and women should stay home." By the 1990s, only 40 to 60 percent of Japanese still clung to these attitudes.[13] Among the young, marriage rates dropped precipitously and a new social type emerged: the *parasaito shinguru*, or "parasite singles," as many Japanese commentators call them.

According to stereotype, a typical *parasaito shinguru* is a young career woman who lives rent free with her parents. Dressed in designer clothes and jewelry, she frequently travels to Europe, New York, or Thailand with girlfriends for shopping or vacation, always staying at the best hotels and resorts. Those who are more sympathetic to such young women say that they avoid marriage because, under Japanese custom, they would become responsible for caring for their husband's aging parents as well as their own.[14] Others note that young Japanese are burdened by high taxes and extraordinary real estate prices that put traditional marriage and family beyond reach. The rigors of the Japanese education system, which drive many parents to enroll their children in expensive cram courses, also raises the economic cost of parenthood, and perhaps erodes its joys as well. Tellingly, among Japanese women with children aged 0–14, only 9 percent report deriving pleasure from child rearing, as compared with 40 to 70 percent in other industrial countries.[15]

Still other commentators blame young Japanese men for a loss of self-confidence and masculine drive that leaves them unappealing as marriage partners. Whatever the explanation is for the phenomenon of *parasaito shinguru*, there is no doubt that it is widespread and rising. In 2001, Japan's Youth Research Institute asked schoolgirls around the world their opinion of the statement "Everyone must get married." Only 12 percent of Japanese schoolgirls agreed. By contrast, 78 percent of American schoolgirls affirmed that marriage is for everyone.[16]

Given such circumstances, it is hardly surprising that Japan has among the lowest fertility rates on earth—just 1.4 children per woman.[17] Despite suffering two nuclear attacks and the near total destruction of all its major cities during World War II, Japan was able to rebuild itself into the world's preeminent industrial power by the 1980s. Its subsequent experience shows, however, that national power and prosperity ultimately depend not just on efficient factories, powerful memory chips, and driven office workers, but on the intimate decisions that individual men and women make when they stare into each other's eyes and ask, "Should we make a baby?"

4–2–1 Societies

Since the 1990s, conventional wisdom has shifted from holding up Japan as the world's most ascendant nation to predictions that China will become the new economic powerhouse of the twenty-first century. But once again, those who are shrewd enough to look beyond current industrial trends and examine the conditions of family life know that China is in deep trouble. If current rates of economic growth were to continue, the output of the Chinese economy would indeed rival that of the United States by 2020. But before China can emerge as a true economic powerhouse, it will have to contend with a demographic challenge even more severe than that currently facing Japan.

The reality of China's birth dearth is hard to square with what any casual observer will see on the streets of the country's fast-growing cities today: throngs of humanity crammed into tenements or camped out in railroad stations, armies of unemployed youths prowling for work. No wonder most people in China and around the world still believe that overpopulation is the country's biggest problem, and why so many foreign companies believe that China will supply them with an inexhaustible source of low-cost labor. Today, for the first time in its history, even college graduates in China are having trouble getting jobs, which only strengthens China's allure to companies seeking a quality workforce at a reasonable price. Way down Mexico way there's a great sucking sound in the air these days. It is not the sound Ross Perot once warned would be made by U.S. jobs rushing south of the border. It's the sound of Mexican jobs speeding off to China in search of lower wages.

But beneath the surface of ordinary life in China, a more profound truth is unfolding. The consensus among Beijing's population experts is that the average woman in China today bears somewhere between 1.5 and 1.65 children, whereas 2.1 are needed to replace the population. The total fertility rate in some large cities such as Shanghai, Beijing, and Tianjin is among the lowest that has been recorded in a sizeable population (around 1.13).[18] There is still population momentum left over from the days when Chairman Mao Zedong urged citizens to help build the country by making babies, but the momentum is fast fading. China's labor pool (persons aged 15–60) currently is expanding by 12.1 million workers a year. But this rate of increase will slow to 6.2 million a year during the second half of the decade before essentially flattening out during the 2010s and declining rapidly thereafter, according to projections by the State Family Planning Commission of China.[19]

Meanwhile, the population of elders will be exploding. By 2040, according to official estimates, 26 percent of China's population will be 60 or older, giving China an age structure similar to Florida's today.[20] Increasingly, China is becoming what demographer Xiaochun Qiao calls a "4–2–1" society, in which one child must support two parents and four grandparents.[21] Chinese writer Lin Ying observes: "Whereas the now-developed countries first got rich and then got old, China will first get old."[22] By contrast, the Asian "tigers"—South Korea, Taiwan, Singapore, and Hong Kong—all had become moderately developed countries before they began to age rapidly.

These projections assume that birthrates will rise by 30 percent in the future, instead of continuing the downward trend now seen nearly everywhere in the world. If China's birthrates remain unchanged, notes Robert Stowe England, a China expert for the Center for Strategic and International Studies in Washington, D.C., China will join the ranks of Japan, Germany, Russia, Italy, and Spain—countries that stand to lose 20–30 percent of their populations over the next 50 years. If the U.S. Central Intelligence Agency is correct in its estimate that China will have 10 to 15 million HIV/AIDS cases by 2010, the loss of population could be greater still.[23]

As alluded to in Chapter Two, China also faces a worsening "shortage" of women, or "surplus" of men, if you like. The scarcity of women has already fostered a brisk trade of women sold into marriage or slavery, as well as a flourishing prostitution industry. This in turn has led to a pandemic of venereal disease, including a mounting incidence of HIV/AIDS and chlamydia, which causes infertility in about 8 percent of women who contract it.[24] By 2015, assuming just a mild spread of the HIV virus, new AIDS cases in China could erupt at a pace of nearly 100,000 per month, according to estimates by demographer Nicholas Eberstadt.[25]

In some major provinces, such as Hainan and Guangdong, the surplus of male over female infants exceeds 30 percent.[26] By 2020, the number of unattached young men in China could reach 33 million.[27] The few other examples in history of societies in which sex ratios became imbalanced in this way—third century Rome, for example, or the American Western frontier in the mid-nineteenth century—tended to be highly volatile and violent.

Though one might think that the social status of women, and of feminine values, would improve when many suitors have to compete for each bride, the opposite appears to be true. As Rodney Stark has observed, a shortage of women creates a situation in which women are "enclosed in repressive sex roles as men treat them as 'scarce goods.' Conversely, to the extent that females outnumber males . . . women will enjoy relatively greater power and freedom."[28]

Even if China can manage its surplus of unmarriageable men, it is still woefully unprepared for the coming wave of elderly. The first problem is a legacy of communism. In the 1950s, Mao established an elaborate employee benefit system as part of what he called the "iron rice bowl." Following the Soviet model, workers in state-owned enterprises received low wages, but generous promises of future pensions and postretirement health care benefits. Unfortunately, as has happened in many capitalist countries as well, no money was put aside to defray the future cost of these promises. As workforces aged or were downsized, huge legacy costs thus emerged.

The government has tried at times to get out of paying the benefits it has promised to laid-off workers and retirees, but it has been met with large-scale protests and riots, most notably in the northern cities of Liaoyang and Daqing in 2002.[29] Political stability requires that the government pay these benefits at least in part. Indeed, in response to the riots, Labor Minister Zhang Zuoji in March 2003 promised to expand the number of people covered by the pension system from 100 to 150 million, and to double the number of people with medical insurance.[30] Yet even before such expansions in coverage, the debts of the country's social security system, which covers only a fraction of the population, exceeded 145 percent of its gross domestic product.[31] In other words, the entire labor force would have to commit 100 percent of its output for nearly a year and a half just to pay off the pension debts the country has already accrued, and still the vast majority of the country's citizens would be left with no provision for their own retirement. In comparison, writing off all the bad loans in China's technically insolvent banking system would require "only" 20 percent of the gross domestic product.[32]

The fragility of China's banking system heightens its vulnerability to aging. The U.S. is also threatened by a retirement crisis, but at least a substantial portion of Americans have actual savings or are covered by private pension plans that contain actual assets, such as stocks or real estate. In 1997, China took the advice of the World Bank and created individual retirement accounts for younger workers, similar to 401(k)s in the United States—a good idea, except that in practice each worker's account amounts to little more than a bookkeeping entry. Contributions do not go for investments in the real economy, but wind up being spent by local social security bureaus to pay benefits to current retirees. If the population were not aging, the system might work just fine. But with fewer and fewer workers available to support each retiree in the future, it amounts to a Ponzi scheme.

Even if workers try to save on their own for retirement, their investment options are hardly attractive: either invest in an illiquid stock market wracked by scandals, or in an insolvent banking system offering returns below inflation. Since 1997, a fledgling private life insurance industry has emerged, but the average Chinese citizen still has little hope of being able to save enough on his or her own to provide for old age.

Adding enormously to the challenge of China's population aging is the rapid disappearance of the traditional extended Chinese family in which several generations lived under one roof. The massive migration of some 100 million, mostly young people from the interior parts of the country to coastal cities, is leaving behind millions of aging parents. China's social security system never extended to the country's rural population, so most of these elders receive few if any health and pension benefits, let alone formal nursing-home or long-term care. At the same time, the breakup of the extended family often leaves young urban women unable to draw on the help of older relatives in raising their children, making the effective cost of childbearing extremely high.

For now, China's rapidly falling fertility and rapid urbanization is a boon to the economy. With fewer children to feed, clothe, and educate, there are more resources available for investment and adult consumption. At the same time, when young people move from primitive farms to factories, their productivity rises enormously.

But both trends obviously have their limits as sources of economic growth—and if taken far enough, start working against the prospects for prosperity. Depopulation of the countryside leaves behind masses of dependent elders stranded in dying towns and villages. And although a falling birthrate may at first leave more resources available for adults to enjoy, soon enough there are fewer and fewer productive workers and consumers as well. The world does not have much experience with population aging of the scale or speed China is soon to experience, but the country that comes closest to matching it is Russia, which is hardly reassuring.

Mother Russia's Empty Cradle

The fall of the Soviet empire provides another object lesson on the hazards of population aging. The Soviet system obviously had many faults, including excessive military spending, corruption, and an inefficient command-and-control economy. Still, it is important to remember that the Soviet Union performed well by many measures throughout much of the Cold War. Its economic growth rate from 1950 to 1960, though exaggerated by Soviet propaganda, still rivaled that of the United States. Russians enjoyed a higher life expectancy than Americans into the late 1950s. And of course, the country was capable of pulling off technological marvels. On October 4, 1957, when the Russians launched the first artificial satellite from the Baikonur Cosmodrome in Kazakhstan, Americans were thrown into a panic. *The New York Times* declared that the United States was "in a race for survival." Lyndon B. Johnson, majority leader of the Senate, said, "Soon, they will be dropping bombs on us from space like kids dropping rocks onto cars from freeway overpasses."[33]

During this period the Soviets had a high fertility rate compared with many European countries—a fact that Soviet officials cited as an example of the advantages inherent to a socialist society. But during the 1960s, the Russian family began to break apart. The marriage rate dropped by 19 percent, the divorce rate doubled, and the number of Russian babies born each year declined by 34 percent.[34] By 1964, Soviet women no longer produced enough children to replace the population.

Fertility rates fell continuously through the 1970s. Concurrently, Soviet society aged and stagnated. The virtual birth strike staged by Soviet women no doubt deeply embarrassed the regime, which was fond of lecturing the rest of the world about the socialist utopia it had created for mothers and children. "Our country's experience in resolving the question concerning motherhood and childhood is of great international significance," proclaimed Nikolay Aleksandrovich Tikhonov, chairman of the Council of Ministers, in a 1979 speech. "It shows that socialism alone is capable of ensuring a happy childhood, lavishing care on mothers and creating all the conditions which make it possible to combine production and public activity with the commitments of motherhood."[35]

But Soviet women did not agree. It is hard to know what exactly caused the continuing decline in fertility rates during this era. One proximate cause was certainly the stunning rise in abortions. By the 1970s, Russian women had a lifetime average of four abortions.[36] Other likely candidates include the large migrations from farms to cities and the acute housing shortages faced by young couples. Also, low fertility around the world is strongly correlated with high rates of educational attainment and workforce participation among women, which the Soviet system had achieved. More subjectively, these were dispiriting years in Soviet life, when real living standards were declining and men were increasingly turning to alcohol. But whatever the reasons, the effects of the birth strike were soon obvious, and deeply threatening to the regime.

In just one decade (1965 to 1975) the percentage of Russians under age 15 dropped from 30 to 23 percent.[37] Significantly, the loss of youth was concentrated in the core of the empire, the Russian Republic. Soviet demographers projected that ethnic Russians would become a minority group by 2000, while Muslims' share of the population would rise from 14 to 25 percent by the turn of the century.[38] Alarmed by the trend, Soviet leaders began pronouncing in the late 1970s against loss of morals and the decline of the family. "Our common responsibility for the country's future requires us to strengthen the family, to elevate the prestige of motherhood and to increase the demands made on the parents as to how their children are growing up," announced Politburo ideology chief Andrei Kirilenko at a Kremlin rally in 1979.[39]

By the early 1980s, with the birthrate continuing to slip, the Soviets launched a host of pro-natalist policies, included partially-paid maternity leave, special housing, tax breaks, and other public benefits for families with three or more children. Women over 55 who had raised five or more children were given special pensions, as well as the usual "Motherhood Medal," awarded to highly fertile women. It was a last-gasp effort to avoid a demographic meltdown, and it did not work. In retrospect, we can see that these policies persuaded many Russian women to have their children earlier, but not to have more children.[40]

With fewer workers in the pipelines, and ever more retirees, the cost of pensions skyrocketed, reaching 6 percent of all budgeted state expenditures by 1986. By 1991, nearly one in five Russians was receiving a pension, with pension levels set between 50 and 100 percent of the recipient's best year of wages.[41] No reserves stood behind these pension obligations, which meant that the system, had it endured, would have put crushing burdens on younger workers. By 1995, there would be only 2.8 workers available to support each retiree, down from 4.96 in 1959.[42]

Indeed, the demographic pressure on the Soviet system was even more intense than these numbers suggest. As Russian demographer Anatoly G. Vishnevsky points out, the decline in fertility among ethnic Russians was unprecedented in Russian history and deeply destabilizing to its political system. "In the course of many centuries," notes

Vishnevsky, "Russia has typically sent population beyond the limits of historical Russian territory. Centrifugal migration flows were the condition sine qua non of the colonization of new regions of the Russian and Soviet empire."[43]

That is for sure. For four centuries, the Russian Empire expanded at an average rate of some 55 square miles per day, fueled by rapid population growth.[44] By 1900, Russian women were still bearing, on average, more than seven children in a lifetime. But by the end of the Soviet era, they averaged just 1.7. As a result, Russia, along with the other Slavic republics, was aging more rapidly than either the Caucasus or Central Asian republics. As demographer Cynthia Buckley has pointed out, this meant the demographic future of the Soviet regime, had it survived, would have been one in which non-Slavic workers (mostly Muslims) would be supporting primarily Slavic pensioners.[45] In other words, the Soviet Union would not only have been divided by deepening ethnic and religious differences, but by generational conflict as well. Population aging did not seal the fate of the Russian people, but it defined the realm of the possible, which did not include sustaining the empire.

Today, a vicious combination of low fertility and diminishing life expectancy within the shrunken boundaries of the Russian Federation has become a huge obstacle to the country's future. As demographer Nicholas Eberstadt has noted, "Russia's health profile no longer remotely resembles that of a developed country."[46] By now Russian men live shorter lives than Indian men did in the 1970s. With deaths exceeding births by well over half, current projections show Russian population will fall by 29 percent by 2050.[47] In order to preserve the current ratio of workers to retirees, Russia would have to either raise the average retirement age to 73, or import 308 million immigrants by 2050, which would leave native Russians a minority group constituting only 27 percent of the population.[48] President Vladimir Putin has spoken about the problem in apocalyptic terms, telling his government: "we are facing the serious threat of turning into a decaying nation."[49]

Europe's Eclipse

Shortly after World War II, a special commission assembled by Britain's King George VI issued a lengthy report on the implications of Britain's falling birthrates. The commission noted that during the Industrial Revolution, "the proportion of the world's population living in Europe increased considerably," and that this "was accompanied by a more than proportionate increase in the relative importance of European civilization." The commission went on to note that "The increase in population provided both a motive for, and a means to, the development of the modern techniques of production, trade and communications on which present day European standards of living are based, for it provided both an expanding market and an expanding labour supply."[50] The Royal Commission strongly encouraged measures to encourage more births as a means of preserving the empire, but by then Britain had lost its demographic momentum, due not only to falling birthrates, but also to its tremendous casualties during two world wars. The collapse of the British Empire came soon afterwards, for the sufficient reason that Britain no longer produced enough people to occupy and rule its teeming colonies.

Today, most European countries have already passed a demographic tipping point that virtually assures not only rapid population aging, but also absolute population decline. In Spain, for example, the cohort now in its infancy (ages 0–4) is more than 42 percent smaller than the cohort now in its prime reproductive years (ages 30–34).[51] What will happen when this tiny younger generation reaches adulthood? In order to replace all members of the previous generation, each female would have to bear close to four children, as compared to the average 1.15 children produced by their mothers. Since this hardly seems likely without an extraordinary transformation in both cultural values and in the economic cost of children, the native population of Spain is all but fated to decline rapidly throughout at least the first half of this century. Together with Italy, Spain is experiencing the lowest fertility rates ever seen in recorded history.[52]

According to demographer Massimo Livi-Bacci, never in the past—not even after the plagues of the 1300s, or the slaughter of the last two world wars—has Europe's ability to renew and sustain its population been more compromised by a dwindling supply of youth.[53] The United Nations projects that Europe as a whole will lose 3.2 million in population between 2000 and 2005. In the following ten years, the population will decline by more than 11.3 million. After 2025, population loss continues compounding. Even after assuming a 33 percent increase in fertility rates over today's levels, the UN projects a loss of 28 million Europeans in just the 2040s.[54]

Already, Europe's population has become so old that it is highly vulnerable to environmental threats that in the past would have been far less lethal. In France, for example, where already 16 percent of the population is over age 65, a heat wave during the summer of 2003 caused a stunning 11,000 deaths. Dehydrated bodies, most of them elderly, overwhelmed morgues and the country's deficit-ridden health care system, forcing a soul-searching national debate over what had happened. Some critics blamed families for leaving elderly relatives alone at home while they took August vacations; others blamed France's 35-hour workweek for causing a shortage of health care personnel. "These dramas again shed light on the solitude of many of our aged or handicapped citizens," said President Jacques Chirac.[55] They also shed light on the future of aging societies, in which a working-age population must devote more and more resources to care for the increasing number of frail elders.

If European fertility rates remain unchanged, the only European countries that will avoid population loss by 2050, according to UN projections, are France, the United Kingdom, Ireland, and Luxemburg, and even these countries will face rapidly aging populations. Without an increase in its fertility rate, France's working-age population (15–64) will decline by more than 9 percent by 2050, while its elderly population will increase by 79 percent.[56]

The financial implications are staggering. In Europe there are currently 35 people of pensionable age for every 100 people of working age. By 2050, on present demographic trends, there will be 75 pensioners for every 100 workers. In Spain and Italy the ratio of pensioners to workers is projected to be one to one. Since in most major European countries pensions are financed out of current revenues, tax rates will have to soar if benefits are not cut. The Deutsche Bank calculates that average earners in Germany are already paying around 29 percent of their wages into the state pension pot, while the figure in Italy is close to 33 percent.[57]

The social implications are also staggering. By mid-century, if current trends continue, Europe will be a society in which most adults have few biological relatives. In Italy, almost three-fifths of the nation's children will have no siblings, cousins, aunts, or uncles—only parents, grandparents, and perhaps great-grandparents.[58] Even among immigrants, families with more than one child are becoming increasingly rare throughout Europe. Among foreign-born women living in Germany, for example, the total fertility rate had dropped to just 1.51 children by 1996, as compared to 1.39 among the native born.[59]

Leading minds in Europe today believe that the Continent's salvation from population aging and decline depends in large measure on attracting more women into the workforce. An extraordinary European Council meeting in 2000 adopted a ten-year plan that calls on Greece and Italy, for example, to increase their percentage of working women from 40 to 60 percent.[60] But what would such a shift mean for future fertility rates?

Among Western European countries it is true that those in which large numbers of women are in the workforce, such as Sweden, currently have higher fertility rates than those in which gender roles are more traditional, such as Italy. Even among conservative politicians, this reality has prompted the thought that, as Britain's shadow secretary of state for work and pensions, David Willetts, has proclaimed, "feminism is the new natalism."[61] Build more day care centers, offer more generous maternity leave, create more part-time jobs, and otherwise make it easier for both men and women to combine work and family, and birthrates will rise.

However, there are good reasons to be skeptical. Through generous pro-natalist policies (tax write-offs for parents, paid parental leave, and state-sponsored day care), Sweden, for example, did manage in the 1980s to move its fertility rate barely up to replacement levels. But during the 1990s fertility fell dramatically, to just 1.54 children per woman by 2000.[62] At the same time, marriage became rare in Sweden, with the annual number of marriages dropping from 109,000 in 1989 to just 39,895 in 2000.[63] Meanwhile, as in other Scandinavian countries, the rate of illegitimacy soared, to the point that, by 1995, more than half of all Swedish children were being born out of wedlock.[64] Indeed, if there is any single reason why the more traditional Catholic countries of southern Europe have lower fertility rates than the Scandinavian northland, it is probably because in countries like Spain and Italy, being a single mom still carries significant stigma. In Italy, only 8 percent of children are born out of wedlock.[65]

Achieving higher rates of fertility *and* higher rates of female workforce participation would indeed be a great boon for Europe's aging economy, especially if it did not lead to large increases in the numbers of children being raised by single parents. But is this vision really obtainable? As Richard Jackson of the Center for Strategic and International Studies notes, "Even as more women go to work, they are expected to have more babies."[66] Nor has the European Commission considered how much the female labor force participation rate would push up budgets for long-term elder care, most of which, in Europe as elsewhere, is today provided informally and for free by women.

Even after assuming no further significant declines in birthrates, the United Nations projects that the population of Sweden, which currently is the fifth oldest of any nation, may shrink by as much as 13 percent between 2000 and 2050.[67] Realizing its peril, Sweden, unlike most other Western European countries, has courageously scheduled significant future cuts in its public pension system and added a supplementary system of mandatory and funded individual retirement accounts. Imitating Sweden's once-generous cradle-to-grave welfare state thus hardly seems a solution to the Continent's fertility crisis.

Europe does still have a considerable labor supply it could tap, at least theoretically, to help close its deficit of young people. Across Europe, only 39 percent of men aged 55 to 65 still work, according to the Organization for Economic Cooperation and Development. These early retirees are beneficiaries of extremely generous pension and disability systems that were designed to ease older workers out of the workforce to make room for the young. Now, not only are these early retirees living far longer than expected, but also the supply of younger workers is shrinking. Raising retirement ages would seem the obvious reform.

Yet in large measure because of the high taxes required to pay for the pensions of those already retired, the youth unemployment rate in many European countries is in the double digits, and in nations where the populations are the oldest, such as Greece, Spain, Belgium, and Italy, more than a fifth of all younger workers are unemployed. Thus, even though raising retirement ages might seem like an obvious countermeasure to population aging, it is not necessarily achievable politically. In both France and Italy, proposed pension reforms caused governments to fall during the 1990s, and with each passing year a higher proportion of the voting population is receiving a pension. In the summer of 2003, after weeks of strikes and street protests, France did at last manage to pass a modest pension reform, but it funds only a third of its likely pension deficit through 2020.[68]

The former Communist countries of Europe at least have the advantage that their old pension schemes have already collapsed, allowing for some significant pension reforms. But a combination of dwindling fertility rates and comparatively little ability to attract new immigrants (or prevent emigrants) means that population throughout many former Warsaw Pact nations is already falling. Among the least fertile nations on earth are Armenia, where the average woman gives birth to 1.02 children; the Czech Republic, with a total fertility rate of 1.1; and Slovakia, Latvia, and Slovenia, which each have a fertility rate of 1.2. Latvia's rate of native population growth has already turned negative, as has Bulgaria's and Poland's. By 2002, the average number of births in Poland was just half what it had been in 1983, and it was no longer sufficient to offset the decline in population caused by death and emigration.[69]

Some voices on the Left in Europe have imagined that population aging and decline will actually work to empower workers. In an article for the *New Statesman*, Anthony Browne predicts that:

> A declining population—and this is why businesses fear it—will involve a gradual but significant redistribution of power from the owners of capital to the owners of labor. A declining workforce puts those who work in a far stronger position—and for those marginalized in the workforce, it can have a very dramatic effect. Companies will be forced to train the unskilled, provide family-friendly policies to retain women and to entice the elderly to stay on rather than forcing them out. People who own properties will have to rent them out at lower rates, while those who rent can choose bigger places to live.[70]

These are pleasant thoughts, but they do not bear scrutiny. If they did, younger workers, particularly in rapidly aging countries like Germany, Japan, Italy, and Spain, would be enjoying rising real wages and falling unemployment, instead of being mired in a generational depression. European labor movements would be successfully pushing to expand the welfare state instead of fighting rearguard street actions against cuts in both social benefits and labor protections demanded by socialist governments.

In the abstract, gradual population decline may seem a pleasing prospect, until one remembers that it is inevitably accompanied by rapid population aging. To meet the swelling cost of supporting a growing population of older voters, governments must either raise taxes on the young, or cut their current and future benefits, or both. Meanwhile, businesses have many ways to respond to a shrinking domestic labor supply short of raising wages, all of which are abundantly in evidence across Europe today. Faced with a shrinking or slow-growing domestic market, businesses may cut investment plans. Or they may respond with automation, or by shifting to foreign labor, either by moving jobs overseas or pressing their home government to allow more immigration. Under all these scenarios, workers in an aging society are more likely to lose their jobs than to be able to make a striking blow against capitalism.

Then, too, Europe doesn't face the prospect of gradual population decline; it faces the prospect of rapid and compounding loss of population unless birthrates soon turn upward. Like population growth, population decline operates on a geometric curve that compounds with each generation. If Europe's current fertility rate of around 1.5 births per woman persists until 2020, this will result in 88 million fewer Europeans by the end of the century.[71] To adopt a somewhat poignant metaphor: If Europe were a woman, her biological clock would be rapidly running down. It is not too late to adopt more children, but they won't look like her.

Japan, China, Russia, and the European nations have all experienced a succession of violent societal upheavals in the twentieth century, ranging from war and famine to brutal social engineering. Yet the ultimate force behind their undoing is now present in virtually every nation: the persistent fall of fertility rates and rapid population aging that comes with a breakdown in family life.

7

The Cost of Children

The casual observer of American life in the early twenty-first century might easily conclude that the country was poised for another baby boom. "Oh, baby! Look how your ranks grow," proclaims the headline of a recent newspaper article, which notes (falsely) that American fertility rates are now the highest in 30 years.[1] Add to this the abundant signs of "baby lust" we see in the culture today: the crowded waiting rooms at fertility clinics, the elaborate baby showers, the emergence of designer baby clothes, the celebrity moms like Calista Flockhart flaunting their long-awaited "trophy babies" in press releases, or the celebrity dads like Paul Reiser writing bestselling paeans to the joys of fatherhood. Over the years, the polling firm Yankelovich Partners has repeatedly asked respondents whether having a child is an experience that every woman should have. In 1979, a mere 45 percent of baby-boom women agreed with that statement. When Yankelovich measured it most recently among Gen-X women, 68 percent, more than two-thirds, agreed.[2]

Then there is the abundant evidence that significantly more women are placing commitment to family over the demands of a career. The labor force participation rate for mothers with infant children fell from

a record high of 59 percent in 1998 to 55 percent in 2000, the first significant decline since the Census Bureau developed the indicator in
1976.[3] The number of children being raised by stay-at-home moms rose
by 23 percent between 1993 and 2000.[4] The trend is already leading
some observers to herald a prestige reversal among American mothers.
"Ten years ago," notes cultural commentator Neil Howe, "a jobless
mom was more likely to be poor, single, and on welfare than a mom
with a job. Today, the jobless mom is acquiring a new reputation for
leisure, for affluence, and for dedication to hearth and home."[5]

Husbands and wives in two-parent families are also spending more
time with their children today than 20 years ago, according to new research, but spending less time on sleeping.[6] At all levels of society, we
also see growing and unprecedented concern for the safety and welfare
of children. These range from Arnold Schwarzenegger's statement
that "I think that children should have first call on our Treasury," to
"Amber alerts," "Megan's laws," mandated child seats, "zero tolerance"
school codes, and the proliferation of wireless devices like the "Wher-
ify" bracelet for tracking children by satellite. Similarly, the spread of
homeschooling, record toy sales, and the high place of educational reform on the national agenda all demonstrate that today's children are
increasingly prized and protected.

But what do these trends mean for the future direction of American
fertility rates? Could it be, for example, that the growing prestige in
some circles of the full-time mom, as well as the mounting societal
preoccupation with child safety, reflect the relative scarcity and high
"price" of children, rather than presage a coming return of large families? As children account for a declining share of the population, there
comes a predictable increase in concern, by both parents and society
as a whole, about the quality of their individual lives. Each child becomes celebrated, protected, as well as pushed and prodded as never
before to succeed in all realms of life. Think of that new social type,
the harried suburban working mom, who chauffeurs her children from
one organized event to the next—soccer, ballet, cello lessons, Prince-

ton Review classes—even as she uses her cell phone to explain to her office why she's running late and beseeches her husband to pick up a meal at Boston Chicken. With this level of parental investment now approaching the norm among middle-class American families, how much surplus time, energy, and money is left for rearing additional children?

Parenthood, to be sure, is often a great source of joy, companionship, and pride. Many parents also profit socially through their children. In our insular society, there are few easier ways to meet and befriend other like-minded adults than by arranging play dates with each other's children, or by volunteering at school. After the birth of a first child, a young couple may also find their own parents much more interested in helping out with a down payment for a first house and with other forms of assistance. As one demographic study concludes, "Children create social capital by establishing new relations among persons (parents, grandparents, aunts, uncles, siblings, friends) that are then available to parents as resources that they can use to achieve their interests."[7]

For all these reasons and more, few people intentionally remain childless. According to studies by demographer Robert Schoen and others, among unmarried white women, only those who place both a very low value on the importance of friends and extended family, and a very high value on their own careers, are likely to say they never want children.[8] Yet what does this prove? There are many expensive, high-status consumer items most people yearn to possess—lakefront vacation homes, yachts, racehorses, best-of-breed show dogs, to name a few. Owning such items might enormously increase your social capital, giving you access to whole new networks of approving, well-connected friends and long-lost family members. But just because such consumer items may have enduring value doesn't mean that you can afford even one of them, let alone two or three.

It would be foolish to suppose that money alone can explain a question as subtle and mysterious as what motivates human beings to procreate. Yet it would also be foolish to ignore the economic dimension of a decision involving, even on the low side, many hundreds of thousands of dollars. As I will demonstrate in the rest of this chapter, the cost of children is now rising so rapidly in the United States and elsewhere that long-term population loss will become nearly inevitable without a more equitable sharing of the economic burdens and benefits of parenthood.

Million Dollar Babies

What does it cost to raise a child in the United States today? Assuming no inflation, and not counting the cost of prenatal care and childbirth, a typical, middle-income, husband-wife family in the United States will spend $211,370 to raise a single child born in 2001 from age 0 to 17, according to estimates by the U.S. Department of Agriculture.[9] This calculation does not include any provision for college.

If America were still a society in which women had few economic opportunities outside the home, the cost of children might include only such direct expenses. But as women's economic opportunities expand, so does the opportunity cost of motherhood. Consider Sherri and Mike, a hypothetical middle-class, dual-income/no children ("DINK") family. Two years into their marriage, both were 30 years old and working full-time, each making $45,000 a year. But then came baby. Sherri immediately quit her job to stay home with Mike Jr., causing their family income to fall by half. After Mike Jr. reaches kindergarten, she hopes to begin working half-time. But remembering her own high jinks as a "latch key" kid growing up in the 1980s, she does not plan to return to full-time work until Junior goes off to college.

What is the opportunity cost of these life choices? Let us assume, optimistically, that Sherri's job skills do not become obsolete during the years she takes off to be a stay-at-home mom, and that she is therefore able to make as much money per hour when she returns to part-time work as she did before. But let's also assume, realistically, that because of her part-time "mommy track" status, her average annual wage increases come to 2 percent instead of a possible 4 percent she could have earned as a childless and committed full-time professional. In that event, her commitment to motherhood will wind up costing her $823,736 in forgone income by the time her child reaches 18. Combined with the $200,000 the Department of Agriculture estimates this couple will likely spend on their child's clothing, health care, and other needs, their economic sacrifice will come to more than $1 million even before the child finishes high school (see Table 7.1).

By then Sherri will be 48. It's possible she will instantly be able to go back to full-time employment and earn as much as she would have had she never taken time off for mothering. But it's not likely. And because of that, the opportunity cost of motherhood will most likely continue

TABLE 7.1 **Cost of Raising a Single Middle-Class Child in the United States (dollars)**

Age of Child	Total Cost	Housing	Food	Transportation	Clothing	Health Care	Child Care and Education	Miscellaneous	Forgone Wages
0	56,197	4,191	1,352	1,438	533	756	1,711	1,215	45,000
1	57,997	4,191	1,352	1,438	533	756	1,711	1,215	46,800
2	59,869	4,191	1,352	1,438	533	756	1,711	1,215	48,672
3	62,101	4,154	1,562	1,401	521	719	1,897	1,228	50,619
4	64,126	4,154	1,562	1,401	521	719	1,897	1,228	52,644
5	43,732	4,154	1,562	1,401	521	719	1,897	1,228	32,249
6	45,472	4,042	1,984	1,562	583	818	1,215	1,277	33,989
7	47,290	4,042	1,984	1,562	583	818	1,215	1,277	35,808
8	49,191	4,042	1,984	1,562	583	818	1,215	1,277	37,708
9	51,090	3,757	2,344	1,649	645	893	794	1,314	39,694
10	53,165	3,757	2,344	1,649	645	893	794	1,314	41,769
11	55,332	3,757	2,344	1,649	645	893	794	1,314	43,937
12	58,527	4,067	2,356	1,798	1,079	893	583	1,550	46,201
13	60,892	4,067	2,356	1,798	1,079	893	583	1,550	48,566
14	63,361	4,067	2,356	1,798	1,079	893	583	1,550	51,036
15	66,189	3,497	2,616	2,282	967	955	1,004	1,252	53,615
16	68,882	3,497	2,616	2,282	967	955	1,004	1,252	56,308
17	71,694	3,497	2,616	2,282	967	955	1,004	1,252	59,120
Total	$1,035,107	$71,126	$36,642	$30,392	$12,983	$15,103	$21,613	$23,510	$823,736

NOTES: Direct expeditures are drawn from United States Department of Agriculture estimates for husband/wife families earning between $39,100 and $65,8000.

* Assumes mother or father quits a $45,000 a year job to stay home with the child from ages 0–4. When the child is age 5, one parent returns to half-time employment at same hourly wage, but receives 2 percent instead of 4 percent annual wage increases.

mounting throughout her lifetime. Even in retirement, any pension in-come will likely be reduced because of her lower life-time earnings.

But what if Sherri, or any woman in her position, decided instead to hire a nanny or place her child in day care? Then the opportunity cost of her having a child would be diminished, but by no means elimi-nated. Working women with children earn substantially less than working women who are childless. Much of this is easily explained by the fact that working mothers are more likely to take time off from their careers, to work part-time, or to gravitate into low-paying "fe-male" professions that are mother friendly. Yet even among women who are equally educated, equally experienced, equally committed to the workforce, and work in the same profession at the same level, those who have children suffer lower wages on average than those who don't.

Researchers estimate, after controlling for all these factors, that the wage penalty for motherhood runs about 5–9 percent per child in the United States. How much of this is due to exhaustion, or employer discrimination, or other factors, we are free to speculate. But as ap-plied to Sherri, this finding suggests that even if she had remained fully committed to her career, she could have expected her cumulative wages over the 17 years following the birth of her only child to be re-duced by anywhere from $57,700 to $100,800, simply as a result of her decision to become a mother.[10]

And that would still leave her with large bills to be paid for child care. In 2000, a 50-state survey by the Children's Defense Fund found that child care costs an average of $4,000 to $6,000 per year, and in some places much more. In 1998, average annual cost of child care for a 4-year-old in Boston was $8,121, or more than double the average annual tuition cost of attending a public college in Massachusetts at the time.[11] According to a study by the Urban Institute, among the 48 percent of working families with children under 13 that pay for child care, the average monthly expense amounts to 9 percent of family in-come, making child care most likely the second largest budget cate-gory after housing.

Some economies of scale are available to parents who have more than one child. Later children can wear hand-me-downs and can share toys and a bunk bed. Closely spaced children may be able to share a nanny. A stay-at-home mom may be able to raise more than one child without forgoing more than a few extra years of paid employment. But if children truly are "cheaper by the dozen," they are not much so. A typical middle-class family that produces the 2.1 children required to sustain the population clearly faces a financial sacrifice measured in the millions.

Accounting for the Baby Boom

In the 1920s and 1930s, birthrates were also declining rapidly in most Western countries. Major economists at the time, such as Harvard's Alvin Hansen, brooded darkly that fewer babies meant shrinking consumer demand, and correctly blamed declining population growth for deepening and prolonging the Great Depression.[12] Demographer Enid Charles, in her 1934 book *The Twilight of Parenthood*, wrote that "in place of the Malthusian menace of over-population there is now a real danger of under-population." Blaming the low fertility of the time on what she called the "acquisitive society," Charles observed, "Statistics clearly show that the choice between a Ford and a baby is usually made in favor of the Ford."[13] But then came the great American baby boom.

Could it happen again? Maybe, but the economic and social conditions most demographers believe created the baby boom generation are absent today. In the early post-war years, millions of young men and women with wedding and family plans long deferred by the war had a chance to catch up. Moreover, the early post-war years were also marked by two trends that rarely come together. First, having grown up during the Great Depression and endured the privations of World War II, young adults of the 1950s had comparatively low consumer expectations. Many people expected the economy would slump back into recession as soon as the war ended. Yet instead, the economy boomed, and real wages, particularly among young men, rose sharply.

Indeed, young men of the early to mid-1950s, even after just a few years in the workforce, frequently found themselves earning as much as, if not more than, their fathers. In 1956, for example, men age 25–34 earned 97 percent as much on average as men aged 45–54. By comparison, in 1980 men aged 25–34 earned only 79 percent as much.[14] One reason young men did so well compared to their fathers in the 1950s may have been that they were in relatively short supply due to the low birthrates of the 1920s and 1930s. Other reasons include a strong labor movement and the educational benefits offered under the GI Bill, which created the largest one-generation jump in educational achievement in American history.

Generous veterans benefits and other government subsidies also helped make homeownership in rapidly expanding, child-friendly suburbs easily within reach of millions of young couples. Meanwhile, with educational and career opportunities for women still quite limited, the perceived trade-off between raising children and fulfilling one's consumer expectations came to seem nearly nonexistent. Indeed, with many new labor-saving products coming into the home—automatic washers and dryers, vacuum cleaners, and frozen foods—housewives had more time to invest in children. Unlike almost all other times in American history, most young couples could easily have more children than their parents did *and* enjoy a rising standard of living undreamt of during their own childhood years.[15]

This widespread experience of rapid and unexpected upward mobility began to fade by the late 1960s. The absolute level of affluence enjoyed by most Americans, young and old alike, continued to increase almost without interruption, but the gap between what young males took home and what men in their 40s and 50s made widened dramatically. There are many reasons why this might be so, ranging from the increased competition from women's labor, to widening premiums given to seniority in a complex society, to a lower differential in educational achievement between fathers and sons. But whatever the reasons, the phenomenon continues to create a sensation among many young couples that they will be lucky to ever live as well as their parents do, particularly if both do not work. As demographer Diane Macunovich notes, since 1970 young white men in the United States have experienced, on average, a 40 percent decline in their income relative to their fathers, while young African American men experienced a 60 percent decline. Today, a typical 29-year-old man in the United States earns less than 50 percent of his father's current income.[16]

Empty McMansions

Americans who raised children during the 1950s are frequently impatient with complaints from today's young people that they cannot afford to start a family. How can a husband and wife who live in a house with three times the floor space of a typical Levittown starter home of the 1950s, with central air, a Jacuzzi, and a three-car garage, claim that they can't afford to have children? Why not just get a smaller house, or forgo those Caribbean vacations?

The answer often is that they could, but the psychological and social costs would be daunting. The first reason is that poverty and affluence are relative terms. People feel affluent not when they achieve some absolute standard of living, but when their material wealth exceeds their expectations. In 1949, a young couple moving out of the city into a $350-down $30-a-month starter home in Levittown felt upwardly mobile. The house might be cramped and sterile, but it was a big step up from living in a tenement. Owning it meant providing for your children in a way your parents probably never could provide for you—the essence of the "American Dream."

But today the same house has a different social meaning, at least for the millions of younger Americans who grew up in similar houses during the last forty years or so. For them, such a house is no longer a symbol of success and upward mobility, but of middling accomplishment—of doing no better than one's parents—even though the house may by now have been upgraded with central air, a finished attic, and redwood deck. And if it turns out that a young Gen-X couple moving into this fifty-year-old house cannot make the payments on one paycheck alone, then they might very well feel financially stressed and unable to "afford" to have children.

The prevalence of two-paycheck families today also creates a circumstance under which economic growth itself actually reduces incentives for childbearing. In a traditional, one-income family, in which the wife concentrates on child rearing and household management, her role benefits her husband by allowing him to work longer hours and concentrate on his career more than he otherwise could. As such, when her husband earns a raise, the economic value of her role increases because her husband (and the household) would have to give up more money should she cease to fulfill it. Under these circumstances, any increase in family income tends to encourage more births because the family is better able to afford children. By contrast, in two-paycheck families, an increase in family income tends to discourage fertility, by driving up the opportunity cost (in both free time and forgone wages) of either spouse tending to children.

Fear of divorce is another major disincentive to having children. Here again, the emergence of the two-paycheck family discourages fertility by reducing the material incentives to remain married (or even get married in the first place). In a traditional family, in which the spouse with the lower earning potential works in the home, both husband and wife are better off materially than if they lived in separate households. But when both husband and wife work, this is not necessarily so, particularly if they earn roughly the same income. They may face the added expense of maintaining two households if they divorce, but neither spouse is threatened by a substantial loss of income.

Adding to the incentives to avoid or defer parenthood is the rising minimum threshold of investment society expects parents to make, and that they themselves often want to make, in their children's education. In 1947, Americans were going to college in record numbers, but still only 10 percent of men aged 20–24, and 3.4 percent of women, were enrolled in school.[17] By 2000, the numbers had reached 64.9 percent for men and 68.7 percent for women.[18] When the baby boom was occurring, the majority of parents did not expect to have to pay for their sons' college education, let alone for their daughters. Today, even many parents who themselves have never finished high school feel responsible for at least trying to help their children through college, because college education has by and large become a middle-class norm—indeed a near requirement for reaching or remaining in the middle class.

This is no small difference. When combined with room and board fees, the annual cost of attending a state university as of this writing averages $9,663 and is rising by 9.6 percent a year. The average cost of attending a private 4-year institution during the 2002-2003 school year was $23,751.[19] For some families, these costs may be offset in part by scholarships, but the vast majority must rely primarily on student loans or their own savings. Moreover, the cost of raising a college-educated, middle-class child may well not end there, especially if his or her education is largely financed through student loans. In 2002, surveys of graduating college seniors found that 60 percent anticipated returning home to live with their parents, and 21 percent intended to stay for more than a year.[20] Today, according to Census Bureau data, 12.5 percent of men and 7.9 percent of women between the ages of 25 and 34 live with their parents—double the rate of 50 years ago.[21]

The ever-increasing cost and importance of higher education works to undermine fertility in another way as well: It means that many young couples in their prime reproductive years feel compelled to put off having children so that they can complete college or graduate school, or pay off their student loans. Consider the case of Jean A. Schoonover, a 32-year-old doctor practicing in southern Maryland. Married to an ophthalmologist, Schoonover and her husband together owe more than a quarter of a million dollars in student loans, after four years of college, four years of medical school, and four years of residency. They live in a low-cost suburb, but can barely afford a $400-a-month payment for their Ford Escape pickup truck. "When I am 47, I hope to be out of debt and to begin saving for retirement," complains Schoonover. "It is not clear yet when we will be able to afford to have children."[22]

Similarly, changing social norms about child safety increase the minimum threshold of investment parents must make in children. In the 1950s, a harried mother who failed to buckle up her four-year-old was the norm; cars did not have seatbelts. Now if she doesn't have a properly installed child-safety seat she's in violation of the law. And if she doesn't drive a heavy, late-model SUV or minivan with childproof door locks, back-up sensing system, airbag shut-off switch, integrated child booster seats, and crash-resistant door pillars, she herself may feel she is recklessly endangering her children's safety. In the 1950s, young children routinely rode their bikes in the streets, played unattended in parks and sandlots, and made their own way back and forth to school. Today, even parents who have paid big bucks to live in "safe" suburbs feel compelled to monitor their children's movements (or pay someone else to do so) as never before in history.

Finally, today's parents face tax burdens that would have been unthinkable during the baby boom years. In 1950, the Social Security tax rate was 1.5 percent for the employer and 1.5 percent for the employee, with all wages above $3,000 tax free. This created a maximum tax of $144 per worker (about $1,100 in today's money). By 2003, the Social Security tax rate had increased more than fourfold, and the threshold of taxation had risen to $87,000, creating a maximum tax of $11,136—a 912 percent increase even after adjusting for inflation. Medicare, which didn't exist before 1965, now consumes an additional 2.9 percent of payroll, with no wages of any amount free of taxation.

In recent years, parents have gained a new federal child care credit and a few other targeted tax benefits (Hope and Lifetime Learning Education Credits, for example), but these measures still leave the tax burden on families many times higher than it was during the years of the baby boom. In 1955, the median American family with one earner paid 17.3 percent of its income in taxes. By 1998, largely because of the increase in state and local taxes, as well as in the cost of Social Security and Medicare, the median family with one earner paid 37.6 percent of its income in taxes, and 39 percent if it was a two-paycheck family.[23]

Families will pay much more in the future if the costs of Social Security and Medicare continue to rise. By the time children born in 2000 turn 30, a payroll tax as high as 28.25 percent may well be required just to finance the cost of Social Security and of Medicare's hospital insurance program alone, according to official projections. These projections assume no new benefits, such as for prescription drugs.[24]

Social Security and Medicare certainly relieve many young couples of responsibility for directly supporting their own aging parents, and in that way may help to make the cost of children more affordable for some. But a huge proportion of the benefits distributed by Social Security and Medicare go to seniors who otherwise would not be receiving financial aid from their children. Many don't have children, or are estranged from them. Many more are well-off enough that they wouldn't think of taking money from their kids. Moreover, to the extent that Social Security and Medicare allow seniors to live independently of their children, the programs help reduce what was once an important source of support for parents: the free child care once commonly provided by grandmothers and other older members of the extended family. Finally, because these programs distribute benefits to parents and nonparents alike, they effectively transfer much of the wealth parents create by investing in their children to those who remain childless. In all these ways, Social Security and Medicare undoubtedly make children less affordable.

Are DINKs Selfish?

Falling male wages, high divorce rates, rising expectations of what it means to be a "responsible" parent, rising educational standards, rising taxes, and the loss of grandparents as a significant source of child care, go a long way toward explaining why so many of today's young couples feel they have to at least defer the cost of raising children. It is easy to dismiss such people as "selfish yuppies." It is also easy to be jealous of the lifestyle enjoyed by many dual-income/no kids couples, or "DINKs." Without the multimillion-dollar liability of children, even young couples of comparatively modest means can often afford many big-ticket luxury items. These might include a fair-sized McMansion, two BMWs, and regular vacations to the Caribbean, all of which could easily cost less than raising 2.1 children. As new and creative uses of leisure time mount—adventure tourism in Belize, high-cuisine restaurants, casino gambling, mountain biking, bed and breakfasts—those stuck at home with kids sometimes cannot help but be envious of those "selfish DINKS" who are not.

The charge of selfishness is hardly new. In 1893, the American physician John Billings argued that the declining fertility rates of that era could be explained by

> the great increase in the use of things which were formerly considered as luxuries, but which have now become almost necessities. The greater temptations for expenditure for the purpose of securing or maintaining social position, and the corresponding greater cost of family life in what may be called the lower middle classes, lead to the desire to have fewer children in order that they may be each better provided for, or perhaps, in some cases, from the purely selfish motives of desire to avoid care and trouble and of having more to spend on social pleasures.[25]

Yet the charge of selfishness is often misplaced. As shown before, few Americans intend to remain childless. The more common reason people wind up without children, or with only one child, seems to be that they defer parenthood until they believe they are economically and emotionally ready for children, and then it is too late. In the typical pattern, today's young men and women wait much longer than their parents did before marrying or even committing to a relationship, and then don't plan to have children until their late 20s or 30s, when they hope life will favor them with secure careers and a comfortable home appropriate for raising a family. Yet for many, separation, job loss, or infertility upset their best-laid plans.

Strong evidence of this pattern emerges from recent poll data. Today in the United States, for example, only 4 percent of adults say they will be satisfied if they never have children, according to a recent Gallup poll, and among those who have reached middle age without producing children, the vast majority express regret. Among the childless Americans aged 41 years and older in 2003, for example, 76 percent say they wish they had had children, up from 70 percent in 1990.[26]

Clearly, there is a large and growing frustration with the rising cost and difficulty of family formation, not only among the childless, but among parents as well. In the United States and in every European nation, for example, women aged 40 in 2000 were coming to the end of their reproductive years having produced fewer children than they intended, according to surveys. American women born in 1960, for instance, desired an average of 2.3 children, but wound up producing only 1.9. In Europe, the gap between the number of children women of this generation wanted and the number they actually produced is even greater. Indeed, if European women now in their 40s had been able to produce their ideal number of children, the continent would face no prospect of population loss.[27]

Adding to the increase in childlessness are common misperceptions about how quickly fertility declines with age. According to one study, 88 percent of American women overestimate by 5 to 10 years the age at which female infertility begins.[28] Even among health care professionals, nearly 40 percent believe that a woman's ability to bear children does not begin declining until age 40.[29] Yet the most recent studies show that a woman's fertility begins to drop at age 27, and by age 30 can decline by as much as 50 percent.[30]

Another factor surely must be the ease with which, under current divorce laws and reigning cultural norms, fathers can skip out on their wives and children. Nature may want women to have their first child while they are still in their late teens or early 20s. But any woman who defers her education to get married and raise children at that age faces high odds of winding up an uneducated single mom dependent on child support payments that rarely, if ever, come. The contribution of the "deadbeat dad" phenomenon to poverty among women and children may be exaggerated, but the fear of abandonment that many young women feel is nonetheless real, justified, and a powerful disincentive to motherhood. As author Ann Crittenden has noted, "The main cause of poverty in the United States is motherhood."[31]

Childlessness is thus not always, or even often, a sign of selfishness or excess materialism. Most people want to provide for their children at least as well as their parents provided for them. Most people also want their children to enjoy at least the same opportunities, security, and luxuries as their neighbors' children enjoy. Many young couples, not wanting to put their children through the ordeal of divorce, defer starting a family until they are sure that their marriage will work. These goals may be ever more difficult to achieve while still of child-bearing age, but they are not necessarily self-centered: Indeed, they may well be altruistic—born of a moral sense that one should not have children until one has the security to raise them according to society's prevailing norms.

Individuals have no control over the economic and social forces that make the cost of forming a traditional family or of being a responsible parent seem increasingly beyond their reach. They also have no control over the grief and emptiness that often results when one realizes one has missed the chance to have children. The high cost of parenthood largely results from institutional arrangements designed to better society—equality for women, expanding educational opportunities, income support for the elderly, and heightened concern for child safety and welfare. If these arrangements lead to a breakdown of the family, falling fertility rates, and unsustainable population aging, that's a political problem, not a moral failing.

The Future of Marriage

Today, another social trend is emerging that may further drive down marriage and fertility rates in the United States and elsewhere. Among the current younger generation, women are outperforming men in school. As *Business Week's* Michelle Conlin notes: "Now, in every state, every income bracket, every racial and ethnic group, and most industrialized Western nations, women reign, earning an average 57 percent of all BAs and 58 percent of all master's degrees in the U.S. alone."[32] In the United States there are now 136 women enrolled in graduate schools for every 100 men—a number that will rise to 146 women per 100 men by 2012, according to the U.S. Department of Education.[33]

What are the implications of this trend for future fertility? We know that today young people in the United States express a much higher preference for parenthood than did their counterparts 30 years ago. Particularly striking is a recent Gallup poll that asked Americans, "What do you think is the ideal number of children families should have?" Among Americans aged 18–29, a stunning 42 percent said 3 or more. The desire for large families is much stronger among this age group than among older generations. Only 29 percent of Americans aged 50–64, for example, think 3 or more children is ideal.[34]

There are also emerging signs of increasing social conservatism among the young, and a preference for more distinct gender roles. William Strauss and Neil Howe, in their studies of today's young Americans, label them a "GI redux, a youthful update of the generation against which the Boomers fought 30 years ago." Since the early 1990s, they note, the rate of violent crime among teens is down 70 percent, the rate of teen pregnancy and abortion is down 30 percent, and the rate of sexual activity in high school is down 20 percent. All these trends suggest an emerging generation that is highly conformist, and that will yearn to form traditional families.[35]

But against all this we have not only the mounting cost of children, but also the increasing mismatch in educational attainment between young men and women. Because of their superior education, many of today's young women will likely find it difficult to find a husband who is as well credentialed. Put alternatively, many of today's young men who are dropping out of school will find that a high proportion of the women they are attracted to either are unimpressed by their accomplishments or are too intimidating or assertive to consider taking as a wife.

No doubt, both sexes within this generation will figure out how to readjust their expectations for love and family. Women may begin to give more weight to physical appearance in selecting a mate; men may give more weight to the economic security an accomplished wife can offer. Yet as any sociology textbook will affirm, women tend to be reluctant to "marry down," and both sexes seek marriage partners who will enhance their social standing.[36] The dramatic relative decline of male achievement within the so-called "millennial" generation thus appears from this vantage point to pose a major obstacle to any large-scale renewal of traditional marriage and family life, no matter how much today's young adults may yearn for it.

Consider that the low-fertility countries of Europe all have an even greater gender gap in educational attainment. In Italy, for example, only 19 percent of men aged 22–24 are still in school, as opposed to 27 percent of women the same age. In Spain among 18–21 year olds, only 28 percent of men have not dropped out, as opposed to 40 percent of women.[37] Similarly, consider that in the United States, the relative decline in male educational attainment first emerged among African Americans and, as many commentators have noted, it led to steep declines in marriage rates and more recently in fertility rates.[38] Among African Americans, 30 percent of 40- to 44-year-old women have never married (as compared to 9 percent of white women of the same age) owing in part to the lack of black men with the same academic credentials and earning potential.[39] Albeit for a different reason, the United States and Europe thus may face the same problem of "unmarriagable men" that China does, and with the same stark implications for social stability and population aging.

"A Handmaid's Tale"

With the benefit of hindsight, we can see how anomalous the post-war baby boom phenomenon was. In the United States, fertility rates have fallen almost without interruption since 1810. After the baby boom peaked in 1957, fertility rates simply returned to their long-term downward trend. Though we can expect slight increases in the fertility rate from time to time, there simply is no reason to expect any reversal of the larger downward tendency without a dramatic change in the economics of parenthood and in institutional arrangements. As the experience of more and more nations shows, there is no law of nature ensuring that humans will create enough children to replace any given population. When the economic and social incentives to procreate and raise families are weak or negative, as they increasingly are in most nations, and when people know how to achieve sexual gratification without producing children, we have no reason to assume that birthrates won't continue to fall below replacement level.

Historically, the way societies maintained population size was not by counting on "mother love" but on coercion. Norms against premarital sex and homosexuality, taboos on abortion and infanticide, restrictions on women's ability to own property or participate in the paid labor force, and a denial of status to individuals deemed too "immature" or "selfish" to reproduce often drove members of both sexes into loveless marriages that produced large numbers of children. Call it the "Taliban solution." Even when the Taliban ruled Afghanistan, the average Afghan woman still bore fewer children than mother or grandmother did, but such a regime of sexual repression was able to keep fertility rates well above replacement levels.[40] The question is, can egalitarian societies find egalitarian solutions to the fertility crisis, or is the future a "Handmaid's Tale" of coerced reproduction and rising fundamentalist domination?[41]

8

The Cost of Aging

I f it's true that there will be fewer babies in the future, is it not also true that most of us are going to wind up living much longer than our parents and grandparents? With the human life span expanding so dramatically, maybe society doesn't need as many babies. We can all just work into our 90s and beyond and not worry that there are fewer younger workers in the pipeline.

It is, indeed, common to hear these days that human beings are in the midst of a "longevity revolution." In his popular book by that title, Theodore Roszak, once know for his celebrations of the 1960s youth culture, turns his eye to aging baby boomers and predicts that "by the middle of the twenty-first century, those who fail to reach the age of one hundred (unless by reason of accident) are apt to fall into a new medical category: *premature death.*"[1] Yet while such predictions of pro-longevity are made in every generation, the assumption that today's adults can look forward to living dramatically longer lives turns out to have little substance. "The gap between what gerontologists know and what the public believes has never been wider," notes gerontologist Harry R. Moody of the International Longevity Center. "Whatever the scientific evidence, prolongevity is an idea that simply will not die (no matter how often actual human beings do)."[2]

Yes, we are living in a graying world. But the overwhelming reason that populations are aging is not because adults are living substantially longer, but because they are having fewer children.

It is easy to understand how most people derive the opposite impression. How often have you heard statistics such as, "The life expectancy of Americans has increased by more than 30 years in just the last century"? That statistic is literally true, but highly misleading. The limits of the human life span have hardly changed in centuries. Even if Methusulah did not really live to be 969, many individuals survived to extraordinary old age long before the miracles of modern medicine were available. To cite just one example, the longest-living member of the U.S. Senate to date is not Strom Thurmond, who died in 2003, but Cornelius Cole, who was born in 1822 and lived to be 102. Of all U.S. senators born in the eighteenth and nineteenth centuries, a total of eighty-eight lived to be 90 years or older. What has changed since the nineteenth century is that, mostly because of dramatic reductions in infant mortality, many more humans are surviving childhood and thereby getting a chance to become elderly.

In 1900, more than one out of ten children born in the United States died before age 1. Today, less than 1 in 140 does.[3] This is the revolutionary change—largely completed in the developed world by the mid-twentieth century—that accounts for nearly all the reported gains in life expectancy. Because people are so much less likely to die as infants, they have substantially improved chances of living to, say, age 65. But from this it does not follow that old people are living substantially longer than in the past. Indeed, since 1950 life expectancy for those who have already reached age 65 has increased by just 3.45 years in the United States, and the rate of increase has been slowing dramatically. In the 1970s, life expectancy at age 65 improved by 7.2 percent; in the 1980s, by 5.2 percent; and in the 1990s by only 2.6 percent. Indeed, according to the Social Security Administration, life expectancy among women over age 65 actually declined by a few months between 1992 and 2000. By 2002, life expectancy for women over age 65 was still shorter than it had been in 1991.[4]

The increase in life expectancy at older ages, as modest as it has been, has profound implications for the cost of pensions, to be sure. Since the mid-twentieth century, Germany's increase in life expectancy at age 50, for example, has added nearly a third to the total cost of the public pension system. But much more than increased life expectancy, the significant factors causing the aging crisis around the globe are the fall in birthrates and the massive increases in health care spending that result in little gain in productive life.

Especially in the United States, with its expensive and stunningly ineffective health care system, even modest increases in the size of the elderly population can bring about huge increases in health care expenditures without producing any improvement in public health. Indeed, the current course of modern medicine in the United States is in many ways reducing the health of the population through overtreatment, medical errors, and the fostering of widespread overconfidence in the ability of medicine to overcome behavioral and environmental threats to health. To understand this, it is necessary to recognize the many false impressions that inform most people's thinking about the history and future of medicine.

Why We Live

In 1966 *Time* magazine surveyed medical leaders to get their predictions regarding what the health of the American people would be like by the year 2000. "Nearly all experts agree," the magazine reported, "that bacterial and viral diseases will have been virtually wiped out. Probably atherosclerotic heart disease will also have been eliminated. Cells have only a few secrets still hidden from probers, who are confident that before the year 2000, they will have found the secret that causes cancer."[5]

Today, as *Time* and similar publications still report, some medical researchers continue to promise an imminent breakthrough in extending human life spans, this time by using gene therapies and other exotic technologies. I hope to persuade you in this chapter to be skeptical about such claims. In the face of falling fertility rates and rapid population aging, it is very tempting to believe that increases in longevity will save the day. We may not produce enough babies to reproduce ourselves, so goes the comforting thought, but thanks to the marvels of modern medicine, we will all just work that much longer. Yet while there are many ways to promote more productive aging and to increase human life expectancy, they barely involve medicine per se.

In order to think clearly about the future of old age, it is important to be free of a common misperception about health care. During the twentieth century the health and life expectancy of the average American improved dramatically. But what role did improvements in medicine play in this achievement? A surprisingly small one. Experts in public health widely agree that medical care contributed no more than 5 of the 30 extra years of life expectancy achieved during the twentieth century.[6]

This finding may seem counterintuitive, but with a little reflection on how living and working conditions have changed over the last one hundred years, we see it is common sense. In cities across America at the turn of the twentieth century, the air stank of coal dust, manure, and rotting garbage. Lacking indoor plumbing, most people still used latrines and outhouses. In the work place as late as 1913, industrial accidents were killing 23,000 Americans a year, a fatality rate since reduced by 90 percent. The only available milk or meat was often spoiled; the water supply was untreated. Fully 16 percent of the population was infected by trichimella, a dangerous parasite found in meat, while food-borne bacteria such as such as salmonella, clostridium, and staphylococcus killed millions—especially children, 14 percent of whom died before their first birthday.[7]

During the first half of the twentieth century, living and working conditions vastly improved for most Americans, and this, combined with public health measures such as mosquito control, quarantines, and food inspections, led to a dramatic decline in premature death. In 1900, 194 of every 100,000 U.S. residents died from tuberculosis. By 1940, before any effective medical treatment for tuberculosis had become available, reduced overcrowding in tenements combined with quarantine efforts had decreased the death rate by three-fourths.

In the second half of the twentieth century, medical care became enormously more sophisticated and effective, particularly in managing pain and preventing sudden death from traumatic injury, infection, and heart attacks. Yet the overall gains to public health were still modest. The greatest gains came from strategic vaccination campaigns, which virtually eliminated diseases that previously were common in the United States, including diphtheria, tetanus, smallpox, measles, mumps, rubella, meningitis, and polio. But these triumphs involve treating people before they are sick. If one looks at the actual ability of modern medicine to cure people, the results are depressing. The consensus estimate, accepted by the Centers for Disease Control (CDC), is that medicine has contributed only two of the seven years in added life expectancy achieved since 1950.[8]

How can this be? Don't we all know someone whose life was saved in a hospital? Probably. Strictly speaking, however, no one's life is ever really saved; at best it is extended. The life span of my son, for example, who spent the first 60 days of his life in a neonatal intensive care unit, may have been extended by medical intervention 90 years or more. But the potential extension of life is much less for a 50-year-old, and still less for a 90-year-old.

What does this have to do with the role of medicine in improving public health? The resources of the medical system are concentrated on the elderly, who consume approximately 38 percent of all health care dollars in the United States. Yet persons over age 65 account for only about 12.4 percent of the population, and, regardless of how effective the medical system may be, they have fewer possible years of life remaining than do the young. This harsh reality of the human condition goes a long way toward explaining why medicine has had such a modest role in improving the life expectancy of the population as a whole. It cannot, despite frequent claims, cure aging, much less prevent death. Moreover, as a greater percentage of the population becomes concentrated in older age groups, the ability of medical intervention to prolong life expectancy for the population as a whole diminishes simply because there are fewer potential years of human life to be saved.

There is also the reality that even when medicine helps us dodge a life-threatening condition, there is always another one ready to weaken or kill us. Chemotherapy, for example, may put a man's skin cancer into remission. But having escaped death from that cause (at least temporarily), he lives on to face the risks of dying from heart disease or other chronic diseases largely determined by his previous behavior and environment, including the insults done to his body by the chemotherapy itself. Even if he had managed to avoid getting skin cancer in the first place, this fact would have raised his odds of contracting Alzheimer's and other chronic diseases of old age. This reality of "competing risks," as epidemiologists call it, is another important reason why high-tech medical intervention has little positive effect on the health of the population as a whole. As psychiatrist and medical ethicist Willard Gaylin notes, "It is often difficult to appreciate that good medicine does not reduce the percentage of people with illnesses in our population. It increases that percentage."[9]

Death by Doc

Another reason the medical system plays such a modest role in extending life is that, frankly, it kills so many people. For example, each year nearly two million patients in the United States get infections in hospitals, and about 90,000 of these patients die as a result.[10] The largest preventable cause of these infections, according to the CDC, is the failure of doctors and nurses to wash their hands.[11] Then there is the well-publicized finding of the Institute of Medicine, that "more people die in a given year as a result of medical errors [98,000] than from motor vehicle accidents (43,458), breast cancer (42,297) or AIDS (16,516)."[12]

Among the tragic and cautionary stories behind those statistics is that of Betsy A. Lehman, a health columnist for the *Boston Globe* and the mother of two young daughters. Betsy died in 1994 at age 39 while in the care of Boston's prestigious Dana-Farber Cancer Institute. In her battle with breast cancer, Lehman and her husband, a senior research scientist at Dana-Farber, had decided she should submit to a regime of high-dose chemotherapy followed by a stem cell transplant from her blood.

The treatment might have killed her anyway. Though it was highly popular in the mid-1990s, with hospitals devoting entire wings to this treatment and regularly netting $18,000 to $20,000 per patient, recent studies have found that it offers no better chance of survival than conventional treatments, while directly causing many painful deaths.[13]

As a health care columnist Lehman was presumably a savvy health care consumer and knew as much as anyone about the risks in her treatment. But there was nothing she could do about the ambiguous prescription ordered by one of her physicians, which called for "cyclophosphamide 4g/sq m over four days." What the doctor apparently meant was that she should receive a total of 1 gram per square meter of body mass every four days. What she received was a total of 1 gram per square meter of body mass during *each* of the next four days. After vomiting up sheets of tissue, she died an agonizing death three weeks later, when the massive overdose at last caused cardiac failure.[14]

Though Lehman's tale is more egregious than most, such medical errors, according to the Institute of Medicine, cause 2 to 4 percent of all deaths in the United States. This loss of life, even with the conservative estimate, is equivalent to a jumbo jet crash every three days.

Another reason the medical system has so little effect on the general health of the population is that so many of the treatments it offers are unnecessary. Sometimes this is a matter of greed. More often, unnecessary surgery and testing result from honest treatment of what epidemiologists call "pseudo disease." Medical researchers Elliott S. Fisher and H. Gilbert Welch define this as "disease that would never become apparent to patients during their lifetime were it not for diagnostic tests."[15] Most Americans have a binary view of illness. Either you have a disease or you don't. But the truth is often much more subtle. Autopsy studies have shown that a third of adults have cancer cells in their thyroid; as many as 40 percent of women in their 40s have ductal carcinoma in situ in their breasts, and half of men in their 60s have adenocarcinoma of the prostate.[16] All of the subjects in these studies died of other diseases. In other words, they died with their cancer, not from it, suggesting that many people who have small cancers will not develop symptoms, either because their cancers are slow growing or because they will die of something else before their cancers become noticeable.

Yet if your doctor performs a diagnostic test and tells you that you have cancer, there will be two likely results. First, you will experience extraordinary and prolonged stress from hearing such a diagnosis, along with the risks to health brought on by stress. Second, both you and your doctor will likely begin trying to fight the disease, which may result in your receiving radiation, chemotherapy, or surgery for a condition that may well have never presented any symptoms, let alone caused you to die. Though it is often impossible for an individual doctor and patient to know, even after the fact, whether or not such treatment is necessary, it is possible to see that for the population as a whole the spread of diagnostic testing is leading to the epidemic of "pseudo disease" and to vast commitments of medical resources resulting in very little, if any, gain to public health.

For people who do not show any symptoms, even an annual physical exam—that ultimate standard of "preventive medicine"—offers no measurable improvement in health, according to a series of studies sponsored by the Agency for Healthcare Research and Quality.[17] These studies have turned up no evidence, for example, that routine pelvic, rectal, and testicular exams make any difference in overall survival rates for those with no symptoms of illness. Yet such tests often give false alarms, setting off rounds of expensive and sometimes risky follow-up tests. The consensus of public health experts now is that patients would be better off if doctors spent less time testing them and more time counseling them on such issues as quitting smoking, eating and drinking moderately, using seat belts, and having working smoke alarms in their houses.[18]

Why has it taken modern medicine so long to determine the effectiveness of even such routine and long-established procedures as an annual physical? In 1939, the young Scottish doctor Archie Cochrane fell into the hands of the Nazis. He spent four years as a medical officer in a prisoner-of-war camp, charged with treating as many as 20,000 underfed prisoners. Epidemics of typhoid, diphtheria, jaundice, and sandfly fever regularly swept through the camp. According to Cochrane's autobiography, however, only four prisoners died during this time. The Germans shot three of them.[19] This experience taught Cochrane two lessons that have great bearing on the question of how an aging society should think about medicine. First, the experience taught him to appreciate the exceptional recuperative powers of the human body. Second, it inspired him to commit his future career to researching the question of which medical therapies actually benefit patients, and which do not—a completely revolutionary idea at the time, and one that is still largely unrealized, for many reasons.

The volume of medical research, much of it financed by pharmaceutical companies and medical device manufacturers, grows year after year. Very little of this research explores what the actual "best practices" of medicine are. Cochrane, who is today remembered as one of the fathers of modern epidemiology, wrote in 1979, "It is surely a great criticism of our profession that we have not organised a critical summary, by specialty or subspecialty, adapted periodically, of all relevant randomized controlled trials."[20] Today, this is still largely true. It is why, for example, a whole industry could spring up in the 1990s to treat breast cancer victims like Betsy Lehman with highly lethal high-dose chemotherapy and stem cell transplants, causing thousands to suffer needless painful deaths. It is why, if you ask your doctor whether Beta-blockers would be a better treatment than Captropril for your hypertension given the history of stroke in your family, he or she is unlikely to give you an answer based on science. Even if a specific randomized, controlled trial exists that addresses the question (in this case one does), your doctor would have to spend hours researching MED-LINE to find it, and even then would probably still have to guess who paid for it.

In recent years a new movement, known as "evidence-based medicine," has tried to put more science into health care practices. But the movement is tentative. Many doctors denounce it as "cook book" medicine. No government agency has authority to enforce standards for best practices, and only a tiny fraction of government research money goes toward figuring out which procedures are better than others. The media is uninterested in the question and the public knows even less. And so the practice of medicine is driven by many forces, with the actual effectiveness of treatment being among the least determinative. In the real world, the largest forces determining how a doctor will treat any given condition are the traditions he or she learned in a particular medical school, the casual advice of colleagues, the patients' own ideas for treatment (which are often determined by advertising and naïve Web surfing), and the influence that various pressure groups (drug makers, device makers, and disease-victims groups) exert over what drugs and procedures are covered by insurance.

But what if we could wring out all the systematic errors in the medical system and adopt sensible, evidence-based medicine that solves the problems of overtreatment, overmedication, and adverse drug reaction? Wouldn't this dramatically improve our health care system and help prepare it for the coming wave of elders? Yes it would. But the overall effect on the health and life expectancy of the American people, and on the future demand for health care, would still be startlingly small. That's because (to borrow an image from the poet Joseph Malines) the health care system is, at best, like an ambulance waiting at the bottom of a cliff. By the time most people come in contact with it, their bodies are already compromised by stress, indulgent habits, environmental dangers, and injuries. The ambulance can help some people who go over the cliff, and a few it can help a lot. But, as Malines writes in his poem, "A Fence or an Ambulance,"

> If the cliff we will fence, we might almost dispense
> With the ambulance down in the valley.[21]

Why We Die

In a recent issue of *Health Affairs*, researchers from the Robert Wood Johnson Foundation surveyed scores of studies back to the 1970s on the various factors that cause people to die before their time in the United States. The consensus of this literature, they report, is that genetic predispositions account for 30 percent of premature deaths; social circumstances, 15 percent; environmental exposures, 5 percent; behavioral patterns, 40 percent; and shortfalls in medical care, 10 percent. As they are quick to point out, these proportions are easily misinterpreted. Ultimately, everyone's health is determined by a combination of factors. So, for example, while only about 2 percent of human diseases are caused by inherited genetic mutations alone, nearly all of us carry various genetic dispositions that, when combined with a hazardous environment or unhealthy lifestyle, can contribute to ill health. But this nuance only underscores the relatively weak role medicine plays in preventing premature death, and the overwhelming importance of behavioral and environmental factors.[22]

If this assertion seems far-fetched, consider the startling difference in mortality between Utah and Nevada. These two contiguous states are similar in their demographics, climate, access to health care, and average income. However, infant mortality in Nevada is 40 percent higher than in Utah, and adult men and women in Nevada face a comparably increased chance of premature death. As health care economists Victor Fuchs and Nathan Rosenberg point out, it's hard not to attribute much of the difference to the fact that the vast majority of Utah's population follows the strictures of the Mormon Church, which instructs followers to abstain from tobacco, alcohol, premarital sex, and divorce. Nevada, with its freewheeling, laissez-faire culture, has the highest incidence of smoking-related deaths in the United States, Utah has the lowest. Utah has the nation's highest birthrate, but the lowest incidence of unwed teenage mothers. Culture and behavior, this example suggests, trump access to health care in improving human life span.[23]

Similarly, when one compares life expectancy in the United States with that of other countries, it quickly becomes evident that the vast sums the United States spends on health care buys very little health. The United States spends far more on health care than any other country—roughly $4,500 per person annually.[24] Yet three-fourths of developed countries outrank America in life expectancy and infant mortality. Even some Third World countries have life tables comparable to the United States, despite miniscule spending on health care. In Costa Rica, total health care expenditures per person come to just $273 a year in 2000.[25] And there are little more than half as many doctors per capita as in the United States.[26] Yet life expectancy at birth in Costa Rica is 76.1 years, virtually the same as in the United States.[27] Moreover, the adult population in Costa Rica has a substantially better chance of becoming elderly. In the United States, the chances of dying between age 15 and 59 are 14.4 percent for men and

8.3 percent for women.[28] In Costa Rica, the chances are 13.4 percent for men and 7.8 percent for women.[29]

How do Costa Ricans get so much health for so little money? It is not that they deny themselves superfluous treatments from enterprising specialists. The country's plastic surgeons and cosmetic dentists are so renowned that they attract thousands of "medical tourists" every year, even from the United States. And it's not because the Costa Ricans can see a doctor whenever they want. The country offers free, universal access to its modern, state-run system of hospitals and clinics, but there are long lines and waiting periods for the majority who cannot afford to see private physicians.

No, the biggest reasons have to do with behavior and environment. Per capita cigarette consumption in Costa Rica is roughly half that in the United States, and largely as a result, its age-adjusted death rate from lung cancer is more than four times lower.[30] A full 27 percent of the population lives in poverty, but even in rural areas all have access to clean water and sewage systems, and, of course, clean, balmy tropical air.[31] The rate of car ownership (and accidents) is rising, but most Ticans spend much of their time walking up and down steep hills. There are more McDonalds and KFCs all the time, and obesity among children is starting to be a problem, but with a traditional diet based on rice, beans, plenty of fruits and vegetables, and moderate amounts of fried food, the number of overweight people is still strikingly less than in the United States. A peaceful, friendly, democratic country with no army and little political strife, Costa Rica enjoys one of the world's lowest rates of heart disease and other stress-related illness.

Or consider that Jamaica, an underdeveloped country with one of the world's worst murder rates, still outperforms the United States in the health status of its senior citizens. There, according to the World Health Organization, life expectancy at age 65 is roughly the same as in the United States, and at age 85 it is nearly a full year longer for men and a few months longer for women.[32] An argument for medical marijuana? No, it is an argument for walking. Dr. Denise Eldemire of the University of West Indies Department of Social and Preventive Medicine notes that 60 percent of Jamaica's elderly live in rural areas, and "a certain amount of physical activity is usually unavoidable as walking is the only reliable means of transport." According to her studies, 78 percent of Jamaican elders take a walk every day.[33] In contrast, only 60 percent of the U.S. adult population as a whole ever engages in exercise.[34] Social and behavioral factors such as smoking, diet, alcohol use, and sedentary lifestyles contribute to approximately half of all deaths in the United States, according to the Institute of Medicine.[35]

The next generation of elders in America will presumably have access to more sophisticated medical interventions, but there is little medicine can do to combat the chronic diseases of aging among people who embrace modern habits of living. Scientists estimate that up to 75 percent of all cancer deaths are caused by human behaviors such as smoking, poor diet, and lack of exercise. This is why the percentage of the U.S. population dying of cancer is higher than it was when President Nixon first declared "war on cancer" in 1970. And it is why the age-adjusted incidence of many specific forms of cancers, including female breast and lung cancer, is growing year after year. Though modern medicine can help some people put off the day they will die from the consequences of their behavior and environment, rarely can it make those consequences go away.

Largely because of such realities, access to low-cost, high-quality health care turns out to have far less effect on health and life expectancy that most people imagine. Rand Corporation's multimillion dollar health policy study—the largest in U.S. history—compared two groups of families over 15 years, one group with full medical coverage and the other with a large deductible. The families with full coverage consumed 40 percent more health care dollars than did the families with the large deductible, but researchers were unable to detect any measurable differences in health between the two groups.[36] These results may seem too strange to be true, until one considers that all eight leading causes of death in the United States are closely related to living conditions and individual behavior: heart disease, cancer, stroke, pulmonary diseases, accidents, pneumonia/influenza, diabetes, and suicide.

Health and Inequality

In contrast, large-scale changes in social arrangements or the environment have profound effects on population health. A mother's level of education, for example, has a positive linear correlation with her child's chances for survival, even in parts of the world where there is no access to health care. According to demographer John C. Caldwell, "The mechanisms at work seem to be a greater likelihood that the mother will foresee danger to the children and forestall it, and the adoption of approaches to sickness, like insisting on rest or shelter, that make recovery more likely."[37]

There is also powerful statistical evidence that social hierarchy and inequality are themselves among the major contributing factors in premature death, both in the United States and elsewhere. The first hint of this came in a classic study of British civil service workers conducted in 1967. Michael Marmot, who now heads the department of epidemiology at London Medical School, found that within a given office, mortality rates increased step by step each level down the organizational hierarchy. Those at the bottom of the hierarchy faced three times the death rate as those at the top. Since all had equal access to health care under Britain's universal socialized system, the study strongly suggested that relative socioeconomic status is a key determinant of health.[38]

Since then, a cascade of studies has confirmed a strong relationship between equality and health. In the United States, the healthiest states, such as Utah, Iowa, and New Hampshire, are also the states with the least disparity in income levels among citizens, while states such as

Louisiana, Mississippi, Alabama, and New York lead the nation in both poor population health and income inequality.[39] Similarly, wealthy nations with a high degree of income equality among their citizens, such as Sweden and Japan, have higher life expectancy than wealthy countries in which income is less evenly shared, such as the United States and Britain.

This is not a phenomenon caused simply by concentrations of extreme poverty or wealth. Across nations and races, under single-payer systems providing universal health care and under market-driven systems, life expectancy increases gradually according to one's socioeconomic status. There is a raging debate over why this is so. Some researchers suggest that a widening gap between the rich and everyone else leads to deepening stress, frustration, and ultimately self-destructive behavior among large numbers of people struggling toward the top but not succeeding. (Think of the unhappy, striving American salesman who tries to relieve his stress with booze, cigarettes, and maybe occasional compulsive, unprotected sex with strangers.) Others speculate that political support for government services that are critical to the health of populations, such as education and police protection, erodes when a very high share of a society's resources are controlled by a narrow elite.

Still others try to turn the question on its head by suggesting that the reason the rich get ahead is that they are, on average, healthier than everyone else to begin with and smart enough to know how to stay that way. But there is one point of agreement among all serious students of public health: Environmental, social, and behavioral factors play an overwhelming role in determining the prevalence of diseases and premature death in any human population. Indeed, a study published in the *Journal of the American Medical Association* estimates that some 40 percent of all deaths are caused by behavior patterns that could be modified by preventive interventions.[40] In spite of this, approximately 95 percent of the trillion dollars the United States spends on health goes to direct medical care services, while just 5 percent goes to population-wide approaches to improving health.[41]

Old Soldiers and Children

How long will people live in the twenty-first century? How many will be able to work past age 65 or otherwise remain productive members of society? One's first instinct might be to ask experts involved in the cutting edge of bioengineering. Many can be counted on to give optimistic answers, followed by calls for more funding. In 1998, *The New York Times* asked Jim Watson, co-discoverer of the structure of DNA, how long it would take for new compounds known as "anti-angiogenic factors" to result in a cure for cancer. Watson's answer, printed on the front page of a Sunday paper, was "in two years."[42] However, with the majority of all deaths in the United States linked to social and behavior factors and accidents, the future of old age will likely have very little to do with rearranging molecules, and will have much more to do with rearranging society. Indeed, a better way to think about the future of old age is to look at past sources of progress, which have been overwhelmingly social and behavioral, and ask how well we are currently improving upon them.

Historically, as we've seen, most of the gains in life expectancy at birth have been due to declines in infant mortality and improvements in the health of children. A growing body of evidence confirms that the gains in life expectancy at older ages are due largely to the same factors.

Though this may seem paradoxical, consider, for example, the life experience of Civil War veterans. Because veterans of the Union Army were the first to become eligible in large numbers for disability pensions, vast records exist documenting their medical histories through old age and death. Records of Union veterans who survived the war show that by 1900 those who had contracted infectious diseases while in the army were far more likely to suffer from chronic illness or death in their 50s and 60s than those who had not. If one survived a case of malaria as a young soldier, for example, one was left with a highly elevated chance of having respiratory problems at older ages. If one had contracted syphilis in a wartime brothel one was also far more likely to develop arteriosclerosis later in life. Similarly, those who had lived in diseased-filled cities before joining the army, and those who had been prisoners of war, also suffered high rates of disability and death in their 50s and 60s.

From these correlations, it is possible to gain strong insights into just how much of the increase in life expectancy among the elderly in the twentieth century resulted from their decreased exposure as children and young adults to infectious disease and other health risks. Economic historian Dora Costa of the Massachusetts Institute of Technology has been able to demonstrate, based on the experiences of Civil War veterans, that some 26 percent of the increase in life expectancy among 50- to 64-year-old American males in the twentieth century was caused by improvements in their health status as children and young adults.[43]

Costa has also found, by comparing the medical records of Civil War veterans with the experiences of today's elderly, that between 1900 and the present the prevalence of respiratory conditions at older ages fell by 70 percent; arrhythmias, murmurs, and valvular heart disease by 90 percent; atherosclerosis by 60 percent; and joint and back problems by 30 percent. What accounts for this improvement? Again, it is largely the result of improving social and environmental conditions experienced at earlier ages. The shift from blue-collar to white-collar work explains 15 percent of the decline in joint problems, over 75 percent of the decline in back problems, and 25 percent of the decline in respiratory difficulties. Reduced exposure to infectious disease while young accounted for at least 10 to 25 percent of the decline in chronic conditions in old age.[44]

Other researchers have shown that the environment we experience in the womb turns out to have profound impacts on our life expectancy in old age. Low birth weight children, for example, tend to develop high blood pressure and have a highly elevated risk of heart disease at older ages. In populations in which pregnant women suffer iodine deficiencies, the distribution of IQ can be skewed downward by as much as 10 percent.[45]

How could low birth weight affect your health as a 60-year-old? The exact mechanism is not known, but more and more studies show that when the fetal environment is stressful, due, say, to a mother's illness, malnourishment, or drug abuse, the fetus will use the resources it has available primarily for brain development at the expense of other organs. This in turn leads to greater vulnerability to disease later in life. The phenomenon is sometimes known as the Barker effect, after the British physician and epidemiologist David Barker, whose studies have established that people who had low birth weights, or who were thin or stunted at birth, have high rates of coronary heart disease, stroke, diabetes, and hypertension in adult life.[46]

Further evidence of how important conditions in the womb are to subsequent life expectancy comes from looking at the life histories of British aristocrats born between 1800 and 1880. If there is any scientific basis for astrology, it probably has to do with the unusual finding that women among this group who were born in May and December lived 2–3 years longer on average compared to those born in February. Specifically, if one graphs the life spans of women born in different months, starting with February, an M-shaped pattern emerges. Lifespan gradually increased the later in the spring one was born; gradually declined for those born during the summer months; gradually rose for those born in the fall, and then dropped back down for those born in January and February.

What could possibly explain such a pattern? Maybe not the movement of the planets, but quite possibly the movement of the Earth around the Sun. It is well known that vitamins B12, B6, C, and E, folic acid, and niacin are critical to fetal development. Researchers in the biology of aging speculate that, in an era before canning and refrigeration, the lack of fruits and vegetables containing these vitamins in the late winter and early spring had a significant effect on fetuses and babies. Specifically, the lower life spans among those born in August and February may be explained by the coincidence that such people were deprived of critical vitamins during one of the two most critical periods in fetal or child development (the third month of pregnancy and the first months after birth).[47]

Obviously, these findings bolster the case for investing more in neonatal and infant care, and for working harder to eliminate childhood poverty. But they also send a strong cautionary message about how much improvement in health and life expectancy among the future elderly is likely to occur in developed nations over the next several decades.

Will 55-year-olds in 2020 live substantially longer than people who are 55 today? One reason to be doubtful is that it is no longer possible to replicate the kind of dramatic improvements in the health of children that occurred in the early twentieth century. Americans who reached age 55 in 1960 were born into a highly infectious environment in which 14 percent of children died before age 1. Those who reached age 55 in 1995, by contrast, were born when only 6 percent of children died during the first year of life. That 8-percentage-point decline obviously cannot happen again without dropping infant mortality rates below zero. This means that one of the most important sources of improving life expectancy among the elderly over the last 100 years—the sweeping improvements in children's health—will be much diminished in the twenty-first century. The last cohort of Americans that experienced a significantly improved health environment in youth were first-wave baby boomers. The percentage of Americans under age 18 reported by their parents to be in excellent or good health has hovered around 80 percent for the last 20 years.[48]

Yet there remains abundant opportunity for disability rates and life expectancy at all ages to worsen in the next 30 to 40 years, even with more and more of the economy committed to health care. Americans over the last several decades have come to face many increased risks to their long-term health. The percentage of children living in poverty, for example, averaged more than 20.6 percent during the 1980s and

1990s, as compared to 15.7 percent in the 1970s. Income inequality also became more severe during this period in most industrialized countries. Smoking has declined, but illicit drug use by teenagers increased throughout the 1990s and, of course, was extremely high during the baby boomers' youth.

In the last 20 years, the population has also grown much more sedentary and prone to obesity. The number of fast-food restaurants per capita in the United States doubled between 1972 and 1997, while the amount of time children spend exercising continues to diminish.[49] In 2001, fewer than 15 percent of students between the ages of 5 and 15 walked to or from school, and a mere 1 percent biked. In 1969, by contrast, 48 percent of students walked or biked to school.[50] A survey by the Centers for Disease Control and Prevention has found that even among children who live close to school, most wind up being driven back and forth; only 31 percent of children aged 5 to 15 who live within a mile of school walk or bike—down from 90 percent in 1969.[51]

The growth of auto-dependent, sprawling suburbs not only discourages routine walking, but leads to greater levels of social isolation, which also has a strong correlation with poor health. As Robert Putnam, a professor of public policy at Harvard University, has shown in his well-known book *Bowling Alone*, for every 10 minutes spent driving to work, involvement in community affairs drops by 10 percent. What is the public health implication? A large volume of literature shows that the health risks of being socially isolated are comparable to the risks associated with cigarette smoking, blood pressure, and obesity.[52] Indeed, Putnam finds that an isolated individual's chance of dying over the next 12 months is cut in half by joining one group and cut by two-thirds by joining two groups.[53]

The decline of marriage rates will also likely be a major new source of premature death. Epidemiologists have long known that married people live longer than unmarried people. Recent research indicates that in the United States, for example, those who have never been married face almost twice the mortality risk of those who are married. Similarly, those who are divorced or separated run a mortality risk more than half again as high as do those who are married.[54] Divorce reduces male life expectancy as much as a pack-a-day cigarette habit does.[55] What are the implications for life expectancy in the future? The U.S. Census Bureau projects that among men age 25 in 1996, 14 percent will never marry. Among those who do, 53 percent will see at least their first marriage end in divorce. By contrast, the Census Bureau estimates that among men who were 60 in 1996, only 3 percent will end their lives having never been married, and only 36 percent have seen or will see their first marriages end in divorce.[56]

In addition to these increasing behavioral and environmental risks, exposure to infectious disease continues to mount. At least 20 infectious diseases that were once thought conquered, ranging from tuberculosis to malaria and cholera, have reemerged, and today's humans are afflicted by at least 30 new infectious diseases, including HIV/AIDS, Lyme disease, hepatitis C, and infections caused by the Ebola virus and the SARS corona virus.[57] After reaching a historic low in 1980, the death rate from infectious disease in the United States has nearly doubled, to some 170,000 annually.

At the same time, antibiotic-resistant strains of all sorts of microbes are cropping up. The World Health Organization reports that "in the struggle for supremacy, the microbes are sprinting ahead and the gap between their ability to mutate into resistant strains and man's ability to counter them is widening fast."[58]

The Cult of Youth in an Aging Society

Meanwhile, our expectations for what constitutes good health, and for what the heath care system can deliver, continue to inflate. In recent decades, Americans in particular have steadily broadened the definition of insurable health care to include whole new realms, from psychiatric counseling for troubled youths to impotence and infertility treatments. The media, and especially the Internet, further inflates the demand for health care by making citizens almost instantly aware of new treatments and medical technologies, no matter how experimental or unproven.

Shannon Brownlee, a health care journalist and New America Foundation fellow, nicely describes the combination of hope and hype that drives the media's coverage of health care:

> Like the rest of America, we medical journalists seem to think that if it's new it must be improved. And the market for happy talk is only growing. There's an unwritten rule in mass-market magazines and television: If your ratings are low run a medical story. If your ratings are really low, run two. If I want to dish out yet another hope-filled piece about how biomedical research is going to make us live for a century, there are plenty of editors to lap it up. In general, editors love stories about the bright, bold future of medicine, undoubtedly because that's what readers love.[59]

Mass media advertising by drug companies fuels the demand for new prescriptions still more—even for products that purport to treat conditions that most people would not otherwise even be aware of, such as "generalized anxiety disorder." The spike of media stories about this previously hidden epidemic occurred after the spring 2001, when GlaxoSmithKline launched a public relations blitz to sell the disease, which it promised could be treated by its anti-depressant drug, Paxil.[60]

Moreover, as society becomes both older and more affluent, people's willingness to accept their own aging seems to diminish. According to *American Demographics* magazine, one out of ten American baby boomers is contemplating plastic surgery. In 2001, 125,000 Americans had face-lifts; 275,000 underwent liposuction to remove midriff bulge; and 220,000 went in for breast enhancements. That year, Americans underwent 1.6 million Botox injections—a 2,356 percent increase over 1996.[61] Those who cannot accept aging are even less likely to accept mortality. In the United States, writes Willard Gaylin, "Death with dignity" and "growing old gracefully" have come to mean "dying in one's sleep at 92 after having won three sets of tennis from one's 40-year-old grandson that afternoon and having made love to one's wife twice that same evening."[62]

These are the trend lines that will have the most bearing on the future of old age, and they appear to be conspiring to create the worst of all possible combinations: a world in which, despite ever-mounting spending on health care, most people enjoy little or no improvement in productive life over the previous generation, but become more and more vulnerable to infection, chronic disease, and disabilities as a result of their over-rich diets, sedentary, isolated lifestyles, and mounting exposure to globe-trotting microbes.

Fortunately, as we will see in Chapter 12, there are many ways to arrest these trends and promote more productive aging. But for now we must accept that the cost of aging, like the cost of children, is on an unsustainable course.

9

The Slowing Pace of Progress

From Capitol Hill to Wall Street to Silicon Valley, a chorus of voices in the late 1990s proclaimed America on the threshold of a new age of superabundance. In Washington, politicians debated what to do with huge projected budget surpluses. Investors meanwhile continued to pump up stock prices beyond all traditional measures of value, expecting that a "new economy" of infotech, biotech, and nanotech—to say nothing of global trade, zero inflation, and world peace—would eventually generate unprecedented corporate earnings.

The new buzz phrase that summed up all these high expectations was "the long boom." In a cover story by that title published in 1997 in *Wired,* authors Peter Schwartz and Peter Leyden proclaimed, "We are watching the beginnings of a global economic boom on a scale never experienced before." The authors then took the reader on a time journey through a twenty-first-century world so superabundant that mundane problems like war and poverty simply disappeared.[1]

Optimism, particularly about the promise of technology, is in the American spirit and is no doubt a source of national strength. And yet time and time again, swelling expectations for the future get Americans in trouble—particularly when it comes to thinking about the future of old age.

An anecdote from the boom years of the 1960s helps to illustrate the point. In the go-go year of 1966, the National Commission on Technology, Automation and Economic Progress issued a report warning of a "glut of productivity." Juanita Kreps, who would later become Jimmy Carter's secretary of commerce, coauthored part of the study, which made bold predictions about what life in the United States would be like in the mid-1980s. Productivity was growing so rapidly, the study concluded, that by 1985 the economy would provide Americans with any one of the following three choices:

A universal twenty-two-hour workweek
A twenty-two-week standard vacation
A standard retirement age of 38[2]

Kreps was in good company in making these predictions. Policy intellectuals at that time were infatuated with the idea that America had become an "affluent society" and that the problems of economic scarcity had essentially been solved. In 1966, *Time* magazine surveyed leading futurists and reported their consensus view: "By 2000, the machines will be producing so much that everyone in the U.S. will, in effect, be independently wealthy." So bountiful would the economy become by 2000 that only 10 percent of Americans would be needed in the labor force, and the rest, *Time* reported, would "have to be paid to be idle" with inflation-adjusted government benefits of up to $40,000 a year.

Influenced by such ideas, Congress dramatically increased deficit spending and entitlement programs during this era, convinced that future taxpayers could easily afford the bill. "Our grandchildren will be able to produce in one day as much as we do in a 40-hour week," proclaimed Social Security Commissioner Robert Ball in the course of his successful arguments for a vast expansion of the system. Yet such utopianism would soon enough meet with a reality check.

By 1977, for example, a sputtering economy and falling birthrates had rendered the Social Security trust fund insolvent, and Kreps found herself, as a key player in the Carter administration, struggling to come up with a bailout plan. Her ironic proposal: raising the retirement age to 68. Carter instead opted for what was then the largest tax increase in American history, proclaiming that it would save the program for the next 75 years. In another 5 years, the system was broke again, and another massive bailout, this time involving both huge tax increases and benefit cuts, was required to keep the checks flowing.

The pattern repeats throughout American history. Prominent voices in every generation pronounce that they are living on the threshold of a new age of mass leisure, abundance, and longevity—that never quite arrives. In 1890 when the Columbian Exposition opened in Chicago, millions thronged to see and hear about what the coming century would be like. By the year 2000, theologian Thomas De Witt Talmag told an audience, "Longevity will be so improved that 150 years will be no unusual age to reach." Reformer Mary E. Lease promised, "Three hours will constitute a long day's work by the end of the next century. And this work will liberally furnish infinitely more of the benefits of civilization and the comforts of life than 16 hours' slavish toil will today."[3]

Such predictions simply echoed the techno-utopianism that has always been a defining feature of American culture. In 1842, the proto-futurist John Adolphus Etzler traveled the lecture circuit raving that the steam engine would allow man to "live in the most magnificent palaces, in all imaginable refinements of luxury, and in the most delightful gardens; where he may accomplish, without labor, in one year, more than hitherto could be done in thousands of years."[4]

Today, the facile answer to the prospect of global population aging and decline is simply to assume future breakthroughs in technology. If projections show there will be fewer workers to support each retiree, then just assume that each worker "will be able to produce in one day as much as we do in a 40-hour week." If the aging of the population implies that health care costs will devour an ever-greater share of national output, then just assume that our grandchildren will produce everything else so efficiently that they won't mind the mounting cost of tending to sick elders. If the solvency of Social Security seems to require bumping up the retirement age, then just assume that the marvels of modern medicine will render most septuagenarians well able to compete in the global economy of the mid-twenty-first century.

The purpose of this chapter is not to dispute the possibilities of such assumptions. It is, rather, to suggest some reasons why it is dangerous to act as if such outcomes were guaranteed. Even after the great technology bust of 2000, each week still brings headlines about faster chips, speedier relays, new wonder drugs, and anti-aging cures. In such an environment, it is all too tempting to believe that we are on the threshold of a Buck Rogers future that will make worries about labor shortages and how to pay for old people seem as quaint as sixteenth-century fears of sailing off the edge of the earth. But a powerful case can be made that we are living in an age of declining inventiveness, and that although the world of tomorrow will bring marvels of new technology, it will not bring gains in productivity sufficient to overcome the life and labor lost to an ever-falling birthrate.

Time Traveling with Ozzie and Harriet

One way to gain an intuitive sense of how today's technological marvels compare with those of the past is to flick on *Nick at Nite* and watch any of the family sitcoms from the 1950s. When Ozzie and Harriet made their television debut on October 3, 1952, they didn't have Internet access or a cell phone, but their living conditions were otherwise very close to those of today's middle-class families. They had indoor plumbing, electric lights, car, television, telephone, refrigerator, blender, vacuum cleaner, and probably an automatic washer and dryer.

If a time machine magically transported the Nelsons to a typical middle-class household in 2000, they would find most of the technologies of ordinary life improved in quality but otherwise familiar. They'd recognize the telephone and need only a second to realize we now use push buttons instead of rotary dials. They'd recognize the television even if, like most everyone else these days, they'd have trouble programming the VCR. The air conditioning and high-quality sound systems available in today's cars might please them, but they would have no trouble knowing how to fuel or drive one. Picking up the morning newspaper, they might be puzzled by references to AIDS and genetically modified food but would understand references to nuclear power, plastics, antibiotics, jet airplanes, rockets, radar, lasers, and even computers.

Yet suppose that a time machine magically transported Ozzie and Harriet half a century in the opposite direction. As viewers of the PBS series *The 1900 House* can attest, even middle-class existence at that time was extraordinarily arduous. Life expectancy at birth was only 47.3 years, compared with 68.3 years in 1950. Lack of refrigeration and poor sanitary conditions meant millions died from spoiled or tainted food, while epidemics of scarlet fever, yellow fever, and smallpox offered constant reminders of life's fragility. Women used rags for tampons, and only a brave man dared shave himself.

Affluent households were illuminated with gaslights that were expensive to run and prone to explosion. Without electricity, there were no laundry machines, vacuum cleaners, or other mechanical means to purge the household of dirt and germs. Only the super-rich could afford a car, and the vast majority of families did without indoor plumbing. Further deprived of access to a telephone, and without even a radio to provide entertainment, Ozzie and Harriet would have felt nearly as stifled and out of place in the dark and chilly rooms of *The 1900 House* as would their great-grandchildren.

Measuring the rate of technological progress over time is hardly easy, but one statistic strongly suggests why Ozzie and Harriet probably would have found it more disorienting to travel 50 years into the past than 50 years into the future. The statistic tracks how efficiently the economy uses labor, capital, raw materials, and new technology. Economists call it "total-factor productivity." Between 1913 and 1972, it grew by an annual average of 1.08 percent. Then between 1972 and 1995, for reasons economists are still debating, the rate of improvement collapsed to less than one fiftieth that of the previous era, despite a widespread adoption of computers.

The rate of productivity growth in America quickened during the late-1990s boom, but the official statistics are deceiving because they mask the dramatic disparity in how different sectors of the economy were performing. In a much-discussed piece for the *Journal of Economic Perspectives*, Robert J. Gordon, a respected economist from Northwestern University, performed a careful analysis of U.S. productivity trends from 1995 through 1999, adjusting for changes in the business cycle, quality of the labor supply, and other technical factors. He found, predictably enough, that we had become very efficient at making computers and, to a lesser extent, other durable manufactured items. But such production accounts for only 12 percent of the U.S. economy, Gordon noted. For the other 88 percent, comprising banks, stores, and other service providers, rates of productivity growth were actually falling slightly.[5]

In a subsequent study, Gordon found that much of the 1990s boom was fueled by several factors: a high dollar value that kept down the cost of imports, low energy prices, a temporary slowdown in medical inflation coincidental with the introduction of managed care, and the stimulus created by spending to avert the feared "Y2K" computer glitch. The contribution of new technology to the boom was real, but for the most part temporary.[6]

There is another way to grasp how comparatively undramatic today's high technology has been in its effect on ordinary life. Think of the life experience of a relative who was born near the beginning of the twentieth century. My grandfather, who came into this world in 1905, used to tell me about how, when he was a boy growing up in Cincinnati, his schoolmates would rush to the window and gawk if an automobile happened by. Lester Longman, who was born 20 months after the Wright brothers' first flight, lived to see not only men walk on the moon, but also the explosion of the space shuttle Challenger.

Where is the invention today that makes schoolchildren rush to the windows? In the mid-1960s, a Rand Corporation study concluded, after surveying 82 leading scientists, that by 2000 a permanent lunar base would be established and that men by then would have flown past Venus and landed on Mars.[7] Given the pace of the technological progress that was occurring at the time, the projection was not unreasonable. But as of this writing it has been 30 years since any human being has even left Earth's orbit, and a second shuttle (constructed at a time when 35 percent of the current U.S. population was yet to be born) has exploded and fallen to earth. Meanwhile, there has been virtually no advance in jet propulsion systems save to make them quieter and more fuel efficient, and air travel times have actually lengthened. Until the final cancellation of the Concorde flights in 2003, it was possible to cross the Atlantic at speeds of up to 1,350 mph, albeit in a plane that was 33 years old. Now the fastest available flight goes less than half that speed.

Similarly, though automobiles now contain microchips and some can talk to you, in most parts of the country it actually takes longer to drive from point A to point B than it did 30 years ago, because of worsening congestion. Between 1992 and 2001, time spent in traffic jams increased by 650 percent in large and medium-sized urban areas.[8] Proposals, common in the early 1990s, to build automated highways are dismissed as impractical.

In 1938 the 20th Century Limited, pulled by a steam engine, sped from New York to Chicago in sixteen hours. Today, Amtrak's version of the train, drawn by a high-tech fuel-injected diesel-electric locomotive with computer diagnostics on board, takes five hours longer. In

Los Angeles and many other cities around the country, governments are spending billions to replace trolleys, interurbans, and mainline passenger trains that were abandoned more than half a century ago. In Tampa, the new trolleys are literal replicas of those that ran before World War II. No one can think of a better idea for relieving the pollution and congestion caused by the century-old automobile than by going back to a technology first introduced in the United States in 1827. Proposals to build high-speed magnetic levitation trains, once championed by the late Daniel Patrick Moynihan, gather dust—too expensive, too technologically risky.

As we know from the last chapter, the pace of progress in health care is also diminishing. Ozzie and Harriet would dramatically shorten their life expectancy by traveling 50 years into the past, but not appreciably improve it by moving 50 years into the future. Since 1950, life expectancy at age 45 has increased by just 5.7 years, and most of that improvement, as we've seen, is not the result of medicine. Traveling to our time might give them the benefit of hearing more about the dangers of smoking, excess drinking, lack of exercise, or fatty diet. But writers as ancient as Aristotle have taught the virtues of moderation.

Perhaps the best bottom-line indicator of the slowing pace of progress is how hard and long Americans must work today. In 1910, President William Howard Taft proposed a two- to three-*month* vacation for American workers. Today, American workers get by with an average 8.1 vacation days after a year on the job, or 10.2 days after three years, according to the Bureau of Labor Statistics.[9]

Yes, we have come a long way since 1890, when a major campaign by the American Federation of Labor's Carpenters Union successfully achieved an 8-hour workday in 137 American cities. Yet three generations after the 1938 Fair Labor Standards Act established the norm of a 40-hour work week, the average "full-time" American worker in 2001 was on the job nearly 43 hours a week, and nearly 1 out of 12 worked 60 hours a week or longer.[10] That same year, Republican Senators Judd Gregg (N.H.) and Kay Bailey Hutchison (Tex.) proposed legislation to allow employers to schedule workweeks of up to 50 hours without having to pay time and a half for overtime.

Far from becoming a leisure society, the United States has a labor force that has swollen to include some 66 percent of the civilian population, up from 58 percent in 1948. An even higher portion of the U.S. (and European) population would have to be put to work today were it not for the shiploads of products imported from Third World factories and sweat shops, where men, women, and children toil as hard today as did their American and European counterparts in the nineteenth century.

Bill Gates vs. Thomas Edison

There is a distinction between inventions that are merely sophisticated (such as, say, personal digital assistants) and those that fundamentally alter the human condition. The invention of the light bulb created more useful hours in each day for virtually everyone. The electric motor directly raised the productivity in every sphere of life, from speeding up assembly lines to creating many labor-saving devices in the home. The steam engine allowed for mass, high-speed transportation of both people and freight while also opening up vast regions of cheap land to development. The materials revolution that brought us petroleum refining, synthetic chemicals, and pharmaceuticals involved learning to rearrange molecules in ways that made raw materials fundamentally more valuable. Without the genetically improved seeds that brought us the "green revolution" of the late 1960s and 1970s, there would be mass starvation. Can we make any parallel claim about personal computers or any other recently emerged technology?

One technological feature of our time that Ozzie and Harriet would find extraordinary is the gadgets we throw out. In 1954, it took the average worker 562 hours of labor to earn enough to buy a color TV. The machine was so expensive that only a few families owned one, and if it broke, as it frequently did, it was repaired. By 1997, the average worker earned enough in just 23 hours to purchase a 25-inch color TV, and if it broke, as it infrequently did, it most likely went in the trash.[11] The Bureau of Labor Statistics predicts that the ranks of "electronic home entertainment equipment repairers" will continue to decline by at least 1 percent a year through 2010, owing to decreased demand.[12]

In the history of technology, what most distinguishes the present age is not the creation of great new inventions but our genius for reengineering and manufacturing existing machines and gadgets with ever-greater efficiency, so that their price declines even as their quality improves. According to calculations by the Federal Reserve Bank of Dallas, the average worker in 1997 could earn enough to buy a new Ford Taurus in just 1,365 hours, whereas a worker in 1955 needed to work 1,638 hours to afford the celebrated but much inferior Ford Fairlane. Stoves, dishwashers, refrigerators, washers and dryers, window air conditioners, and most other accouterments of modern middle-class life have fallen in real price even more dramatically since the 1950s.[13]

In their time, Ozzie and Harriet lived much better than the average American family; now their material standard of living would be average or even below average if one accounts for the inferior quality and high price of the electrical devices and appliances that filled their home. That the mass of American families now has access to television at all, let alone one in every bedroom with 130 channels, is in itself an amazing achievement, as is the ability of the global economy to provide millions of American teenagers with their own cars, computers, and picture phones. But this democratization of access to existing technology, although it has obvious and mostly salutary social implications, is hardly the mark of a great age of invention. Perhaps another Thomas Edison is hard at work, using nanotechnology or bioengineer-

ing to invent new machines that are truly revolutionary and trans-
forming. But he or she has not succeeded yet.

The New Boutique Economy

Suppose these trends are temporary and that the pace of scientific
progress will soon compound at rates that would amaze today's most
optimistic champions of technology. Indeed, suppose that trust, interest, and investment in science rebounds so dramatically that within
the next ten years a revolution in materials and manufacturing techniques occurs. Suppose this revolution reduces the cost of making a
car to $50 and reduces the financial and environmental cost of driving
one to near zero. Suppose further that with bioengineering, beef
comes to cost less than cereal, and smoked salmon can be had for a
penny a pound. How far would such scientific breakthroughs go in reducing the financial burdens of an aging society?

Far less than you might think. The greatest gains in labor productivity over the last century have come in manufacturing and agriculture.
Largely as a result, both sectors account for an ever-diminishing share
of the American economy. The fraction of American workers employed in production work declined to less than 7 percent in 2003.[14]
Today less than 2 percent of Americans are farmers or commercial fish-
ermen.[15] The good news about this trend is that the price of food and
most manufactured items is remarkably low by historical standards. But
the bad news is that when people go from working on tractors or assembly lines to serving tables or lawsuits, their output per hour almost always goes down.

That is because, as economist William Baumol famously argued,
service sector jobs are inherently less subject to automation than fac-
tory or farm jobs. One day, perhaps, we will turn over our entire legal
system to a network of computers programmed to decide cases, but

even then we'd probably wind up suing each other over who gets to input what facts, or what to do when the system crashes or catches a virus. Computers and robots may play ever-larger roles in hospitals, but if we know anything about medicine it is that hospitals at best play a weak role in improving public health, and that patients often respond far more to the hope and compassion offered by a nurse or doctor than to any mechanized process. The biggest opportunities for improvements in productivity probably reside in transportation, where most of the work done is by auto drivers who receive no compensation for their time and effort. Yet there are few signs of people anywhere in the world wanting to give up their automobiles, no matter how much time they may waste behind the wheel.

The continual stream of workers migrating from highly productive manufacturing jobs to less productive service sector jobs seems to be part of a natural evolution of all economies as they develop. In recent years, even such manufacturing giants as Japan and South Korea have seen the percentage of their work forces employed in services begin to rise. This is progress of a kind, but the process puts real obstacles in the way of easy, economy-wide productivity increases, even if some sectors become super efficient.

The reasons for this course of evolution are not mysterious. As Fred Hirsch pointed out more than two decades ago in his prescient book *Social Limits to Growth*, as societies become more productive in their ability to manufacture goods, the relative prices of these goods declines and so does their status.[16] A middle-class couple who once would have been proud to order a brand new dining room set from Sears now wants antiques or handcrafted furniture. People who once would have been thrilled to own a VCR and a crock pot for their Perdue chicken now flaunt their ability to hire nannies and personal fitness trainers, and to afford organic vegetables raised on small plots by college graduates.

The use of the automobile itself reflects a social preference for the least safe, least fuel-efficient, and most labor-intensive transportation technology available. Because it squanders so much time and energy, driving alone to work has more status than ride sharing, much less taking the bus, even when the bus is faster. For many people, SUVs have high status precisely because they are expensive gas guzzlers. If SUVs were to cost $50 and get a million miles per cubic foot of hydrogen, hip junior executives would start arriving to work in old-fashioned chariots, boasting about their well-bred steeds and stable boys.

Shortly after the technology boom went bust, I participated in a conference on the future of technology. There, leading technologists from Google, Hewlett-Packard, and AOL-Time Warner bragged to me that they never use instant messaging and consult their e-mail only once a week at most. No one at the conference sported a cell phone, much less a picture phone. The retreat itself was held in a rustic setting amidst California's redwood trees, where rooms go for $500 a night precisely because there are few modern amenities—no broadband access, no supermarkets, no television.

The effect of this phenomenon is to lower the economy's long-term growth potential. Each time we get more efficient in manufacturing mass consumer items, people are drawn toward new frontiers of consumption, where productivity gains are harder or impossible to realize—from personal services and gourmet food to clean air, primitive art, antiques, and ecotourism. In her recent book, *Against the Machine*, Nicols Fox celebrates the living space of a man who lives in a yurt in Maine. His "door handles are beautifully polished pieces of wood. Everything speaks of a certain patience: the ability to wait for the right piece of wood, the perfect object, the strength to spurn the unnecessary, the inferior, the ugly. Selectivity is the key to life."[17] This is the new Luddite consumerism, exemplified by *Real Simple*, the glossy consumer magazine which attracts 4.8 million upscale readers a month with its celebrations of hand-engraved garden tools, $6-a-pound Old Time red salt (a mixture of Hawaiian clay and sea salt), and hand-woven hala-leaf mats on which to enjoy your homegrown hibiscus tea as you survey your very own Hawaiian hobby plantation. Never mind that mass merchandisers like

Banana Republic, Patagonia, Anthropologie, and Pier 1 are in a constant race to deliver low-cost, efficiently produced substitutes for such experiences. Precisely to the extent they succeed, they fail.

This is not to suggest that we should cease striving as a society to boost our productivity. According to one estimate, raising the economy's long-term rate of productivity growth from just 1 percent to 1.5 percent will reduce the amount of payroll taxes needed to support Social Security benefits in the next century by more than 7 percent. But such an achievement will be by no means easy, and even if it occurs, it is likely to leave many wants unmet.

Aging and Innovation

There is a final reason to be skeptical of claims that a revolution in productivity will overcome the challenges created by population aging and shrinking labor supplies. Abundant evidence suggests that these very population trends work to depress the rate of technological and organizational innovation.

Cross-country comparisons imply, for example, that after the proportion of elders increases in a society beyond a certain point, the level of entrepreneurship and inventiveness decreases. In 2002, Babson College and the London School of Business released their latest index of entrepreneurial activity by country, known as the Global Entrepreneurship Monitor.[18] The index measures the percentage of a country's population that is involved in planning new businesses or in owning or managing businesses that are less than 42 months old. As Sylvester Schieber, a pension expert for Watson Wyatt Worldwide, has shown, there is a distinct correlation between countries with a high ratio of workers to retirees and countries with a high degree of entrepreneurship as measured by the index. Conversely, in countries in which a large share of the population is retired, the amount of new business formation is low. For example, among the most entrepreneurial countries on earth are India and China, where (at least for now) there are roughly five people of working age for every person of retirement age. Meanwhile, Japan and France are among the least entrepreneurial countries on earth and have among the lowest ratio of workers to retirees. Countries such as the United States, Canada, Italy, and Germany have levels of entrepreneurial activity that correlate closely to the age of their populations. "At least at a high level," concludes Schieber, "there seems to be some relationship between entrepreneurialism and the age structure of society."[19]

There are many possible reasons for this correlation. One, of course, may be that aging workers and investors tend to be less flexible and more risk averse. Both common sense and a vast literature in finance and psychology support the claim that as we approach retirement age, we become more reluctant to take risks with our careers and nest eggs. It is not surprising, therefore, that aging countries such as Japan, Italy, and France are marked by exceptionally low rates of job turnover, and by exceptionally conservative use of capital.

Because prudence requires that older investors take less risk with their investments, we can expect that as populations age, investor preference will shift toward safe bonds and bank deposits and away from speculative stocks and venture funds. As populations age further, we can expect an ever-higher share of citizens to be cashing out their investments and spending down their savings. Neither of these trends is consistent with a future marked by high levels of high-risk investment in new technology.

Population aging could retard innovation in another way as well. Because of the mounting costs of pensions and health care, government-financed research and development expenditures and educational spending will be under increasing budgetary pressure. Moreover, massive government borrowing could easily crowd out financial capital that would otherwise be available to the private sector for investment in new technology. Projections by the Center for Strategic and International Studies (CSIS) show, for example, that today's old-age benefit promises will eventually consume an additional 12 percent of the gross domestic product a year in the typical developed country. As CSIS reports: "Were these imbalances permitted to accumulate, by the mid-2020s, budget deficits in the rich countries would consume all of their savings, making them dependent on capital flows from the third world to fund domestic investment. Long before this happens, of course, capital shortages and default risks would spill over and disrupt growth everywhere."[20]

There are no easy ways to avoid such deficits. Raising taxes on capital would discourage savings at a time when individuals need to save more to protect themselves against reduced pensions, rising health care costs, and fraying safety nets. Raising taxes on labor would encourage unemployment at a time when more workers are needed to support each retiree. Increasing the workforce by putting more women to work would probably result in fewer babies, when it is higher fertility that is ultimately needed. Cutting pensions and health care benefits, even if politically possible, would reduce consumer demand at a time when demand will already be falling, due to a dwindling supply of younger citizens.

Even if government deficits in aging nations are kept under control, and even if there turns out to be huge investment opportunities over the coming decades in emerging markets and new technologies, the aging savers of Europe, Japan, and the United States are likely to want to keep their capital safely deployed in mature industries at home or in government bonds. Theoretically, a highly efficient global financial market could lend financial resources from rich, old countries that are short on labor to young, poor countries that are short on capital, and make the whole world better off. This is the vision of the high priests of the global economy in places like the World Bank and The International Monetary Fund. But for this to happen, aging citizens in the developed world (and their pension fund managers) would have to be persuaded of the wisdom of risking their nest eggs on investment in places that are themselves either on the threshold of hyper-aging

(China, India, Mexico) or highly destabilized by religious fanaticism, disease, and war (most of the Middle East, sub-Saharan Africa, Indonesia), or both. Maybe someday, smart mutual-fund managers will produce golden retirements for their clients by snapping up start-up firms from warlords in Afghanistan, or investing in nanotech plants in AIDs-ravaged Botswana, but the day seems remote.

And even then, the question would remain, who exactly would buy the products produced by these investments? Japan, Korea, and the other recently industrialized countries relied on massive exports to the United States and Europe to develop. But if the population of Europe and Japan is falling away, while the only population growth in the United States comes from old people (who by then may be living on reduced benefits and paying a far higher percentage of their income for health care), where will the demand come from to support development in places like the Middle East and sub-Saharan Africa?

It also stands to reason that as the preponderance of people in a society become middle-aged or older, there will be increasing political resistance to the kind of "creative destruction" that economist Joseph Schumpeter once identified as the dynamo of capitalistic and technological progress.[21] Why doesn't Japan reform its sclerotic banking sector? Why don't France or Spain eliminate job guarantees, stop protecting inefficient industries, or rein in their unsustainable pension costs? Why does Germany allow a pattern of ingrown corporate governance, high taxes, and increasingly mediocre universities to smother the country's former prowess in engineering? Why does the United States spend time debating how to expand its unsustainable Medicare program, rather than reforming its staggeringly inefficient health care system? In part, it must be because a critical proportion of the population is old enough to be highly invested in the status quo, and too old to recover from the deep structural changes in society that would be required to reintroduce entrepreneurial and technological dynamism.

An aging workforce may also be less able or less inclined to take advantage of new technology. This seems to be part of what is behind

Japan's declining rates of productivity growth in the 1990s. Before that decade, the aging of Japan's highly educated workforce was a weak, but positive, force in increasing the nation's productivity.[22] Older workers "learned by doing," developing specialized knowledge and craft skills, as well as the famous company spirit that made Japan an unrivaled manufacturing power. But by the 1990s the continued aging of the workforce contributed to Japan's declining competitiveness.

No longer did the Japanese firms with the oldest workers show the strongest rates of productivity growth; instead they showed the weakest. Japan was able to use information technology to compensate for its vanishing supply of low-skilled younger workers, but did not succeed in using it to boost the productivity of its highly skilled older workers. Yoshiaki Nakamura of the University of Tokyo and other economists have found that during the 1990s Japanese firms reached the limits of what productivity increases could be achieved by the deepening skills and experience of Japan's manufacturing workers, who were essentially hardworking, but aging, craftsmen. Aging went from having a mildly positive effect on productivity growth to having a negative effect that technology could not overcome.[23]

Aging works against innovation in another way as well: As growth in population dwindles, so does the need to increase the supply of just about everything except health care. That means there is less incentive to find ways of making a gallon of gas go farther, building houses more efficiently, or increasing the capacity of existing infrastructure. Population growth is the mother of necessity. Without it, why bother to innovate when you could be contentedly enjoying an ample supply of affordable houses, open roads, and comparatively abundant natural resources? An aging society may have an urgent need to gain more output from each remaining worker, but without growing markets, individual firms have little incentive to learn how to do more with less—and with a dwindling supply of talent, they have fewer ideas to draw on.

Instead of assuming that technology will overcome the challenge of population aging and decline, we need to concentrate on the human factors in the economy—adequate fertility rates, strong families, life-long education, and more productive aging. These are the most important raw materials that make technological progress and prosperity sustainable.

10

Home Economics

"The battle to feed all of humanity is over," proclaimed Paul R. Ehrlich in his 1968 bestseller, *The Population Bomb*. "In the 1970's the world will undergo famines—hundreds of millions of people are going to starve to death in spite of any crash programs embarked upon now."[1]

Ehrlich was wrong about at least the timing of his predicted catastrophe. Today food is cheaper and more abundant than ever, even if many still go hungry. Indeed, according to the World Bank, the price of food, adjusted for inflation, declined by 53 percent between 1980 and 2001. The amount of food calories available per person has increased some 20 percent since the 1960s, even as fewer and fewer people still work as farmers.[2] The United Nations reports that "the most rapid increase has been in the developing countries where population more than doubled and daily food calories available per person rose from roughly 1,900 to 2,600 calories."[3]

In 1998, welfare economist Amartya Sen won the Nobel Prize in large measure for his demonstrations that speculators, as well as corrupt or genocidal governments, are the cause of almost all modern-era famines. Famine today is a political problem—a matter of fair distribution of food, not of inadequate supply.[4]

As with food, other commodity prices have declined significantly since 1980. The price of crude oil, adjusted for inflation, declined by 46 percent between 1980 and 2001, while metal and mineral prices fell by 35 percent. Such declines are imposing real hardships throughout the developing world. Declining food prices are ravaging most rural economies, forcing mass migrations of impoverished peasants into cities. Declining real energy prices help to foster turmoil in the Middle East. But whatever dislocations to the world economy and culture may be set off by such trends, the root cause is a growing surplus of raw materials relative to demand.[5]

Why have natural resources become cheaper over the last generation, even as consumption and human population continued to expand? Every additional dollar of the gross national product, it turned out, required fewer natural resources to produce. Thanks to improved efficiency, producing a ton of steel in the United States, for example, now requires 45 percent less energy than it did in 1975.[6] Due to soaring yields per acre, producing a bushel of soybeans in the United States required 36 percent less land in 2002 than in 1970.[7] Moreover, with the growth of the service sector, all natural resources—water, energy, food, and minerals—account for an ever-smaller share of economic activity. Hospitals, for example, use far less energy and far fewer minerals than steel mills. Law offices use far less water than farms or steam engines, and they produce less pollution, too.

Yet we still do face a "population bomb" of a different sort. Shortages of raw materials may or may not appear in the future, depending on such factors as who controls access to Middle Eastern oil, how changing weather patterns or plant diseases may affect agricultural production, and how quickly alternative energy sources and new materials are developed. But what makes today's economic growth unsustainable is not that it is about to exhaust the Earth's bounty, but that it is consuming more human capital than it produces. When the economy demands more and more education from its workers, while providing them with neither the time nor the money to raise and educate their replacements in the next generation, the stock of human capital falls and is not easily renewed.

Where Do Doctors Come From?

A hospital is a good place to start in considering how this is so. More so than steel mills, hospitals require a high concentration of responsible workers and highly trained specialists. They require doctors whose formal education extends into their 30s. They require highly trained, multitasking nurses with adept social skills. They require administrators and bureaucrats who are masters of law, regulation, and data management. Even the low-skilled workers who distribute the hospital meals and disinfect the bedpans must be highly trustworthy, for if they do their job wrong, patients will die.

What is true of hospitals is also increasingly true for the workplace in general. The clear tendency of economic development is toward a more knowledge-based, networked economy in which decisionmaking and responsibility are increasingly necessary at lower levels. In such economies, children often remain economically dependent on their parents well into their own childbearing years because it takes that long to acquire the panoply of technical skills, credentials, social understanding, and personal maturity that more and more jobs now require.

The most persuasive measure of this phenomenon is the growing economic necessity of having a prolonged education. Increasingly, advanced economies do not provide for those who lack a college degree. In the United States, the wage advantage of people with 16 or more years of schooling over those with just a high school degree skyrocketed from about 45 percent in 1980 to more than 66 percent by 1990. Since then the economy has been demanding an even more highly educated workforce, as shown by the growing income gap between those with college degrees and those with graduate school education. In 1981, holders of advanced degrees (including MBAs, MDs, and JDs) as a group enjoyed no greater income than those with only a college education. By 1997, the economy rewarded advanced degree holders with 34 percent more income than mere college graduates.[8]

But where do these highly educated professionals come from? Human capital does not just spring into being, and it is not simply a product of higher education. Doctors, for example, must first be born. Doctors must also, for many years, be swaddled, fed, and comforted—by someone. Prodigious human effort is further required to teach them to read their first sentence and to add their first sums. Indeed, teaching them to read almost always requires far more adult effort and pedagogical savvy than teaching them biochemistry, the latter of which is usually performed in large lecture halls by teaching assistants and junior faculty members. Moreover, because doctors must be trusted with highly technical life-and-death decisions, they had also better acquire a strong sense of morality, a balanced personality, sober habits of living, and discipline—all of which will most likely require vast commitments of time and money by parents and other nurturing adults.

Yet the adults who sacrifice the most to create and mold this precious human capital, whether they be dutiful parents, day care workers, schoolteachers, camp counselors, or even college professors, retain only a small share of the value they create. Indeed, as a rule, the more involved one becomes in the nurturing of the next generation, the less compensation one is likely to receive. Those who devote themselves full-time to raising their children receive no wages. Day care workers take home less pay than hotel maids. Elementary school teachers could easily make more money as casino dealers. Camp counselors could raise their income by taking a cashier job at the mall. High school teachers would receive more money if they taught stock or real estate seminars. The highest paid college professors are those who teach the least. Even among doctors, pediatricians generally receive far less compensation than specialists dealing with adult illness.

To take another example, becoming a nursery school teacher in most states requires one to have a minimum of an associate's degree with a major in childhood development, to have mastered a certification exam, and to have served as a student teacher. Nonetheless, the average annual wage of nursery school teachers in 2001 was just $20,940. By comparison, the average wage for animal trainers that year, according to the Bureau of Labor Statistics, was $27,280.[9]

Does this disparity prove that teaching a dog to sit is more valuable to the economy than teaching the alphabet to a future worker? Clearly it does not. The opposite is true, and increasingly so: As the population ages, and as the economy makes more intensive use of human capital, those who work at forming this capital become more useful and valuable to all members of society. Simply by having children, parents provide the raw material for tomorrow's workforce, as well as a brake on population aging. Then parents, assisted by other caregivers and educators, transform this raw material, through a process that sometimes takes as long as 30 to 35 years, into the next generation of labor.

The returns to society, if not to individual parents, caregivers, and educators, are huge. Businesses receive a windfall of new workers who arrive on the labor market already endowed with unprecedented amounts of human capital, almost all of which has been formed and paid for by others—including parents, who receive no compensation from their children's employers, and scores of caregivers and educators who could have earned far more money doing something else. As these new workers are also new consumers, businesses receive another windfall in the form of increased demand for their products. Governments, meanwhile, harvest an expanded tax base, allowing government beneficiaries, such as Social Security and Medicare recipients, to receive bigger benefits than they otherwise could.

So how is it that parents, caregivers, and educators continue to receive such a small share of the value they create? One explanation, of course, is that this is all overwhelmingly "women's work," and that therefore broad sectors of society (including men, but also many women employed in the "masculine" economy) devalue it. Another factor is that we (men and women alike) do not want parents or helping professionals to be "in it for the money." We want them to be motivated as much as possible by sympathy, compassion, and a genuine desire to serve others. The nature of their role requires, we believe, that they be caring and warm hearted. Thus, offering them only minimal financial compensation, or even status, helps to ensure that the people who assume these roles will be motivated by idealism, or so we hope.

Yet the low pay and low status of those involved in nurturing human capital is not a sustainable arrangement. The problem is not that parents as well as other caregivers and educators are any less idealistic than in the past. Arguably, those who continue to perform these roles are more idealistic than ever, since there are so many more opportunities available to them than in the past. Women do not become mothers or nursery school teachers today, for example, because they are barred from becoming lawyers or investment bankers. Similarly, since in today's market economy children no longer provide economic benefits to their parents, those who nonetheless choose to bear the cost of raising a family must be motivated largely by their hearts, not their heads.

Instead, the problem is that the value created by the "nurturing sector" of the economy is, in effect, being taxed away to the point that it makes less and less sense for individuals to invest or participate in it, and so increasingly they don't. The initial result is a below-replacement-level fertility rate. The eventual result, if the trend continues to run its course, is an exhaustion of human capital—a harried, overworked society in which there are too few people to support the old or tend to the young.

Are Children Pets?

At first, most people reject the proposition that parents and other nurturers are in any way unfairly burdened. "Don't we all pay school taxes to support *their* kids?" "What about those child care credits, and all the money that goes to mothers on welfare?" "If they can't afford children, they shouldn't have them." These are all common attitudes. Some critics go even further. In her book *Baby Boon*, Elinor Burkett charges that "handing out goodies to parents just because they are parents is affirmative action—the preferential treatment of one group designed to correct real or perceived discrimination or inequality—based on reproductive choice."[10]

What is behind these attitudes? By tradition, of course, parents have been responsible for the cost of their own children. Moreover, in recent times widespread fear and resentment of population growth has fostered the perception that parents are just another kind of selfish consumer, and that we would be better off with less of them—particularly if they are of another race or ethnic group. Thus, it seems to many people that any assistance parents receive in raising their children—public schools, tax credits, family allowances—is a form of subsidy. As economist Nancy Folbre has lamented, the common notion is that children are like pets. "Parents acquire them because they provide companionship and love. Therefore, they should either take full responsibility for them, or drop them off at the pound."[11] The analogy goes further in the popular mind. Just as dog owners are expected to use pooper-scoopers, observe leash laws, and not ask for subsidies, parents are expected to potty train their children, keep them quiet and well behaved, and let the joys of parenting be their own reward.

A corollary of this view is that people who decide not to have children hurt no one, or even benefit society, and so cannot be criticized. As writer Stephanie Mencimer has noted, "Today, we talk about the childless in the casual way we once discussed swingers, as just another group exercising one of the many lifestyle options available in this country."[12]

The problem with these attitudes is that they fail to account for the deepening dependency all people have on both the quantity and quality of other people's children. In this aging society, we have largely socialized the cost of aging, through programs like Social Security and Medicare, for example. But we still leave it to individuals to bear (in both direct expenses and forgone wages) nearly all of the growing cost of raising the children who sustain the system, while allowing those individuals to retain a dwindling share of the value they create. What could you buy with your Social Security check or your IRAs if everyone else in your generation had simply forgotten to have children or had failed to invest in them?

We also live in an increasingly knowledge-based economy. In this economy, the formation of human capital becomes more essential to all sectors. Yet again, we leave the cost of forming this human capital primarily in the hands of individual parents and low-paid caregivers and educators, nearly all of whom could vastly increase their incomes simply by getting out of the "nurturing business."

And many are, as attested by the low birthrate, the high divorce rate, and the growing shortages of caregivers and qualified teachers. Under these circumstances, a child care credit, much less the cost of public education, is not a subsidy to parents. Parents pay school taxes, too, while also making huge additional investments in the next generation. Yet parents do not receive any greater return for their greater investment. Instead, they must share the benefits of whatever human capital they form in the next generation with everyone else.

Consider that in the past parents bore the full cost of raising their children, but also held on to most of the resulting return. How so? To begin with, children as young as five or six started paying dividends to the household economy by performing economically useful work such as tending farm animals, stitching clothes, gathering wood, or, in the early industrial age, working in factories. Young children were particularly lucrative in colonial America. In explaining the rapid economic growth in England's American colonies, Adam Smith noted in the *Wealth of Nations*, "Labor [in North America] is . . . so well-rewarded that a numerous family of children . . . is a source of opulence and prosperity to the parents. The value of children is the greatest of all encouragements to marriage. We cannot, therefore wonder that the people in North America should generally marry very young."[13]

As young adults, well-bred children often benefited their parents by entering into strategically arranged marriages that brought new wealth and station to the extended family or secured alliances with rivals. Moreover, the majority of parents who were engaged in a common enterprise with their children, such as running a farm or a craft shop, derived a direct and exclusive reward for whatever work skills they taught their children, or had others teach them. Finally, adult children provided their parents with at least the prospect of support in old age, which was then, for most people, nearly impossible to secure from any other source.

The system had many brutal features that no equalitarian would wish to replicate, but it did allow parents to reap what they sowed. Today's parents, by contrast, recapture little if any of the return created by their investment in children, even though they typically invest much more, and for much longer, than did parents in the past. In developed countries, the economy provides little opportunity for children to perform useful work, even in the rare circumstances in which it is legal. With the end of arranged marriages, few parents in developed countries make strategic gains from alliances with their children's in-laws, or if they do so it is simply by chance. Moreover, except in the now rare instances in which a son or daughter joins a family business, parents must be content to see the job skills they provided for their children go not to the benefit of a common enterprise, but to the benefit of employers outside the family.

Finally, and just as importantly, parents no longer hold a unique claim on their children for support in old age. Instead the state, primarily through programs like Social Security and Medicare, redistributes an ever-increasing share of the human capital parents create to all members of society.

As economist Shirley P. Burggraf has pointed out, "People who never have children; parents who neglect, abuse or abandon children; deadbeat parents who don't pay child support, all have as much claim (in many cases more) on the earning of the next generation through the Social Security System as do the most dutiful parents."[14] Similarly, corporations that profit from skilled labor or that sell to affluent consumers appropriate the human capital created by parental investment, while paying parents nothing in return.

Even in the twilight of their lives parents continue to subsidize nonparents. As a group, elderly parents impose far less of a burden on public budgets than do childless elders. Mothers with living children, for example, are 40 percent less likely than are childless women to wind up in a nursing home; for fathers the risk is 66 percent less than for childless men.[15] The biggest reason for this disparity is of course the incalculable amounts of free informal care elderly parents receive from their grown children—care that would otherwise have to be paid for by programs like Medicaid, which finances nursing home care for the indigent elderly. Although dutiful parents benefit society in this way as well, they receive no compensating benefits from society. Neither childless people nor those who abandon their children are required at any time in their lives to pay extra taxes to defray extra costs they impose on the public in old age.

The effect of all this is to further erode the incentives to be a parent or otherwise engage in nurturing the next generation. Already the Social Security System (including Medicare) redistributes 1 out of 7 payroll dollars in the United States, and could easily be redistributing 4 out of 10 in another 30 years. Nominally, this redistribution is occurring from one generation to another—that is, from current taxpayers to current beneficiaries. But the larger distribution is ultimately from dutiful parents and others directly involved in forming the human capital that sustains the system, to those who are not. A parallel transfer occurs when employers consume human capital without offering compensation to its producers. In effect, we have placed a very high tax on responsible parents and other nurturers of human capital, and used the proceeds to support the consumption of the population as whole.

The system has so far benefited both business and government in a self-reinforcing cycle. As the human capital the family creates is effectively taxed away, the family discovers it needs two incomes to sustain itself. Mothers join fathers in the paid workforce, thereby providing employers with new workers, and government with new taxpayers, which helps to replace the workers and taxpayers who are not being born because of the increasing tax on parenthood. The economy at least appears to grow, because the work a woman performs as a nanny, a day care worker, or any other paid employee counts in estimates of gross domestic product, while the work a woman performs as a mother and homemaker does not. The two-paycheck family, moreover, creates increased market demand for a broad range of products—processed foods, business attire, takeout service, an extra car—all of which is fully taxable—and measured gross domestic product increases. But the population ages, and the demand for human capital outstrips supply as the family is slowly taxed out of existence and other nurturing institutions are left with insufficient resources to even begin to make up the loss.

The Nurture Tax

What does the tax on nurture look like in day-to-day experience? A young woman faces a choice between becoming a nursery school teacher, a vocation she admires but that pays $7 an hour, or getting a license to be a casino dealer, a calling she finds less noble, but that pays $20 an hour. Is society really trying to tell her that she'll add more value to the world as a casino dealer than as a nursery school teacher? No, nearly everyone would agree (even high-rolling social conservatives like Bill Bennett) that a qualified nursery school teacher plays a more important social and economic role than a qualified casino dealer does. But the problem is, if a nursery school paid her $20 an hour to teach, few parents could afford the tuition, even if she proved to be an extremely effective teacher.

And why is that? It is in large measure because almost all of the economic return on that tuition would go not to the parents who paid it, but would be divvied up by society as a whole, beginning 20 to 30 years later. If you send your child to a high-quality, high-cost nursery school, you may substantially increase the chances that your child will grow up to be a well-adjusted, highly prized employee who pays lots of taxes. The same may be true if you sacrifice your own wages to home-school the child. But either way you will receive little or none of the economic return on your investment, which means you can afford to invest far less in your child than you could if so much of those returns were not appropriated by others.

The same relation applies to the cost of college and all other child-related expenditures. Who would bet in a casino in which, even when you were lucky enough to hit the jackpot, you had to share the winnings with all the other customers? Maybe a few gamblers motivated by pride and the sheer joy of winning, but most gamblers would take their business elsewhere. The answer suggests one big reason why casinos offer better pay than nursery schools. Customers of both face long odds of success. But if you use your money to play in a casino, you get to keep what you win. If you use your money to invest in your child's education, or even in the education of someone else's child, whatever economic returns follow wind up being shared by everyone. Under these terms, casinos will become highly profitable, but nursery schools almost never enjoy a surplus because the value they create is too diffuse. Parents are repaid, if ever, only with pride and joy.

Fortunately there are still many parents for whom pride and joy in their children is enough. Fortunately, too, even as the percentage of voters who are parents declines, the public is still willing to bear the cost of public education, even if it still resists any entitlement to preschool. Yet looking to the future, we can anticipate that as demand for human capital continues to increase, this very process will threaten its own supply. First there is the mounting opportunity cost of compromising one's own education to have children. The young mother who defers college or graduate school in order to start a family is at ever greater risk of poverty if the father of her children abandons her, and in any event forgoes evermore potential income by becoming a mother. Then comes the cost in time and money required to provide her own children with ever higher levels of education, while simultaneously facing the growing burden of supporting the old, both formally through taxes and informally through caring for individual parents. We are headed toward a future in which only rich people will be able to afford to raise and educate a child, and rich people, generally, are not much interested in the work. If they were, they would not be rich.

If we were in the habit of seeing the family for what it is—not as a mere consumption unit, but as the sector of the economy most responsible for human capital formation—we would see that this sector is starved for resources, as more and more of the value it creates is consumed by other sectors, most notably employers and, through government transfers, childless retirees. These are not sustainable trends. An economy that creates disincentives to have children, while undercompensating parents and other caregivers for the essential human capital they create, is living beyond its means.

The Culture Wars

In the village of Calzadilla in southwestern Spain, the mayor takes it upon himself to present each new mother with a live Iberian piglet. This is his way of promoting fertility in a country where births are few. But the reaction is underwhelming. "I'd rather have free day care than a free pig," one woman told a reporter. Though the animal, when fully grown, might be worth as much as a year's worth of diapers, the mayor has had occasion to award only 40 piglets in nine years.[16]

In the United States it is not so different. No, we don't literally present new mothers with a pig. Instead, we offer parents a $1,000 federal income tax credit and some unpaid leave, and, for single parents and two-income families, some write-offs on child care expense. But relative to the million-plus dollar cost of raising a child, that's not much better than a pig.

What is the explanation for this? There are, of course, the objections from religious and social conservatives who are wary of working mothers and who view day care and other social services that might benefit working parents as an encroachment by the "nanny state." *National Review* editor Richard Lowry thunders, "The mass entry of women into the workforce has acted to dissolve the family in general."[17] Neoconservative intellectual Francis Fukuyama warns that "substantial empirical evidence links higher female earnings to both divorce and extramarital childbearing."[18] There are also plenty of people who object to the idea that they should have to pay more taxes so that dual-income yuppies or Murphy Brown–type single moms can have an entitlement to free day care. When not making their case on moral grounds, they cite an avalanche of studies on the health and developmental risks to children in day care. Business interests, meanwhile, consistently oppose any mandate that would require them to pay parents who need time off to take care of an infant or a sick family member.

The antinatalism of the Left is just as important in explaining the status quo. Many early socialists and feminists put great emphasis on promoting family life and on getting the state to relieve mothers of their risks and burdens. A century ago, for example, nothing could be more progressive than supporting mothers' pensions, which in the United States and many other nations became the spearhead of the early welfare state. In a 1911 speech that launched the successful crusade for mothers' pensions, Mrs. G. Harris Robertson, the original "maternal feminist," declared that the beneficiaries of such pensions should even "include the deserted wife, and the mother who has never been a wife. Today let us honor the mother wherever found—if she has given a citizen to the nation, then the nation owes something to her."[19] By 1919, thirty-nine states provided some form of mothers' aid. In 1935, something like mothers' pensions became federalized under the Social Security Act in the form of the program known as Aid to Dependent Children.

But by the 1960s, the idea that mothers should be rewarded for giving "a citizen to the nation" was already becoming an outdated notion. As noted before, Betty Friedan set the tone of the modern feminist movement when, in the first chapter of *The Feminine Mystique*, she fretted about the ongoing "population explosion." She then went on to describe how the typical American mother was smothering her children and helping to create a "comfortable concentration camp" that made both sexes neurotic.

Since then, Friedan's complaint that overmothering was causing male homosexuality to spread "like murky smog over the American landscape" has lost resonance on the Left. But her general critique—that motherhood should not be a woman's highest calling or priority—has not lost its following. And so the preoccupations of modern feminism, and of the Left in general for the last generation, have been with issues of personal liberation, birth control, abortion, and access to the market economy.

Accordingly, the idea that either mothers or fathers deserve unique compensations and protections has dropped off the progressive agenda. Long gone are the days when the labor movement crusaded to force employers to pay men a "family wage" to compensate for the cost of raising the next generation of workers. Long gone, too, are the days when mainstream feminists championed "wages for housework," or when mainstream liberals resisted "workfare" and insisted that poor mothers be allowed to stay home with their young children.

Instead, with rare exceptions, today's Left has joined with market libertarians in deromanticizing motherhood and family life, while at the same time sharing a celebration of hyperindividualism and maximum competition in labor markets. As a result of this ideological cocktail, capitalists are relieved from having to pay anyone a family wage, and are more than happy to watch working mothers and fathers scapegoat each other over who is now responsible for the children.

Across the political spectrum, people harbor private fears and resentments that further complicate their feelings on this subject. If the state offers benefits to parents, won't this encourage the "wrong" people to have or adopt children: single mothers, gays, immigrants, blacks, the poor? Alternatively, if the state offers benefits only to the "right" sort of parents, that is, married, heterosexual, single-paycheck, self-sufficient couples, doesn't this discriminate against alternative lifestyles, foster patriarchy, penalize working women, etc.? Again, there are the deep and unresolved questions about what is really best for mothers and children—the endless debates over the effects of day care verses parental neglect, the worries about fostering dependency among "welfare queens," and "the problem with no name" of isolation and boredom among stay-at-home mothers.

And so the culture wars over work and family result in today's tough bargain for parents: Everyone who wishes may join the paid labor force, but almost no one gets a family wage, or enough help from government to defray the cost of raising children. Employers, and the majority of citizens who are not actively involved in raising children benefit from this status quo, which is no doubt why it has continued for so long. Dutiful parents do not benefit, which is why there are fewer of them.

In the long term, the cost of this bargain is not just the harried, downwardly mobile life faced by most of today's parents. A falling birthrate and an aging population have consequences for every member of society that will soon become more and more apparent. The context of debate over work and family today is a world in which most people still view population growth with alarm, and simply take it for granted that large numbers of mothers and other caregivers will always be available to raise up children for little or no wages. But these mass opinions will shift, and probably quite rapidly, as the reality of population aging sets in. The critical moment will probably come in the next decade, as millions of baby boomers start crashing past the boundaries of old age, and as today's teenagers find themselves saddled with massive student loans, rising taxes, and growing frustration over the increasing difficulty of forming or affording a family. It is none too soon to begin thinking about how the politics of work and family will then change, and about what policies could save the day.

11

Freedom and Fertility

W hat will the future be like? Like the present, only more so, is the most common and usually inaccurate answer. Unsustainable trends end. Generations come and go, each reacting to what went before.

"The family, in its old sense, is disappearing from our land, and not only our free institutions are threatened but the very existence of our society is endangered."[1] This sentiment sounds as if it were voiced by a grumpy social conservative in the late twentieth century, but it was actually written by a contributor to the *Boston Quarterly Review* in 1859. The writer was reacting along with many others to a breakdown in traditional morality that began in England and America in the mid-1700s, and that continued, with rising opposition from outraged moralists and religious conservatives, throughout much of the nine-teenth century. During this era prostitution and pornography flour-ished, divorce rates rose steadily, and the percentage of children born out of wedlock soared, while saloons and taverns came to outnumber churches in most cities. By 1830, per capita consumption of alcohol in the United States had reached a level more than three times higher than today's.[2] By 1860, an estimated 20 percent of pregnancies in the United States ended in abortion.[3]

Threats to traditional morality came from all sectors of society throughout the nineteenth century. Romantic poets like Shelley declared "love is free," Darwin declared man an ape, Nietzsche pronounced "God is dead," while best-selling novelists like George Sands mocked marriage, and social utopians like Charles Fourier argued for a "new system of license." In 1869 the great liberal thinker John Stuart Mill attacked the oppressive nature of the traditional family, which he described as "a school of willfulness, overbearingness, unbounded selfish-indulgence, and a doubled-dyed and idealized selfishness."[4] The long trend toward dissipation and decline of the family would lead to a reaction we today call the Victorian age, with its religious revivalism, cult of mother-worship domesticity, and growing intolerance of divorce, extramarital sex, and birth control.

Could we be on the threshold of a similar reactionary age? It is worth reflecting that, for better or for worse, many of the values one associates with Victorian social gospel have renewed utility in an aging society, and that many of the economic and social trends that underlay late-ninteenth- and early-twentieth-century attitudes are reemerging. These include intensifying market competition and a weakening social safety net; huge public health threats emerging from mass behaviors and population movements; and a growing social impulse to protect children from the perceived decadence of secular society, all accompanied by ambivalent empire building amid growing fear of population decline.

The Victorian Frame of Mind

One of the strongest parallels between the Victorian era and our own is the rising levels of economic insecurity felt by the middle class, as the market economy expands and becomes more competitive and social safety nets become less secure. It is true we do not live in a Dickensian world of debtor's prisons, almshouses, and satanic mills. But around the world, both the labor movement and the welfare state are in retreat, forcing individuals to bear dramatically increasing risks of unemployment and impoverishment, and making the economic consequences of sickness, addiction, excess debt, and disability increasingly harsh.

In China, Eastern Europe, and the former Soviet Union, the collapse of the welfare state has been dramatic, leaving millions of elders living on meager or nonexistent pensions. Elsewhere, population aging and globalization mean that governments and corporations that do not continue cutting back on pension and health care promises face huge deficits and loss of international competitiveness. Sweden, once the vanguard of "cradle-to-grave" socialism, now means-tests its basic pension benefits and has reset benefit formulas so that future pensions will shrink dramatically. Most Latin American countries have engaged in draconian reforms of their Social Security systems, as have many English-speaking countries, including Britain, Australia, and New Zealand. Western Europe will either roll back its spending on pensions and health care, or else face the loss of even more of its economic base to foreign competition.

In the United States, where employers have historically been responsible for providing the lion's share of social benefits, corporations have been retreating from their pension and health care promises with increasing frenzy, and will be scaling back much more in the future. For example, among companies employing 500 or more workers, the share offering health insurance to their retirees plummeted from 40 percent in 1993 to 27 percent in 2001.[5] A mere 11 percent of all private establishments in the United States still offer health care benefits to their retirees.[6] Meanwhile some 75 million Americans go without any health insurance for at least part of the year, and those who remain covered by employer-sponsored plans pay an ever-increasing share of the cost of their care.

The percentage of Americans who can reasonably expect to receive a pension from their employers is also shrinking rapidly. Half of all working Americans do not even have access to a company retirement plan.[7] The number of so-called defined benefit pensions, which guarantee workers a fixed benefit in retirement based on their wages and years of service, fell from 114,400 in 1985 to just 32,500 in 2002.[8] Such plans are now rarely available outside the public sector and a few declining, heavily unionized industries, where they have become a major drain on competitiveness.[9] General Motors now has 2.5 retirees on its pension rolls for every active worker, and an unfunded pension debt of $19.2 billion. Honoring its "legacy costs" to retirees now adds $1,800 to the cost of every vehicle GM makes, according to a 2003 estimate by investment bank Morgan Stanley.[10]

Moreover, an unprecedented number of these pension plans are going broke. In 2002 alone, 144 went under, leaving the federal government to pick up the tab for 187,000 pensioners, many of whom now must get by on severely reduced benefits. Just between 2001 and 2002, the government's projected short-term liability for bailing out failing defined-contribution plans increased from $11 billion to $35 billion, with huge defaults expected from the steel industry.[11] Most workers are now finding that they must bear the full responsibility for their own retirement savings, with many employers no longer even offering to make contributions to their 401(k) plans, much less offering protection from investment losses.

These new realities seep in slowly. Today most Americans understand that they are overburdened with debt, that they will probably have to switch jobs many times in a career, that the stock market goes down as well as up, and that they must save more. Clearly, the aging of the population does not improve the market power of workers. Instead, population aging, especially when combined with globalization, creates pressures to cut back benefits and to move jobs to places where labor is cheaper and younger.

Few Americans understand what they are really up against. Huge segments of the American population are now in danger of being stranded in old age because they grew up in a world in which population growth, and attendant economic growth, were simply taken for granted, while thrift was deemed an archaic "Victorian" notion.

Even among those approaching retirement age, the savings habit is amazingly weak in the United States. Among households headed by a person 55 to 64 (one of the most prosperous birth cohorts in American history), only 62 percent managed to spend less than they earned in 2001. Fewer than 60 percent had any assets in tax-deferred retirement accounts, such as IRAs or 401(k)s, and among those who did, the median balance was just $55,000.[12]

How far will that money go? Here is just one illustrative example of how unprepared most Americans are to cope with the coming crisis of old age. Suppose that the Medicare program continues without cuts in eligibility or coverage. Suppose, too, that despite the extra demands placed on the health care system by an aging, sedentary, and overweight population and by new medical technology, the rate of health care inflation slows down to just 7 percent, as compared to the 14 percent increases that occurred during many years in the 1980s and early 1990s. Now, suppose you retired in 2003 at age 65. How much savings would you need on the day you retired to cover the cost of all your future, out-of-pocket health care expenses or to purchase insurance for bills not covered by Medicare?

According to estimates by the well-respected Employee Benefit Research Institute, if you live to be 80, the amount is $116,000; if you live to be 90, it is $219,000; if you live to be 100 it is $354,000.[13] For younger Americans, health care costs in retirement will be much higher, given even moderate rates of health care inflation and no cuts in Medicare coverage. For example, Americans who retire at age 65 in

2013 and who live to be 90 would need an estimated $426,000 in the bank on their day of retirement to pay for their future health care bills not covered by Medicare. The recently passed prescription drug benefit under Medicare may reduce these numbers somewhat for some seniors, but bear in mind that they do not include any possible costs for long-term nursing home care, which typically runs between $40,000 and $80,000 a year.

The impossibility of these figures suggests another Victorian value that may soon reemerge—not only thrift, but also temperance. If the average American cannot afford to pay these sums, these sums will not be paid. Instead, access to quality health care will diminish, leaving individuals more and more responsible for preserving their own health. Government may succeed in forcing doctors to work for less, but that means there will be fewer doctors or doctors of lesser quality. Government may succeed in forcing drug companies to lower their prices, but as with all price controls, that too is likely to lead to shortages and loss of innovation. Government may jawbone hospitals to lower their rates, but that likely will lead to even fewer nurses per patient and more medical errors, so that as lethal as hospitals are today, they will become more so. Government may shift costs from generation to generation and from institution to institution by, for example, expanding Medicare to cover prescription drugs or by making Americans of all ages eligible. But by insulating more people from the real cost of their care, such expansions only increase the demand pressures on the system as a whole, forcing more tightly managed, or dare we say, rationed care.

All of which means that people in the future will be forced to place much less faith in medicine, and to take more responsibility for their own and other people's risky behaviors. How will these new realities express themselves culturally? Think of the collusion between evangelicals and municipal leaders in the nineteenth century in their common preoccupation with improving public health. The new Victorians, like the old ones, will not oppose drunkenness, gluttony, and promiscuity merely by pointing to the Bible, but by making utilitarian arguments about what is best for the greatest number, and about how the reckless endanger or encumber the prudent. Today tobacco smokers in California face opprobrium equivalent to that once visited upon opium smokers. It does not take much imagination to see a day when evangelical preachers will join together with uniformed public health officials in condemning not only cigarettes and bath houses, but "demon rum," "demon hamburgers," and "demon SUVs." Already, fundamentalist preachers circulate a manifesto asking, "What would Jesus drive?" and answer, quoting both scripture and the Environmental Protection Agency, that The Risen Lord Jesus would have us "walk, bike, car pool, and use public transportation more."[14]

Eight Thousand Harlots

Parallels with history are never exact, nor are historical explanations. But it is fair to say that many of the attitudes that we today associate with Victorians—moral rigidity, thrift, strict gender roles, a cult of motherhood—had two essential origins, both rooted in demography. The dynamic went something like this. First, the Industrial Revolution caused huge shifts in population from rural areas to large, impersonal cities. This shift in turn caused a dramatic increase in the average age of first marriage. Children were of little economic benefit in an urban environment and were instead increasingly costly impediments to upward mobility. As a result, men in particular often aged well into their 30s before they acquired enough wealth and position to make a "prudent marriage."

Urbanization and delay of marriage in turn gave rise to an enlarging pool of unattached young men and women, many of them recent migrants to the city, whose presence led to a steep rise in prostitution, pornography, gambling, and other vices. To resist such temptation, more and more voices began calling for a new regime of social repression, and often knew from personal experience just why it was necessary. Responding to charges of prudery, that eminent Victorian, Cardinal Newman, once retorted, "With eight thousand harlots in London alone, what utter nonsense is such talk. It is clear that many of us are early and profoundly corrupted: no one can tell how small a spark may cause explosion."[15]

At the same time, booming laissez-faire capitalism created stresses that caused both men and women to yearn for a "haven from a heartless world." As factories replaced farms and cottage industries, production in the home dwindled. Husbands and wives no longer worked side by side. Men had to leave the home each morning to face a market world of increasingly ruthless competition and bewildering change. Women, remaining at home with children of diminishing economic utility, needed a new role, which society eventually provided by elevating the prestige of motherhood to near mythic proportions while holding out the ideal of women as moral guardians of a debased, commercial culture.

Thus came the cultural reaction we call the Victorian age, with its exaltations not just of motherhood and domestic bliss, but also of women's special responsibility to crusade outside the home for the moral betterment of society. The proper upper-middle-class woman of the age became not just "the angel in the house," but increasingly a "municipal housekeeper" as well—a crusading activist against brothels, saloons, overcrowded settlements, and other threats to decency. "Woman's place is Home," Rheta Chile Dorr insisted in *What Eight Million Women Want*, "but home is not contained within the four walls of an individual house. Home is the community."[16]

Cradle Competition

By the later part of the nineteenth century and into the twentieth century, another demographic trend was reinforcing cultural conser-

vatism in both Britain and the United States: mounting fear of population decline. By 1900 the birthrate in the United States had fallen
40 percent from a hundred years before, and even more sharply among
the white, Protestant middle class. Among graduates of elite colleges,
the numbers marrying and having children were vanishingly small. At
Harvard, the diminishing number of graduates bringing sons into the
world caused President Charles W. Eliot to despair that children of
alumni would constitute a dwindling share of each year's new class. A
professor at Mount Holyoke College calculated that the percentage of
that school's graduates who never married had more than tripled between the mid-1840s and the early 1890s to an astonishing 50 percent. Of women graduating from Bryn Mawr College between 1888
and 1900, the average fertility rate as of 1913 was just 0.37 children
per graduate. Among the most talented women graduates of Wellesley,
the fertility rate was only one-fourth that required to replace their
numbers.[17]

These trends eventually caused even progressives to question their
support of women's rights. In an interview with the *Ladies Home Journal*
in 1906, Theodore Roosevelt bemoaned the fertility decline among the
"old New England stock." He attributed the trend partly to the "highly
welcome emancipation of woman" but went on to explain that "this
new freedom has been twisted into wrong where it has been taken to
mean a relief from all those duties and obligations which, though bur-
densome in the extreme, women cannot expect to escape."[18]

Roosevelt rallied a movement that came to be known as "positive
eugenics." Unlike many in his class at the time, he did not stress the
need to discourage the poor from breeding, but rather used his "bully
pulpit," both during his presidency and after, to harangue middle- and
upper-class couples to have more children. By 1906 his alarm over the
falling birthrates of America's most educated and accomplished citizens led him to chastise well-born women in his State of the Union
address for "willful sterility—the one sin for which the penalty is national death, race suicide."

Many rallied to his cause, finding that the declining fertility rate among the educated and affluent could be used as a weapon against both materialism and birth control. In a pamphlet published by a Catholic press, entitled *Race Suicide, Birth Control*, Michael P. Dowling attacked what he called a "gospel of greed" that was causing the well-to-do to limit their family size:

> Can it be possible that wealth is the natural enemy of infancy and childhood? And is the instinct of reproduction weaker in the privileged classes, the spirit of self-denial more pronounced? Is it not rather that large families are looked upon with disdain as a plebeian institution, entailing too much sacrifice, debarring the mother from many pleasures she is unwilling to forego? Is it not because every new birth requires the expense account to be overhauled, several chapters of travel to be blotted out, transfers to be made to the side of the nurse and the governess, balls and parties and receptions to be given up?[19]

Dowling, along with many other Catholic and Protestant conservatives, used "race suicide" arguments in successfully fighting off attempts to repeal the Comstock Act, so that information about birth control remained classified as "obscene" right through the 1930s, when the Supreme Court at last struck down this provision. In practice, few men or women heeded Roosevelt's call to procreate, especially among America's upper class. Instead, upper-class opinion increasingly rallied around a different strategy for avoiding race suicide.

"The lack of balance between the birthrate of the 'unfit' and the 'fit,' admittedly the greatest present-menace to civilization, can never be rectified by the inauguration of a cradle competition between these two classes," wrote Margaret Sanger, the founder of Planned Parenthood. Rather than haranguing the well-to-do about their small families, Sanger argued that "the most urgent problem today is how to limit and discourage the over-fertility of the mentally and physically defective.

Possibly drastic and Spartan methods may be forced upon American society if it continues complacently to encourage the chance and chaotic breeding that has resulted from our stupid, cruel sentimentalism."[20]

Sanger, who many today remember as the feminist heroine who tirelessly advocated a woman's right to "choose," repeatedly articulated this emerging vision, eventually winning strong support among the American public. "Birth control itself," Sanger wrote in her 1923 book, *Woman and the New Race*, "often denounced as a violation of natural law, is nothing more or less than the facilitation of the process of weeding out the unfit, of preventing the birth of defectives or of those who will become defectives."[21]

Three years later in an address to Vassar College, Sanger acknowledged that the declining birthrate among women like those in her audience was a national problem, but the solution, she argued, was to keep other people from reproducing: "Our statistics tell us that the birth rate of the college men and women is lower than it should be," Sanger allowed.

> There are some who deplore this condition and would remedy it by abusive epithets hurled at this conscientious group of decent and responsible citizens, who would rather have only the number of children they can decently rear, than to enter a cradle competition with the irresponsible.
>
> There is only one reply to a request for a higher birth rate among the intelligent, and that is to ask the government to first take off the burdens of the insane and the blemished from your backs. Sterilization for these is a remedy.[22]

By the time Sanger spoke, twelve states had already adopted a model eugenics law that called for the sterilization of the "feeble-minded, insane, criminalistic, epileptic, inebriate, diseased, blind, deaf, deformed and dependent"—including "orphans, ne'er-do-wells, tramps, the homeless and paupers."[23] Eventually, some 8,300 people would be sterilized in Virginia alone, including a young single white mother named Carrie Buck, whose alleged promiscuity, mental deficiency, and family history of mental illness was deemed enough to justify the state's cutting her tubes against her will. In the notorious words of Oliver Wendell Holmes, the Supreme Court justice who wrote the majority opinion upholding her conviction:

> It is better for all the world, if instead of waiting to execute degenerate offspring for a crime, or to let them starve for their imbecility, society can prevent those who are manifestly unfit from continuing their kind. The principle that sustains compulsory vaccination is broad enough to cover cutting the Fallopian tubes. Three generations of imbeciles are enough.[24]

The culture war over human reproduction that took place in the late nineteenth and early twentieth century essentially had two sides arguing over means, not ends. There were those, like Roosevelt, who sought to preserve the ruling class by cajoling emancipated white women to give up their clubs and careers to become dedicated mothers. And there were those like Sanger who argued that the same end could be achieved by a combination of universal access to birth control and eugenic measures to "weed out" the unfit, thereby relieving accomplished white women of the need to commit their lives to competitive breeding. The political movement that eventually embraced both sides of this culture war and took them to monstrous extremes was fascism, which engaged in both positive and negative eugenics (breeding farms for Aryans, concentration camps for the unfit) and thereby discredited both forms of eugenics until this day.

It is a sad history that may seem long behind us. Today, Sanger's ideological descendents speak in a language of individual rights, not eugenics—even if they still do point to the prospect of global overpopulation as an ancillary justification for abortion and birth control.

Meanwhile, Teddy Roosevelt's positive eugenics seems to have no surviving descendents among mainstream secularists. I am aware of nascent movements to revive "maternal feminism," but know of no mainstream thinker, much less politician, who openly worries about "race suicide" or who encourages educated women to be more fruitful. If social conservatives have anything at all to say about the subject, it is usually to discourage well-educated women from having babies unless they also have a husband, as when Dan Quayle famously criticized TV's Murphy Brown for daring to raise a child on her own.

Why did Quayle pick on Murphy Brown for having a child, instead of picking on, say, Dick Loudon and his wife Joanna of the popular and contemporary *Newhart* show. Dick and Joanna were just the type of well-educated, happily childless couple—living in Vermont, no less—who once drove Teddy Roosevelt and many other moderate conservatives into fits of recrimination. One obvious reason is that we still live in a cultural era dominated by the consequences of the 1950s baby boom. It is an era in which most members of the public still take U.S. population growth for granted, and accordingly can think of no harm done to society by a childless couple. The Loudons moved to Vermont to escape overcrowded New York, and who couldn't relate to that?

Another obvious reason is that we still live in an era in which there is living memory of the excesses of the eugenics movement, including its hideous expression in fascism. In the ideological struggle against the Nazis, opinion leaders in the United States set about delegitimizing notions of racial superiority and population engineering with amazing haste. Tellingly, the year the Supreme Court began to strike down sterilization laws was 1942, just as American GIs were preparing for their first major battle against the Nazis at El Alamein. At that time, just fifteen years after Oliver Wendell Holmes had upheld Virginia's right to cut the tubes of "imbecile" women, the Court decided that the Constitution did not, after all, allow the state of Oklahoma to sterilize a man for stealing chickens, noting that "in evil or reckless hands [sterilization] can cause races or types which are inimical to the dominant group to wither and disappear." By 1942 that was abundantly clear.[25]

The context of debate over all issues of human reproduction is about to change again. People who have adult memories of the 1930s and 1940s comprise a dwindling share of the population, and those who survive into the next decade will be deep into old age. Meanwhile, in both developed and undeveloped nations, rapid population decline will cause people to pay far more attention to population issues and to look at them differently.

One change to be expected is a revaluation of children, particularly in countries where elders outnumber them. As aging baby boomers in Europe and the United States swell the ranks of the elderly, children will come to seem scarcer and more valuable in many people's eyes. Partly this will be for emotional reasons. There will be unprecedented numbers of senior citizens, for example, and most senior citizens want grandchildren—and probably all the more so if, like the baby boomers, they've had few children themselves. And partly it will be for economic and even military reasons. Each new life will be literally more valuable, because each new person will wind up supporting, and possibly defending, increasing numbers of older people.

Under these circumstances, one cannot help but fear the return of something like the Progressive Era eugenics movement or even of Nazi-like population programs. And this time the population engineers will be empowered with much more sophisticated tools of biotechnology, albeit not with any deeper understanding of the essence of human life.

Already popular culture is increasingly infused with notions of genetic determinism that could well be put in service of a new eugenics movement. As the University of Maryland's Steve Selden has observed, "From news stories about 'novelty seeking' genes, to supposedly academic tomes on intellectual 'bell curves,' to 'reawakened' racist interpretations of American history, the social seeds for resurgent eugenics are still alive."[26] A continuation of subreplacement fertility rates, particularly if the trend remains concentrated among the best-educated members of society, could well make those seeds sprout, and the old debate between Sanger and Roosevelt will begin again.

What might that debate sound like in a modern American context? Americans need not worry, as Sanger did, about the high cost of "keeping alive thousands who never, in all human compassion, should have been brought into this world."[27] As it has turned out, the classes of people Sanger had in mind when she wrote those words went on to do quite well for themselves and for their country. Roosevelt, too, would have to acknowledge that the waves of Irish, Southern Italians, Eastern Europeans, and highly fertile southern blacks did not cause the American gene pool to degenerate or cause a Communist revolution, but made the country and its institutions ineffably stronger, to the point of making the United States the very hegemonic power Roosevelt wanted it to become. But now their children are not having enough children to reproduce themselves, and population aging is creating far greater burdens of dependency, not only in the United States but around the world, than Sanger ever imagined could be caused by too many "feeble-minded" children.

The response of religious fundamentalists to these trends will, of course, be to promote traditional family life, including strict separation of gender roles, while also continuing to oppose homosexuality, premarital sex, divorce, abortion, and birth control. To the extent that religious fundamentalists practice what they preach, they and their progeny will account for an increasing share of the population, both in the United States and elsewhere. What will the secular response be? The example of what happened the last time American secular opinion makers became fearful about "race suicide" should be chilling to those who favor reproductive freedom and human rights. What can we learn from where they went wrong?

The Revolt of Paterfamilias

In 1903, writing in response to Roosevelt's calls for more children from the well-to-do, an author who chose to identify himself only as "Paterfamilias" gave the President a lesson on what had happened to the cost of raising children in the last generation. Writing in the highbrow *North American Review*, this father of four explained:

> It used to be said that it did not cost anything to raise a baby, but that on the contrary it was an investment. Such a proposition can no longer be maintained. . . . Each baby cramps a little all that have come before it, with the result that the mother and father are soon obliged to sacrifice themselves almost entirely on the family altar. They must give up their comforts and pleasure; the mother must give up often even the necessities of life and take up its worst burden in order that the children shall not suffer.[28]

Both Sanger and Roosevelt, as well as other secularists involved in the culture war of the era, failed to grasp how the spread of the market economy was undermining fertility, particularly among the well-to-do. The Victorian age had sentimentalized domestic life, but failed to protect it from market forces that were eroding its economic viability. It championed many values people needed to survive in a world of rapid urbanization and laissez-faire capitalism—including thrift, temperance, and a strong family life based on mutual affection and common interests. It used social coercion and legal barriers to keep as many women as possible out of high-paying professions. But it could not prevent fertility decline because it could not protect the family—particularly the middle- and upper-middle-class family—from the mounting opportunity cost of raising children in an industrialized economy.

There was first the increasing competition for the family's resources created by the expanding consumer market. "The young couple who get married in the city or the small village at this day have become accustomed to many things with which they are not willing to part," Paterfamilias further explained. "They have learned to dress well, to have expensive pleasures, the theatre, concerts, visits and the like, which have been inspirations in their lives. They do not look forward to a life of self-sacrifice. . . . If one or two children are born, it is considered enough among those who are intelligent and even tolerably educated."

Then there was the escalating cost of equipping children with a proper education. By the late Victorian era, as today, the economy eagerly consumed the human capital formed by rising levels of parental investment, but offered parents no compensation save pride. For an upper-middle-class professional, another child was another bundle of bills for tutors, governesses, nannies, doctors, and nurses, the cost of which could easily threaten one's social standing. Paterfamilias counted himself "as fond a father as ever lived." But he worried,

> If a time should come when we had to give up our present style of living (which, practically, means our friends, since in that event we would not and could not continue present relations with them), I would consider it, perhaps, the most serious day of my life. So far as can be judged at present, the only thing that might threaten such an event would be the appearance say of a couple more children.[29]

Paterfamilias no doubt knew that such sentiments would strike many readers as selfish, which is probably why he remained anonymous, as did many others who wrote articles in this era criticizing Roosevelt's pro-natalist views. But there is no doubt that the economic anxiety he felt as an upper-middle-class parent of four was widely shared among his class, and that no amount of moralizing by evangelicals or the President himself was going to change their basic circumstance.

Women's "emancipation" further added to the cost of parenthood, as was well understood at the time. Those well-educated graduates of Wellesley, Bryn Mawr, and Vassar already had opportunities open to them in the arts, professions, and public life that their mothers had never known, making any children they might have cost much more in forgone income and social opportunity. "We have to face the practical certainty," warned eugenicist S. H. Halford, "that the gradual throwing open of trades and professions to women will involve the payment of large salaries to the more capable, and that this will place a premium, in women, upon celibacy or childlessness."[30]

The Victorians had understood that the emergence of industrialized capitalism made the family all the more essential, both as a "haven from a heartless world," and as a fount of what we today call human capital. But Victorians were not able to figure out, nor has anyone since, how to preserve the family so long as either market forces or the state usurps its productive functions. Universal public education helped spread the cost of raising the next generation, but left parents with less control over their children and still stuck with child-related expenses and opportunity costs that were relentlessly rising. The two great socialist experiments of the twentieth century, in Sweden and the Soviet Union, utterly failed to maintain replacement-level fertility rates, because they, too, could not compensate couples enough for the opportunity cost of raising children in an industrialized economy. In the United States and elsewhere, attempts to ameliorate the breakdown of the family through Social Security schemes have only added to the incentives to remain childless. Under all forms of government, eugenics and birth control have not succeeded in sustaining replacement-level fertility among the educated, but have contributed to a worldwide drop in birthrates that will, with cruel irony, leave a rising share of the world's population enfeebled by advancing age and without adequate support from the young. If no alternative solution can be found, the future will belong to those who reject markets, reject learning, reject modernity, and reject freedom. This will be the fundamentalist moment.

But perhaps there is another way. Three progressive, family-based alternatives to a fundamentalist future will be explored in the next chapter.

12

Work and Family

D oes the future belong to fundamentalism? It does if the spread of modernity continues to erode individual incentives to invest in children, while leaving a growing share of the population enfeebled by the chronic diseases of affluence and dependent on unsustainable social benefits. We can now see that in modern societies the root causes of population aging and decline are threefold:

1. The effective "double taxation" parenthood that occurs when programs that depend on increased human capital formation, such as Social Security, extract the same taxes and deliver the same benefits to parents and nonparents alike, thus offering nonparents a chance to "free ride" the system.
2. The mounting cost and declining effectiveness of health care spending in modern societies in which citizens are increasingly sedentary and prone to obesity and other diseases of affluence that limit their productive potential as they age.
3. The decline of the family as a locus of economic activity and mutual welfare, which occurs with globalization and the spread of mass production.

Taken together, these trends increase the dependence of citizens on big government and big business, even as population aging and increasing health care costs force both governments and corporations to retreat from commitments to provide a social safety net.

Can these trends be turned around? Not with incremental policies. In this chapter I lay out several policy prescriptions that address each of the three underlying causes of population aging and decline in modern societies. To many readers, most of these proposals will seem to lack political viability, and they may indeed be right, for now. But political viability is ultimately driven by changes in consciousness. As the reality of global aging and its consequences seeps into public understanding, policies that today might seem bizarre and impractical may well come to seem obvious and overdue.

Parental Dividends

If my first proposal is as good as I think it is, it will not inflame conservative fears about the growth of the "nanny state" or about fostering dependence among the undeserving poor. At the same time, the proposal would make vast new resources available for high-quality day care centers, nursery schools, and after-school programs that liberals favor. It would not require single-paycheck households to subsidize households in which both parents work, nor vice versa. Better yet, over time the proposal could largely pay for itself and benefit all sectors of society. In presenting this proposal, I show how it would apply in an American context, but it would be just as appropriate in any other modern nation.

First, some background. Today, Social Security and Medicare are financed through payroll taxes. For employees, the Social Security payroll tax currently comes to 6.2 percent of the first $87,000 of income. Employees are also liable for a payroll tax of 1.45 percent of all income, which is earmarked for Medicare. Employers contribute an equal amount for each employee, but economists agree that workers really pay both shares, because employers recoup the cost of their payroll taxes by offering less-generous salaries and benefits. If Social Security and Medicare continue on their current course, substantial increases in payroll taxes will be needed to fund future benefits. The cost of the two programs could exceed 30 percent of taxable payroll by 2035, and even 54 percent by 2080, according to the system's actuaries.[1]

My proposal is to offer substantial relief from these taxes to married parents with children under age 18, and to offer higher Social Security benefits to lower- and middle-income parents whose children complete high school. Have one child, and the payroll taxes you pay (and that your employer nominally pays) would drop by one-third. A second child would be worth a two-thirds reduction in payroll taxes. Have three or more children, and never pay payroll taxes until your youngest child turns 18.

When it comes time to retire, your Social Security benefit (and your spouse's) will be calculated just as if you had both been contributing the maximum Social Security tax during the period in which you were raising children, provided that all your children have graduated from high school. For most parents, this would mean an increase in Social Security benefits over what they would receive in today's system.

Notice, first, that the proposal would at least reduce the "double taxation" parents face under the present Social Security system. The system appropriates much of the human capital parents create when they invest in their children, and then requires them to contribute payroll taxes as well. The proposal offers an equitable remedy for this double burden. Because the payroll tax is a flat tax that applies to the first dollar of income, it is particularly hard on middle- and lower-middle-class parents, most of whom pay more in regressive payroll taxes than they do in progressive income taxes.

Notice, too, that this proposal is of no benefit to households in which no one works. It does not create an incentive to have a child just to get a check, as the old welfare system used to. At least one parent must be holding down a job with taxable income for this tax relief to be of value, and the same is true if one is to receive a higher retirement benefit. Under the proposal, middle-income parents would receive greater tax relief than low-income parents, but this is not necessarily unfair, if for no other reason than that the opportunity cost of having a child is higher for the middle class. Moreover, lower-income parents under this proposal would wind up receiving higher Social Security benefits, because their benefits would be calculated as if they had paid the maximum Social Security tax during their child-rearing years. The benefit to high-income families would be less than to middle-income families, both because any income above $87,000 is already free from Social Security taxes, and because they would be receiving no greater retirement benefits than they do currently.

Notice, also, that this proposal does not create a vast new child welfare bureaucracy, nor does it allow government to dictate what is the best way to raise a child. Instead, it takes resources *away* from government and puts them in the hands of individual parents, who decide for themselves how best to raise their children. This means that the family with a stay-at-home mom doesn't have to pay extra taxes just so the dual-income yuppie couple across the street can be entitled to free day care, as would occur if the government simply created an entitlement to day care. But nor do two-paycheck families wind up having to pay extra taxes to support the stay-at-home mom with any kind of government check. Instead, all parents receive a substantial increase in household income, which they can use to pay for more and higher-quality child care and education, if they like, or just to compensate themselves for the income they forgo by staying home with the children.

Of course, some parents might use the extra income in a manner that did not benefit their children—say to buy fancy cars or illegal drugs. But if they neglected their children to the point that their children failed to graduate from high school, they would in most instances forfeit substantial future retirement income. Exceptions would have to be made for parents whose children are too mentally or physically disabled to earn a high school degree, or whose children have died.

In the event of divorce, the benefit of payroll tax relief would be apportioned between the parents according to the terms of their custody agreement, so that, for example, a divorced couple with joint custody of the children would each receive half the payroll tax relief that they received jointly while married. Current law concerning the calculation of retirement benefits for divorced couples could be retained, so that, for example, a divorced wife who never remarried would still be eligible for benefits based on her former husband's earnings. If she has, or has had, full custody of the children she would also be eligible to receive extra retirement benefits if the children successfully complete high school. In cases of joint custody, divorced parents would have to split any extra retirement benefit for which they might be eligible.

Is it necessary to require that parents start off married to be eligible for these parental benefits? Let us have a fine debate about that as a nation. Conservatives can make their best case that only those who commit to marriage should be encouraged to have children, and that only heterosexual couples should be allowed to marry. Those on the opposite side of the culture war can make their best case that children of single or gay parents do just fine, and that the state has no business discriminating against individuals who have or adopt children out of wedlock.

My personal view is that a good compromise would be to sanction gay marriage, but to insist that marriage be at least an initial requirement for receiving parental benefits. Even in an age of easy divorce, the decision to marry signals commitment. Limiting benefits to married couples helps to ensure (however imperfectly) a greater increase in human capital than if the money is shared with those who have not demonstrated such a commitment.

Who Pays?

Wouldn't the Social Security system quickly go bankrupt if this proposal was adopted? The short-term costs to the system would be substantial, however, one must bear in mind the little-known fact that
100 percent of the 75-year projected deficit in Social Security could be
eliminated in a single stroke without causing what most people would
view as a cut in benefits. Just pay future retirees the same sized benefits
(adjusted for inflation) as today's retirees receive.[2]

The formulas used to determine Social Security benefits result in
each new generation of retirees receiving, or being promised, higher
and higher benefits. This is because benefits are linked to wages, and
over time wages consistently grow faster than inflation. Average full-
time wage earners retiring in 2001, for example, received an initial
benefit of $1,051 per month. Under current law, average full-time
wage earners retiring in 2020 will become entitled to a benefit with 21
percent more purchasing power, because of their higher lifetime
wages. By 2070, according to calculations by the Congressional Research Service, retirees with an average full-time wage history would
become entitled to a benefit 84 percent larger than what their counterparts today receive, even after adjusting for inflation.[3]

In the mid-1990s, a poll found that 46 percent of Americans aged
18 to 34 believed UFOs exist, while only 28 percent believed Social
Security would still be around by the time they retire.[4] How
shocked most of these Americans would be to learn that their worries about the future of Social Security are justified, but largely because they are promised much bigger benefits than their parents and
grandparents are receiving. Most would be profoundly surprised just
to receive any benefits, let alone do as well in retirement as today's
seniors.

To be sure, if future Social Security benefits grew only in line with
inflation, while real wages continued to advance, Social Security

would over time wind up replacing a diminishing share of a worker's wages. Typical retirees in, say, 2040 would enjoy the same purchasing power from their Social Security checks as do today's retirees, but instead of receiving a check that replaced around 42 percent of their former wages, as is currently promised, their check would replace only about 29 percent. However, it cannot be emphasized enough that the real choice is not between what's promised today and some lesser amount; it's between benefit levels that are sustainable and those that are not.

In the long run, of course, what most threatens Social Security is the low birthrate, which leaves fewer workers available to support each retiree. So long as that ratio continues to widen, the challenge of financing even reduced benefits continues to grow. This is why it is singularly appropriate to use pro-natalist measures to reform Social Security, instead of simply reducing benefits or raising taxes across the board. Yes, financing such a reform will require raising taxes on some people more than they would otherwise be raised. And it will require holding the purchasing power of future retirement benefits to today's levels for nonparents, while raising benefits above today's levels for a significant share of parents. But in the process, we would be eliminating or reducing the "double taxation" of parenthood, which is the only reform that gets to the root cause of the system's deficits.

Would such a reform create enough human capital to sustain the system? Today in Europe, countries that offer generous family allowances and day care services, notably France and the Scandinavian countries, have higher fertility rates than those in which parental benefits are less generous, such as Italy or Spain. Yet no country in Europe produces enough children to replace its population.

One reason may be that even in countries like France, the amount of compensation offered to parents is still insufficient to overcome the growing opportunity cost of children, or to remove the incentive to let other people's children pay for one's health and pension benefits. A host of cultural, economic, technological, and generational changes also affect attitudes toward children and the amount people are willing to sacrifice on their behalf. Moreover, European economies in general are highly rigid, making it difficult for mothers to find part-time work or flexible hours.

For all these reasons, there is no single policy lever that will automatically raise a country's fertility rate. Changes in the nature of work, in gender roles, in the costs and benefits of the welfare state, and in the economy's demand for human capital are all conspiring to eliminate economic incentives to procreate, and to make the cost of raising children increasingly prohibitive. Offering parents and other caregivers more compensation for the human capital they create may not save the day, but it is surely just and sensible in an aging society.

Health of Ages

The unsustainable cost of old age entitlements is one good reason to encourage younger Americans to have at least enough children to sustain the population. But it is also a good reason to encourage greater health and productivity among older citizens. We know with great certainty how many people will be over age 65 in 2050, because those people have already been born. What we don't know, but can influence, is how many of those 65-year-olds will be, in today's sense, "elderly."

How many will suffer from disabilities? How many will be able or want to continue working? Will the population of 65-year-olds largely consist of isolated individuals enfeebled and impoverished by chronic conditions? Or will large numbers be healthy enough to participate in the job market, become active in their grandchildren's lives, or serve as volunteers or community leaders? Some people age poorly, some gracefully. And some people age both gracefully and productively. If enough people embrace the ideal of productive aging, those looming deficits in Medicare, Social Security, and other entitlements may turn out to be vastly exaggerated, and liberal secular institutions may just have a future.

During our last six months of life, for example, we may consume $50,000 worth of high-tech health care at taxpayers' expense, but if those last six months come when we are 85 instead of 75, and we've meanwhile been able to continue contributing to society, then what's the harm in our increased longevity? In an aging society, there will be fewer children to support. And there could be fewer adults to support as well if the threshold of true old age recedes and the average life span includes more productive years. If baby boomers turn out to be as healthy at age 75 as today's 65-year-olds, and are also able to delay their average age of retirement by ten years, then we have little trouble financing the aging of the population.

Is there any reason to believe this will actually happen? Let's start with the good news. Health and wealth for a vast cross section of those over age 65 are improving, creating what some gerontologists call a "second middle age," or what others call a "third age." People who are experiencing this new life stage are not hard to spot. They are people like Don Q. Davidson who, after stepping down from a 30-year career in publishing, thought he would pass his golden years tinkering in his wood shop. Instead, at age 72 Davidson found himself presiding over a flourishing custom woodworking business in Wilton, Connecticut. "Little did I think that at age 72 I'd have as much energy and interest in a work-related enterprise as I still have," says Don.[5]

They are people like Ashley H. Carter, a former AT&T Bell Laboratories research physicist, who at 75 now directs a program at Drew University that teams retired industrial scientists like himself with undergraduates on research projects.[6] These are folks who contemptuously reject the "golf and drinks" model of retirement. They may have lost some of their youthful drive and vigor, but they don't feel old or out-of-date, and they want to remain productive. Many enroll in flourishing "elder hostel" programs. Many others serve as consultants, volunteers, or small business owners, or launch long-delayed careers in the arts or helping professions.

How broad-scale is this phenomenon of productive aging? There are several indicators. The average age of retirement, after trending downward for 50 years, is now moving back up, at least in the United States. Whereas less than a quarter of all American men aged 65–69 were still in the labor force in 1985, nearly a third are today. Some of this change may be due to less generous pensions and health care plans, but clearly most older Americans are not putting off retirement because they have to. In 1984 the median net worth of households headed by a person 65 to 74 was slightly less than that of households headed by a person 45–54. Now it's the older households that are the wealthiest by far, enjoying exactly double the net worth of the younger group.[7]

There are also many signs that older Americans are less frail than in the past. According to several well-publicized recent studies, disability rates among older Americans declined by between 1.55 percent and 0.092 percent per year during the 1990s.[8] Older Americans are also becoming more involved in the lives of their grandchildren. Between 1970 and 1997, the number of children living in households headed by their grandparents increased by 76 percent. Today's older Americans are also far better educated than the elderly of previous generations, which is very positive, since health strongly corresponds to education.

In the face of all these trends, one might reasonably conclude that we have little to fear from population aging. With fewer younger workers available, employers in the future will pay a higher economic penalty for age discrimination, and will have new incentives to create flexible, part-time jobs suitable for older workers. To keep their classrooms full, universities will be forced to reach out to older students and promote lifetime learning. If all these current trends continue, the percentage of the population over 65 may increase, but the percentage of the population that is "elderly"—that is, frail and economically dependent—may not.

Yet, as we saw in Chapter 8, overshadowing all this good news are other trends that threaten to make promises of productive aging seem like happy talk. They include an alarming decline in physical fitness among young and middle-aged Americans, increasing exposure to infectious disease, increasing inequality, and declining access to health care—all colliding with expanding social definitions of what good health is and inflating expectations of what the health care system can and should do to enhance longevity and quality of life. What can be done?

Persuading Americans to take better care of themselves is by no means easy. As Prohibition and the War on Drugs prove, simply criminalizing unhealthy behavior doesn't work. Similarly, imposing sin taxes on undesirable behavior, although effective, can only go so far without creating black markets. Besides, most Americans are appropriately resentful of government efforts to penalize them for their chosen lifestyles. But what if, instead of trying to punish or castigate citizens for unhealthy behavior, government concentrated on reducing the major environmental causes of premature death (including not just pollution, but poverty and hazardous living arrangements) and then offered to pay citizens to clean up their act? Here are some illustrative suggestions of how this might be done.

Death by Sprawl

On a purely statistical basis, what is more likely to get you killed over the course of the next year: (a) living in Israel in the midst of the Intifada, (b) living in crime-ridden, inner city Baltimore, Chicago, Dallas, Houston, Milwaukee, Minneapolis–St. Paul, Philadelphia, or Pittsburgh, or (c) living in the bucolic outer suburbs of those cities? The answer is overwhelmingly (c). A recent study by William H. Lucy, professor of urban and environmental planning at the University of Virginia, confirmed that the great migration of Americans into sprawling outer suburbs over the last generation is a huge cause of disability and premature death.[9] Yes, in the suburbs you're less likely to be killed by a stranger—unless, that is, you count strangers driving automobiles. To cite just one example, residents of inner-city Houston face about a 1.5 in 10,000 chance of dying during the coming year either at the hands of a murderous stranger or as the victim of an automobile accident. But in Montgomery County, a sprawling suburb of Houston, residents are 50 percent more likely to die from one of those two causes, because of the much higher rate of automobile accidents.[10]

Sprawling, auto-dependent suburbs are unhealthy in other ways as well. In such an environment almost no one walks or takes a bike, and for good reason. Although only 6 percent of all trips are made on foot or by bicycle, pedestrians or cyclists account for 13 percent of all traffic fatalities. Not surprisingly, metro areas marked by sprawling development are the most dangerous regions to walk or bike today.[11] Largely because of the growth of sprawl, the number of trips people take on foot has dropped by 42 percent in the last 20 years.

Rarely walking or biking is even more deadly. Among women, walking ten blocks per day or more reduces the chance of heart disease by a third.[12] Although taking at least 10,000 steps a day (the equivalent of a five mile walk) is widely considered by public health officials to be a baseline for maintaining health, a typical, sedentary American takes only about 3,500–5,500 steps per day. The risk of a sedentary lifestyle is comparable to, and in some studies greater than, the risk of hypertension, high cholesterol, diabetes, and even smoking.[13]

The trend has particularly affected the lives of children. In 1977, children aged 5 to 15 walked or biked for 15.8 percent of all their trips. By 1995, children made only 9.9 percent of their trips by foot or bicycle—a 37 percent decline. Some 70 percent of all trips made by children today are in the back seat of a car.[14]

According to the surgeon general, the direct and indirect economic costs of obesity come to $117 billion a year, or about 9.4 percent of all health care spending.[15] Americans who never exercise cost the health care system some $76.6 billion a year.[16] Sprawl does not fully account for Americans' increasingly sedentary lives, but it is a major factor, and that makes it a leading cause of chronic disease and disability.[17]

One must add that sprawl, in addition to all the auto-related pollution it creates, is also associated with high levels of social isolation—people lacking casual day-to-day contact with neighbors or networks of acquaintances—and with low involvement in community affairs. According to the World Health Organization, "Road traffic separates communities and divides one side of the street from the other. Fewer pedestrians means that streets cease to be social spaces, so that isolated pedestrians often fear attack. Further, suburbs that depend on cars for access isolate people without cars, particularly the young and old."[18] What's the public health implication? A large volume of literature shows that the health risks of being socially isolated are comparable to the risks associated with cigarette smoking, blood pressure, and obesity.[19] In a sprawling environment, many elders who might otherwise be able to work and volunteer cannot when fading nighttime vision and other infirmities prevent them from being safe drivers.

So it turns out that among the biggest policy levers available for improving public health and reducing old age dependency involve reducing subsidies to sprawl. These include gas taxes that are nowhere near high enough to compensate for even the environmental cost of driving, let alone the direct and indirect toll in injury, chronic disease, and premature death. And they include ending overinvestment in new roads and highways, and directing more investment to mass transit, bike trails, and sidewalks. Thanks to warnings from the surgeon general and vastly increased tobacco taxes, millions of Americans have managed with great difficulty to overcome their addiction to nicotine. It's equally important for the federal government to put Americans on notice about the health hazards of auto-dependent sprawl, and to provide them with financial incentives to choose a healthier environment and lifestyle.

Instead of transit users having to feed a fare box, for example, they should receive a dollar's credit on their swipe cards for up to three rides a day, financed by drivers, who will enjoy less traffic, cleaner air, and a smaller burden on the health care system. The government could also offer greater home mortgage deductions to homeowners who move to cities and compact developments served by mass transit. These and other measures described below may seem politically unfeasible, but when sold to an aging population as policies to improve public health and as remedies for a failing health care system, they may gain more political traction than you might at first imagine.

Drugs for Jumping Jacks

The benefits to older people of even moderate exercise are overwhelming. As a report sponsored by the AARP and other leading health and aging groups concludes: "Scientific evidence increasingly indicates that physical activity can extend years of active independent life, reduce disability, and improve the quality of life for older persons."[20] Elders who exercise develop disabilities at only one-fourth the rate of nonexercisers, and incur 25 percent less health care expenses.[21] Yet approximately 34 percent of the population aged 50 and older is sedentary, and fewer than 50 percent of older adults report ever having received a suggestion to exercise from their physicians.[22]

Meanwhile, though the Medicare program is scheduled to go broke by 2030,[23] the program has recently been expanded to cover prescription drugs. There's little evidence that such a new entitlement will add to the health and life expectancy of the elderly. Only 3 percent of the elderly report not getting drugs that were prescribed to them.[24] Meanwhile, overmedication and adverse reaction to prescription drugs remain a leading cause of death in the United States, particularly among the elderly. Medicare enrollees suffered an estimated 1.9 million drug-related injuries a year before the new prescription drug benefit went into effect.[25]

So perhaps if our political system cannot resist expanding Medicare to cover prescription drugs, it can at least extract an ameliorating quid pro quo that will help defray the financial cost while also giving seniors many more years of active, independent life. Offer every American over 50 a voucher he or she can use to join a gym or exercise program. Those who use the voucher, and can demonstrate at least a once-a-week attendance record, will become entitled to subsidized prescription drugs, regardless of financial need. Those who do not use the voucher will also be entitled to subsidized drugs, but only if they lack enough income or private insurance to purchase them on their own.

Better yet, why not apply the same principle to the whole population? Already some private health insurers are offering everything from discounted health-club memberships to European vacations for those who exercise, lose weight, or quit smoking. Why not mandate that all insurers, including Medicare, adjust their premiums on an actuarially fair basis to reward those who can establish regular gym or exercise-class attendance?

Any measures that will lead to more people working at older ages will also bring large dividends in public health. If you doubt that work benefits the elderly, consider the experience of so-called "notch babies." These are people who were born just after January 1, 1917, who, due to a change in Social Security benefit formulas, wound up receiving substantially smaller Social Security benefits than those born during the years just prior to that date. One might imagine that notch babies as a group would suffer poorer health as result of their loss of benefits, but the opposite is true. If one compares the mortality rates of cohorts born in the six months prior to January 1, 1917, with the mortality rates of those born in the subsequent six months, a startling disparity emerges. Up until age 65, these two cohorts showed no difference in their mortality, but after age 65, men in the group with the lower Social Security benefits enjoyed significantly better health. The reason, researchers speculate, is that many notch babies responded to their benefit cut by delaying retirement or taking on part-time jobs, which helped them to avoid the unhealthy consequences of inactivity and social isolation.[26]

Is this an argument for cutting Social Security? Perhaps, especially since the program on its current course offers progressively more generous benefits to each new generation of retirees. But it is also an argument for better job retraining, better mass transit, and reforms to the health insurance market that will make it easier for employers to offer flexible part-time employment to older workers.

Such approaches might seem far fetched, but they would bring far higher returns to public health and do far more to promote productive aging than, for example, expanding Medicare to pay for mood-altering or sex-enhancing drugs. Population aging need not break the Treasury or cause vast poverty among the elderly, but only if we take more responsibility for the rate at which we age.[27]

The Americans Without Disabilities Act

The Americans with Disabilities Act (ADA) mandates everything from how parking lots and public bathrooms are arranged to how employers organize work, but it does nothing to prevent disability. Why not adapt parallel legislation that would attack, with equal invasiveness, the problem of how to keep Americans from getting disabled in the first place. Here are a few examples:

To encourage exercise:

Use abandoned railroad right-of-ways to create an interstate bicycle highway system. Instead of charging tolls, install machines that pay cyclists according to the number of miles they've peddled.

Mandate that all companies employing twenty-five workers or more either provide on-site exercise rooms or tax-free employee benefits covering gym membership. Mandate one hour of daily physical education in all public schools. Limit the size of school districts so that most students can reasonably walk or bike to school. Designate more parking spaces at high schools as handicapped only.

Just as the ADA mandates that a set number of parking spaces be set aside for the handicapped, let the AWDA (Americans Without Disabilities Act) mandate that all new planned urban developments contain a set length of sidewalks and trails per resident. Developments with more than 300 residents should have mandatory community centers to combat social isolation and its adverse health effects.

Offer a $200-a-month increase in benefits to welfare recipients who shed 20 or more pounds to achieve a body mass index appropriate to their height, using the resulting decrease in Medicaid expenditures to meet the cost.

To improve diet:

Require the Food and Drug Administration to develop an operational definition of "junk food" based on fat, salt, and sugar content. Require health warnings on junk food, and make it subject to sales taxes commensurate with those imposed on cigarettes and alcohol. Ban sales of junk food in school cafeterias. Ban junk food advertising on children's television. Ban the use of "Joe Camel" equivalents, such as Ronald MacDonald, in all junk food advertising.

Just as most jurisdictions hold down concentrations of liquor stores through licensure and zoning, do the same for fried meat shacks. Restaurants serving items meeting the FDA's definition of "junk" would require a special license to operate, with the supply of new Burger Kings and McDonalds strictly limited by regional quotas.

Through an expansion of the food stamp program, make the entire population entitled to generous, free weekly allowances of fruits and vegetables. The National Cancer Institute recommends a minimum of five servings of fruits and vegetables a day. However, fruits and vegetables have gone up in price more than any other food category in recent years.[28]

To reduce the adverse health effects of hierarchy and income inequality:

Repeal the regressive Medicare payroll tax. Increase the progressivity of the federal income tax, and finance Medicare through increased gas taxes and general revenue.

Promote small business, particularly in urban areas. Make executive compensation in excess of 30 times what the average American worker makes no longer deductible from corporate taxable income. Promote thrift as an avenue of upward mobility. Invest in improving urban schools. Look for ways to reduce stress and social isolation at a population level, such as by building more parks and offering more opportunities for public recreation.

Redirect the research agenda of the National Institutes of Health to put much greater resources into discovering the biological determinants of addiction, depression, and obesity. Canada's equivalent of NIH now directs research dollars away from high-tech research that, although possibly very beneficial to individuals, does little or nothing to improve public health.

Many of these proposals may lack political viability for now, but there are clear signs that the American people are becoming fed up with the current health care system and open to bold new approaches. Marcus Welby would be shocked, for example, to know what Americans think of doctors these days. In the late 1960s, when millions of viewers tuned in every Tuesday night to watch the avuncular MD offer sage advice to his patients about the root causes of their illnesses, more than 70 percent of Americans told pollsters that they had confidence in medical leaders; today, only 40 percent trust doctors. A mere 29 percent of the public agree with the statement, "The health care system would work better if doctors had full control of the system."[29] According to a poll commissioned by the consumer advocacy group Center for Science in the Public Interest, two-thirds of Americans believe that the financial interests of business and industry drive science, while 64 percent think that the medical judgment of physicians can be swayed by gifts from drug companies.[30]

The more people know about health care, the less faith they have in doctors and their remedies. Fully half the public now says it lacks trust in "scientific solutions" for health care, and nearly 80 percent of health care policy professionals share this doubt. Indeed, according to a study recently published in the *Milbank Quarterly*, the largest single factor driving down trust in doctors—among the general public, but especially among health care policy elites—is the growth of concerns about the ineffectiveness of modern medicine.[31]

These new realities are creating a climate of opinion that may be very receptive to nonmedical approaches to improving health and promoting productive aging. In combination with measures to reduce the problems of overtreatment and medical errors, an increased emphasis on health promotion would not only reduce the demand for health care, but would help free up the resources needed to provide universal access. It's true that we all die of something, and that usually our deaths trigger large expenditures of health care dollars regardless of our age at the time. But the more we can reduce the incidence of chronic disease related to behavior and the environment, the less money we'll have to spend on health care right up until the time death approaches, even as people gain extra years of productive life.

In Greek mythology, the god of medicine, Asclepios, had two daughters: Hygeia was the daughter responsible for prevention, and Panacea was responsible for cure. In our time, we keep expecting modern medicine to produce a panacea, but somehow the namesake goddess never quite delivers. It's time to pay much greater respect to her more powerful sister.

A Homemade Future?

Reducing the cost of children and promoting more productive aging are daunting tasks, but they still may not be sufficient to save the day. The largest and original cause of population aging and decline lies with the scope of the market system itself. Yes, global capitalism is highly efficient. It can produce just about anything far more cheaply than you or your family can for yourselves. But in the process it erodes individual incentives to invest in children—by offering competing and more lucrative uses of time and money and appropriating most of the human capital produced by parents—even as it requires vast amounts of uncompensated parental investment to sustain both production and consumption.

Such a system can continue to thrive even with below-replacement fertility rates, but only so long as population momentum from the past continues to produce an adequate supply of new workers and consumers. In the long term, it is probably not sustainable without population growth, and the long term may get here much sooner than most anyone imagines if the modern market system becomes truly global and drives fertility rates below replacement levels worldwide.

From time to time, various groups in modern societies, from returning American GIs in the 1950s, to upper-middle-class Catholics in the 1960s, to Mormons in the early 1990s, may try to ignore the relentlessly rising cost of children in a mass production economy, but are inevitably punished to the point that whatever baby booms (or boomlets) they produce quickly end. The long-term trend is that mass production and consumption relentlessly suppress fertility, particularly among the most educated and affluent, regardless of their race, ethnicity, or religion, even as it requires more and more highly educated workers to operate. If the global economy runs short on oil or some other natural resource, there is a good chance it can find a substitute. But if it runs short on children, it has no way to correct the imbalance without radical change in its underlying rules. For a while, more machines, more female labor, more immigrants, and eventually more elderly labor may make up for the workers and consumers who are not born, but obviously a system that consumes more human capital than it produces must one day end.

If it is not sustainable, then what might take its place? It may seem far-fetched, but let us consider what might happen if the home, and the children in it, could become more of a locus of economic activity in the twenty-first century. America will never again be a nation of yeoman farmers, and all over the world current trends are threatening small family businesses and discouraging home production. But imagine if, through some combination of changes in law, technology, and consumer preference, these trends began to reverse.

Encouraging home-based employment and family business could help society cope with many of the problems that attend an aging population. For example, just as it is easier to raise a child when you work at home, so it is easier to look after an aging relative. With a return to three-generation households united in common enterprise, the burdens of motherhood could be brought back closer to historical norms. Grandparents would help out with the raising of children, and then children would help out with the care of grandparents, while members of all generations contribute to the family enterprise according to their abilities. Time that mothers, as well as fathers, now lose commuting to work or driving back and forth to the day care center or to look in on grandma could be put to more satisfying and useful purposes. The cost of raising children would decline, and parents would benefit more from the human capital they create by raising and educating children.

To some this may sound utopian; to others it might sound like a return to a benighted past. But regardless of how individuals feel about the constraints or intimacies of family life, population aging itself could well force a large-scale return to home production and family enterprise. In both developed and underdeveloped countries, population aging will likely depress growth of the formal economy. As we can see in Europe today, just because there are fewer young people does not mean jobs will be plentiful. Meanwhile, population aging will cause many pension systems to fold or collapse. These very consequences will force many individuals to fall back either on the traditional family or on other communitarian forms of living.

Many other social factors may increase the appeal of family enterprise. It is worth remembering, for example, that before the growth of mass markets and the decline of home production, Western societies had little concept of the stage of life we now call adolescence, and certainly did not associate puberty with such negative features as identity crisis, alienation, or suicidal tendencies. Certainly Western literature, particularly in the eighteenth century, is replete with descriptions of youths struggling to get free of tyrannical fathers or suffocating mothers. But the angst-filled "troubled teen," typified by Holden Caulfield in *The Catcher in the Rye*, is a modern character whose prominence in the culture is deeply related to the growth of mass production and the attendant decline of family enterprise.

In the modern era, teenagers typically contribute little more to the economic well-being of the family than do infants. Many would be at a loss to describe with any detail what their parents actually do for a living, much less derive an identity by participating in their parents' craft or profession. Long past the age in which they are biologically ready to start families of their own, most teenagers retain the economic and social status of costly dependents—neither asked nor able to play any significant productive role inside the home or in the wider economy. No wonder then that the modern era produces widespread self-abuse among the young and deviant youth cultures. Under the modern system of mass consumption and mass production, young adults remain dependent on their parents far longer and far more extensively than in the past, and yet have little or nothing of economic value to return. Under such conditions, "identity crisis" becomes inevitable as biological maturity does not meet with social maturity.

Obviously, there will always be happy families and unhappy families. But in general both youths and elders could feel less marginalized in families united by a common enterprise, because both would be re-gaining productive roles, even if it only involved looking out for one another. Indeed, for members of such families the economic obstacles to getting married while still of childbearing age could be reduced. A young bride might have to live with her in-laws for some years. But she and her husband could also be gaining free child care and low housing costs, as well as flexible employment, all of which could make the pursuit of a higher education and parenthood much easier to reconcile.

Increased family enterprise and home production would also likely lead to tighter communities as neighbors begin to trade goods and ser-vices with one another. This in turn would further ease the burdens of parenthood, as neighbors who are at home and who have daily deal-ings with each other will naturally look out for each other's children. The importance of such informal child care networks is hard to overemphasize. Indeed, as Sarah Blaffer Hrdy and other social biolo-gists point out, the child care provided by such "allo parents" is a ma-jor factor in human evolution. Why, even under primitive conditions, do women often live many decades after reaching menopause? Be-cause natural selection has apparently favored societies in which older women were available and inclined to help out with the care and nur-ture of the young.[32]

Note, however, that a return to family enterprise does not have to mean a return to patriarchy or traditional gender roles. Fathers who work and live in the same place are more likely to be involved in the lives of their children. The division of labor within a family enterprise would be a matter for each family to decide, with men having no in-trinsic advantages such as a unique right to hold property. On balance, the quality and equality of marriage most likely improves when hus-band and wives work side by side in a common enterprise. Rather than meeting as near strangers at the end of the day, exhausted by their at-tentions to bosses, co-workers, and competing commuters, married couples could reintegrate their lives with each other and with their children, making investment in family life potentially far more re-warding, both economically and emotionally.

An economy reoriented to home production and family business would no doubt have to sacrifice many of the economies of scale of-fered by today's corporate giants. Your neighbor's local hardware store will never be able to compete with Home Depot on the price of drill sets or patio furniture. The family-owned grocery store down the street will be more expensive than Walmart. The handmade vase purchased from a local artisan will cost more than the factory-made equivalent available at Pier 1. But against this, an economy reoriented towards small-scale family enterprise and home production offers the benefits of greater social cohesion, less stress on working parents, and many other practical advantages. Paying your neighbor to look after your frail grandmother during work hours, for example, could well be a far more cost-effective and appropriate solution than paying some nursing home chain $40,000 a year.

Home production, especially if combined with the growth of barter systems and local markets, offers individuals in an aging society an-other potential benefit. In a coming era when payroll taxes may well consume 30–40 percent of a worker's income, being a wage slave will make increasingly less sense for many people, as will participating in the formal economy generally. Why use after-tax dollars to buy a stranger's services if you and your extended family can provide the same service, or can barter it with a neighbor, tax-free? In Italy and many Latin American countries, high payroll taxes have already driven much of the economy underground, making home production and barter systems an increasingly attractive alternative to employ-ment in the formal sector.

Some of the conditions necessary to foster family enterprise will evolve of their own accord, as individuals in aging societies grapple with failing social safety nets as well as diminishing opportunities and returns in the formal economy. Others may come about due to changes in technology. Already, networked computers are making "telecommuting" more feasible, thereby giving more parents the flexibility they need to balance work and family. Which business models will ultimately succeed on the Internet is unknown, but eBay's success demonstrates the Internet's dramatic potential for opening up new niche markets to small-scale producers and empowering small retailers. The Internet is also making homeschooling far less labor intensive, and may eventually lead to a collapse in the price of higher education as virtual campuses replace those made of bricks and mortar, thereby dramatically lowering the cost of children.

Other technological changes could also help to restore the economic basis of family life. For example, could a day be coming when solar power or fuel cells allow each household to produce its own energy? Will advances in bioengineering one day allow the majority of families to raise most of the food they need in their own back yards, or to trade for it with nearby neighbors? Will advances in information technology and nanotechnology one day allow for efficient home manufacture of consumer items, or alternatively, make consumer items so cheap that demand increases for handcrafted goods?

Government could and should play a catalytic role in moving technology in these directions, while taking many other measures to encourage family enterprise. In many areas, for example, zoning laws prohibit or discourage small business. Consistent with the need to reduce sprawl for environmental and public health reasons, government should encourage patterns of development that allow small stores and craft shops in residential areas, as well as small-scale agricultural production. Government could also help by offering low-interest microloans to budding family enterprises, and by reducing regulation and taxation of small business.

Separating health insurance from employment is another key to fostering family enterprise. In the United States, there is no greater barrier to self-employment and entrepreneurship than the cost of health insurance, which cannot be acquired under current arrangements at an actuarially fair price by individuals or small businesses.

This is not the place to debate all the possible ways to reform the financing of health care, except to point out that the current employer-based system in the United States undermines the economic viability of parenting.

Another policy option that should be explored is what Roy Boshara of the New America Foundation calls a new "Homestead Act for the twenty-first century." Essentially, the idea is to endow every baby born in America with a $6,000 "stakeholder account." If invested in a relatively safe portfolio yielding a 7 percent annual return, this endowment would grow to more than $20,000 by the time the child graduated from high school, and to $45,000 by the time he or she reached age 30. The idea, which the United Kingdom is already trying out, would go a long way toward decreasing inequality of wealth, but more importantly, it would help to reduce servility of the next generation to both corporations and the state. It would give more young people the freedom and capital they need to pay for the cost of higher education or vocational training, buy a first home, or start a small family business, and in all these ways would empower more people to have the children they want.

Family enterprise may never be as efficient, in a narrow sense, as a global system of wage slavery, but it does offer the incalculable advantage of not overconsuming its supply of human capital by making material goods too cheap and children too expensive. Will the family become the new locus of production in the twenty-first century? We cannot know, but this much is sure: If free societies have a future, it will be because they figure out or stumble upon a way to restore the value of children to their parents, and of parents to each other.

Notes

Chapter One

1. United Nations Population Division, "World Population Prospects: The 2000 Revisions," vol. 3, figure v.1., 156.

2. Commission on Population Growth and the American Future, *Population and the American Future* (Washington, D.C.: U.S. Government Printing Office, 1972).

3. United Nations International Conference on Population and Development, "Programme of Action of the United Nations International Conference on Population and Development" (Cairo, Egypt, September 5–13, 1994), http://www.iisd.ca/linkages/Cairo/program/p02005.html (accessed November 2003).

4. Edwin M. Hale, *The Great Crime of the Nineteenth Century* (Chicago: C. S. Halsey, 1867), quoted in Reva Siegel, "Reasoning from the Body: A Historical Perspective on Abortion Regulation and Questions of Equal Protection," *Stanford Law Review* 44 (1992): 261.

5. Comments of Rep. Charles Finley (R.-Ky.), quoted in Women and Social Movements in the United States, 1775–2000, "Excerpts from National Committee on Federal Legislation for Birth Control Reports on Interviews with Representatives and Senators, 1931–36," reprinted in "Birth Control and the Good Old Boys in Congress," *Margaret Sanger Papers Newsletter* 26 (Winter 2000-2001): 2–5, http://womhist.binghamton.edu/mwd/doc24.htm (accessed November 2003).

6. Roy T. Englert, Alan Untereiner, and Sherri Lynn Wolson, "Brief of Professors of History George Chauncey, Nancy F. Cott, John D'emilio, Estelle B. Freedman, Thomas C. Holt, John Howard, Lynn Hunt, Mark D. Jordan, Elizabeth Lapovsky Kennedy, and Linda P. Kerber as *Amici Curiae* in Support

of Petitioners," *John Geddes Lawrence and Tyron Garner v. State Of Texas*, U.S. Supreme Court, no. 02–102.

7. Betty Friedan, *The Feminine Mystique* (1963; reprint, New York: W. W. Norton and Company, 1977), 32, http://www.h-net.org/~hst203/documents/friedan1.html (accessed November 2003).

8. Social Security Online, "2003 OASDI Trustees Report," tables IV.B2 and IV.B3, http://www.ssa.gov/OACT/TR/TR03/trLOT.html (accessed November 2003).

Chapter Two

1. David M. Adamson, Nancy Belden, Julie DaVanzo, and Sally Patterson, "How Americans View World Population Issues: A Survey of Public Opinion," Rand Corporation (2000), http://www.rand.org/publications/MR/MR1114/ (accessed November 2003).

2. United Nations Population Division, "World Population Prospects: The 2002 Revision: Highlights" (February 26, 2003), figure 1, http://www.un.org/esa/population/publications/wpp2002/WPP2002-HIGHLIGHTSrev1.pdf; and W. Lutz, W. Sanderson, and S. Scherbov, "The End of World Population Growth," *Nature* 412 (2001): 543–546.

3. U.S. Central Intelligence Agency, "Long-Term Demographic Trends: Reshaping the Geo-political Landscape" (July 2001), http://www.fas.org/irp/cia/product/Demo_Trends_For_Web.pdf; and United Nations Population Division, "World Population Prospects: The 2002 Revision: Annex Tables," http://www.un.org/esa/population/publications/wpp2002/wpp2002annextables.pdf (accessed November 2003).

4. Hideo Ibe, "Aging in Japan," International Longevity Center–USA, Ltd. (2000), http://www.ilcusa.org/_lib/pdf/Aginginjapan.pdf (accessed November 2003).

5. United Nations Population Division, "World Population Prospects: The 2002 Revision: Annex Tables," table 8, http://www.un.org/esa/population/publications/wpp2002/wpp2002annextables.pdf (accessed November 2003).

6. Ibid.

7. Eric Boehlert, "The Arab Baby Boom," Salon.com (Oct. 18, 2001), http://archive.salon.com/news/feature/2001/10/18/arab_population/index_np.html (accessed November 2003).

8. Yeni Yüzul, quoted by Youssef Courbage, "Nouveaux horizons démographiques en Méditerrané," National Institute of Demographic Studies (Paris, February 27, 1995), http://www.ined.fr/englishversion/publications/collections/courbage/chapter3.pdf (accessed November 2003).

9. "Contraception Is Treason, Turkish Islamist Leader Says," *Agence France Presse*, February 16, 2002.

10. Courbage, "Nouveaux horizons démographiques en Méditerranée."

11. Philippe Fargues, "The End of Patriarchy?" *The New Courier*, No. 3 (2003), http://www.unesco.org/courier/2001_11/uk/culture2.htm (accessed November 2003).

12. Yonghong Wang, "What Should China Do about the Gender Imbalance Problem?" *E-Merge* 4 (May 2003), http://www.carleton/.ca/emerge/docs_vol4/articles/YonghongWang.doc (accessed November 2003).

13. United Nations Population Division, "World Population Prospects: The 2002 Revision" and "World Urbanization Prospects: The 2001 Revision," http://www.esa.un.org/unpp (accessed November 2003).

14. Tim Dyson, "On the Future of Human Fertility in India," in "Completing the Fertility Transition: Background Papers," United Nations Population Division, http://un.org/esa/population/publications/completingfertility/RevisedDysonpaper.pdf (accessed November 2003).

15. United Nations Population Division, "World Population Prospects: The 2002 Revision: Annex Tables," table 8, http://www.un.org/esa/population/publications/wpp2002/wpp2002annextables.pdf (accessed November 2003).

16. National Intelligence Council, "The Next Wave of HIV/AIDS: Nigeria, Ethiopia, Russia, India, and China," no. ICA 2002-04D, http://www.cia.gov/nic/pubs/other_products/ICA%20HIV-AIDS%20unclassified%202009230POSTGERBER.pdf (accessed November 2003).

17. United Nations Population Division, "World Population Prospects: The 2002 Revision: Annex Tables," table 3, http://www.un.org/esa/population/publications/wpp2002/wpp2002annextables.pdf (accessed November 2003).

18. Antonio Golini, "Possible Policy Responses to Population Ageing and Population Decline: The Case of Italy," United Nations Population Division, no. UN/POP/PRA/2000/7 (September 26, 2000), http://www.un.org/esa/population/publications/popdecline/Golini.pdf (accessed November 2003).

19. United Nations Population Division, "World Population Prospects: The 2002 Revision: Annex Tables," table 6, http://www.un.org/esa/population/publications/wpp2002/wpp2002annextables.pdf (accessed November 2003).

Chapter Three

1. Benjamin Franklin, "Observations Concerning the Increase of Mankind, Peopling of Countries, etc.," *The Magazine of History*, vol. xvi, no. 61–64 (Tarrytown: 1918; first printed in Boston: 1755), http://bc.barnard.columbia.edu/~lgordis/earlyAC/documents/observations.html (accessed November 2003).

2. Theodore Roosevelt, "Twisted Eugenics," *Outlook* (January 3, 1914): 32.

3. Andrew Hacker, "The Case Against Kids," *The New York Review of Books*, November 30, 2000.

4. Michael Haines, "Ethnic Differences in Demographic Behavior in the United States: Has There Been Convergence?" (working paper no. 9042, National Bureau of Economic Research, July 2002), http://www.emory.edu/COLLEGE/ECON/faculty/curran/Adobe%20Files/Haines2002.pdf (accessed November 2003).

5. Births per 1000 foreign-born women in the United States declined from 93 in 1994 to 85.4 in 2000. See Amara Bachu and Martin O'Connell, "Fertility of American Women: June 2000," *Current Population Reports*, ser. P20–543RV, table 2 (U.S. Bureau of the Census, October 2001), http://landview.census.gov/prod/2001pubs/p20–543rv.pdf (accessed November 2003); and Amara Bachu, "Fertility of American Women: July 1994," *Current Population Report*, ser. P20–482 (U.S. Bureau of the Census, August 1995), table N, http://www.census.gov/prod/2/pop/p20/p20–482.pdf (accessed November 2003).

6. Brady E. Hamilton, Paul D. Sutton, and Stephanie J. Ventura, "Revised Birth and Fertility Rates for the 1990s and New Rates for Hispanic Populations, 2000 and 2001: United States," *National Vital Statistics Reports*, 51, no. 12 (August 4, 2003), table 2, http://www.cdc.gov/nchs/data/nvsr51/nvsr51_12.pdf (accessed November 2003).

7. Brady E. Hamilton, Joyce A. Martin, and Paul D. Sutton, "Births: Preliminary Data for 2002," *National Vital Statistics Reports* 51, no. 11, (June 25, 2003), table 2, http://www.cdc.gov/nchs/data/nvsr/nvsr51/nvsr51_11.pdf (accessed November 2003).

8. T. J. Mathews and Stephanie J. Ventura, "Birth and Fertility Rates by Educational Attainment: United States, 1994," *Monthly Vital Statistics Report* 45, no. 10, supplement (National Center for Health Statistics, April 24, 1997), http://www.cdc.gov/nchs/data/mvsr/supp/mv45_10s.pdf (accessed November 2003).

9. Hans Johnson and Laura E. Hill, "Understanding the Future of Californians' Fertility: The Role of Immigrants" (San Francisco: Public Policy Institute of California, 2002), http://www.ppic.org/content/pubs/R_402LHR.pdf (accessed November 2003).

10. William J. Carrington and Enrica Detragiache, "How Extensive Is the Brain Drain?" *Finance and Development* 36, no. 2 (June 1999), International Monetary Fund, http://www.imf.org/external/pubs/ft/fandd/1999/06/carringt.htm (accessed November 2003).

11. David T. Ellwood, "The Sputtering Labor Force of the 21st Century: Can Social Policy Help?" National Bureau of Economic Research, working

paper no. w8321 (June 2001), http://papers.nber.org/papers/W8321 (accessed November 2003), cited in D. Altman, "Blunt Portrait Drawn of the U.S. Work Force in 2020," *The New York Times*, August 30, 2002.

12. Frederick W. Hollmann, Tammany J. Mulder, and Jeffrey E. Kallan, "Methodology and Assumptions for the Population Projections of the United States: 1999 to 2100" (working paper no. 38, U.S. Census Bureau Population Division, January 2000), tables B and D, ttp://www.census.gov/population/www/documentation/twps0038.html#B11 (accessed November 2003); Campbell J. Gibson and Emily Lennon, "Historical Census Statistics on the Foreign-born Population of the United States: 1850–1990" (working paper, U.S. Census Bureau Population Division, February 1999); and U.S. Census Bureau Population Division, "National Population Projections," table NP-T1, http://www.census.gov/population/www/projections/natproj.html (accessed November 2003).

13. Ibid., middle series data files, http://www.census.gov/population/www/projections/natproj.html (accessed November 2003).

14. Gagadeesh Gokhale and Kent Smetters, *Fiscal and Generational Imbalances: New Budget Measures for New Budget Priorities* (Washington, D.C.: American Enterprise Institute [12th draft], 2003), http://www.aei.org/docLib/20030508–gokhale.pdf (accessed November 2003).

15. Henry George, *Progress and Poverty*, 15th ed. (Robert Schalkenbach Foundation, 1966), 75.

16. Congressional Budget Office, "The Long-Term Budget Outlook," (December 2003) http://www.cbo.gov/showdoc.cfm?index=4916&sequence=0 (accessed January 2004). Though the statistics cited are taken from the gloomiest of six scenarios projected by the CBO, it is worth noting that they nonetheless rest on rather optimistic assumptions. For example, health care spending is assumed to rise no faster in the future than it did between 1960 and 2001, despite significant population aging and the cost of new technology.

17. Office of the Under Secretary of Defense (Comptroller), "Department of Defense Budget Fiscal Years 2004/2005: Military Personnel Programs (M–1)" (February 2003): 22, http://www.dod.mil/comptroller/defbudget/fy2004/fy2004_m1.pdf (accessed November 2003); and Office of Management and Budget, "Budget of the United States Government: Fiscal Year 2004: Historical Tables," table 11.3, http://w3.access.gpo.gov/usbudget/fy2004/pdf/hist.pdf (accessed November 2003).

18. United Nations Population Division, "Replacement Migration: Is It a Solution to Declining and Ageing Populations?" (2000): 73, http://www.un.org/esa/population/publications/migration/cover-preface.pdf (accessed November 2003).

19. Jean-Claude Chesnais, "Below-Replacement Fertility in the European Union (EU-15): Facts and Policies, 1960–1997," *Review of Population and Social Policy*, no. 7 (1998): 83–101; http://www.ipss.go.jp/English/R_S_P/NO.7_P83.pdf.

20. Lothrop Stoddard, *The Rising Tide of Color against White World-Supremacy* (New York: Blue Ribbon Books, 1920).

21. Allan C. Carlson, *Family Questions: Reflections on the American Social Crisis* (New Brunswick and Oxford: Transaction Books, 1988), 69.

22. Enrique Quintana, "Corridinates," *Mexico City Reforma*, June 3, 2003. Quintana is the newspaper's business editor and a columnist. Translation from unclassified Central Intelligence Agency document no. 134249357.

23. Tamar Jacoby, "Too Many Immigrants?" *Commentary*, 113, no. 4 (April 2002): 37–44.

24. United Nations Population Division, "Population Estimates and Projections: 2002 Revision: Annex Tables," http://www.un.org/esa/population/publications/wpp2002/wpp2002annextables.pdf (accessed November 2003).

25. United Nations Population Division, "Population Estimates and Projections: 2002 Revision: Population Database," http://esa.un.org/unpp/index.asp?panel=2 (accessed November 2003).

26. Joel Millman and Carlta Vitzthum, "Europe Becomes New Destination for Latino Workers," *The Wall Street Journal*, September 12, 2003.

27. Jane Sneddon Little and Robert K. Triest, "The Impact of Demographic Change on U.S. Labor Markets," *New England Economic Review*, (First Quarter 2002): 61. http://www.bos.frb.org/economic/neer/neer2002/neer102c.pdf (accessed November 2003).

28. Jean-Pierre Geungant and John F. May, "Impact of the Proximate Determinates on the Future Course of Fertility in Sub-Saharan Africa" (paper, Workshop on the Prospects for Fertility Decline in High Fertility Countries, United Nations Population Division, June 13, 2001), table 3, http://www.un.org/esa/population/publications/prospectsdecline/guengant.pdf (accessed November 2003).

29. National Intelligence Council, "Global Trends 2015: A Dialogue about the Future with Nongovernmental Experts," http://www.cia.gov/nic/pubs/2015_files/2015.htm (accessed November 2003).

30. United Nations Population Division, "Population Estimates and Projections, 2002 Revision," http://www.un.org/esa/population/publications/wpp2002/wpp2002annextables.pdf (accessed November 2003).

31. Tom A. Moultrie and Ian M. Timæus, "Trends in South African Fertility Between 1970 and 1998: An Analysis of the 1996 Census and the 1998 Demographic and Health Survey," Centre for Population Studies, London School of Hygiene and Tropical Medicine (2002), http://www.lshtm.ac.uk/cps/dfid/2002_17.htm (accessed November 2003).

32. United Nations Population Division, "HIV/AIDS and Fertility in Sub-Saharan Africa: A Review of the Research Literature," no. ESA/P/WP.174* (April 2002), http://www.un.org/esa/population/publications/fertilitysection/HIVAIDSPaperFertSect.pdf (accessed November 2003).

33. U.S. Central Intelligence Agency, "The Global Infectious Disease Threat and Its Implications for the United States," NIE 99–17D (January 2000), http://www.cia.gov/cia/publications/nie/report/nie99–17d.html (accessed November 2003).

34. United Nations Population Division, "World Population Prospects: The 2002 Revision: Highlights," 7, http://www.un.org/esa/population/publications/wpp2002/WPP2002-HIGHLIGHTSrev1.pdf (accessed November 2003).

35. W. Lutz, W. Sanderson, and S. Scherbov, "The End of World Population Growth," *Nature* 412 (2001): 543–546.

Chapter Four

1. Daniel Perusse, "Cultural and Reproductive Success in Industrial Societies: Testing the Relationship at the Proximate and Ultimate Levels," *Behavioral Brain Science* 16: 267–322.

2. Alexandre Kalache (remarks to the III Global Forum on Integrated Non-Communicable Disease Prevention and Control, Rio de Janeiro, Brazil, November 11, 2003).

3. José Miguel Guzmán and Ralph Hakkert, "Some Social and Economic Impacts of the Ageing Process in Latin American Countries," http://www.iussp.org/Brazil2001/s00/S02_03_Guzman.pdf (accessed November 2003).

4. CELADE, "América Latina y el Caribe: Estimaciones y proyecciones de población 1950–2050," *Boletín demográfico* 69 (2002), part A.

5. United Nations Population Division, "The Future of Fertility in Intermediate-Fertility Countries," table 2, http://www.un.org/esa/population/publications/completingfertility/RevisedPEPSPOPDIVpaper.pdf (accessed November 2003).

6. Janet S. Dunn, "Mass Media and Individual Reproductive Behavior in Northeastern Brazil" (paper presented at the XXIV General Population Conference of the International Union for the Scientific Study of Population, Salvador, Bahia, Brazil, August 18–24, 2001).

7. Alaka Malwade Basu, "On the Prospects for Endless Fertility Decline in South Asia," United Nations Population Division (March 2002), http://www.un.org/esa/population/publications/completingfertility/BASUpaper.pdf (accessed November 2003).

8. Mary Pride, *The Way Home: Beyond Feminism, Back to Reality* (Westchester, Ill.: Crossway, 1985), 80.

9. Frank Newport, "Desire to Have Children Alive and Well in America," Gallup Poll Tuesday Briefing, August 19, 2003.

10. Natalie Gochnour, "Population Estimates: The Utah Experience," Utah Population Estimates Committee (September 21, 1999), http://www.governor.utah.gov/dea/UPEC/UPECHistory.pdf (accessed November 2003); and Governor's Office of Planning and Budget, "Demographic and Economic Analysis," http://www.governor.utah.gov/dea/Demographics/fertility.html (accessed November 2003).

11. B. E. Hamilton, J. A. Martin, and P. D. Sutton, "Births: Preliminary Data for 2002," *National Vital Statistics Reports*, 51, no. 11 (2003), table 10, http://www.cdc.gov/nchs/data/nvsr/nvsr51/nvsr51_11.pdf (accessed November 2003).

12. See, for example, Monique Borgerhoff Mulder, "The Demographic Transition: Are We Any Closer to an Evolutionary Explanation?" *TREE* 13, no. 7 (July 1998): 266–270.

13. Rodney Stark, *The Rise of Christianity: A Sociologist Reconsiders History* (Princeton, N.J.: Princeton University Press, 1996).

14. I am indebted to Max Singer of the Hudson Institute for this formulation. See his essay, "The Population Surprise," *The Atlantic Monthly* 284, no. 2 (August 1999): 22–25.

15. C. Murray and A. Lopez, "Mortality by Cause for Eight Regions of the World: Global Burden of Disease Study," *The Lancet* 349 (May 3, 1997): 1269–1276.

16. Centers for Disease Control, "Background on Antibiotic Resistance," http://www.cdc.gov/drugresistance/community/; see also Laurie Garrett, "The Collapse of Global Public Health," *Hyperion* (August 2000).

Chapter Five

1. See, for example, Landis MacKellar, "Economic Impacts of Population Aging in Japan," International Institute for Applied Systems Analysis, 31ff, http://www.iiasa.ac.at/Research/SSR/docs/tokyo-rep.pdf?sb=11 (accessed November 2003); see also David E. Bloom, David Canning, and Jaypee Sevilla, "Economic Growth and the Demographic Transition" (working paper no. 8685, National Bureau of Economic Research, December 2001), http://www.nber.org/papers/w8685 (accessed November 2003).

2. Jeffrey G. Williamson, "Demographic Shocks and Global Factor Flows," Federal Reserve Bank of Boston's Conference Series [Proceedings] (2001): 247–269.

3. David M. Cutler, James M. Poterba, Louis M. Sheiner, and Lawrence H. Summers, "An Aging Society: Opportunity or Challenge?" Brookings Papers on Economic Activity, no. 1, The Brookings Institution (Washington D.C., 1990).

4. Neil Howe and Richard Jackson, "Entitlements and the Aging of America: 2001: Chartbook," National Taxpayers Union Foundation, Institute of Public Policy Studies/University of Denver (2001), charts 2–3.

5. Massimo Livi-Bacci, *A Concise History of World Population*, 2d edition (Malden, Mass.: Blackwell, 1997).

6. Ron J. Lesthaeghe, "On the Social Control of Human Reproduction," *Population and Development Review* 694 (1980): 527–548.

7. Angus Maddison, *Phases of Capitalist Development* (Oxford and New York: Oxford University Press, 1982).

8. Paul Johnson, *The Birth of the Modern: World Society, 1815–1830*, 1st ed. (New York: HarperCollins, 1991).

9. Thomas R. Malthus, *An Essay on the Principle of Population*, 1st edition (London, 1798; 6th edition printed in 1826 in two vols.).

10. J. Bradford DeLong, *Macroeconomics* (Burr Ridge, Ill.: McGraw-Hill, 2002), 3, http://www.j-bradford-delong.net/macro_online/ms/ch5/Chapter_5.pdf (accessed November 2003).

11. Ibid., 14.

12. For a discussion of the view of Adam Smith and Karl Marx on population and development, see Nathan Keyfitz, "Population Theory and Doctrine: A Historical Survey," in *Readings in Population*, ed. William Peterson (New York: Macmillan, 1972). Adam Smith believed that the spark that set the engine in motion was an increase in demand for labor. As labor became more valuable, the "supply" of children naturally increased. Karl Marx agreed, but concentrated on the next turn of the cycle, in which he believed that population growth drove down the cost of labor to the point that capitalists could exploit the surplus value created by workers. Both men agreed, in other words, that a growing supply of both workers and consumers was an essential mechanism of capitalist development, even if they differed on how long this engine could run without falling to pieces.

13. Bart van Ark and Marcel P. Timmer, "Computers and the Big Divide: Productivity Growth in the European Union and the United States" (working paper, Information and Communication Technology Spin-off workshop, European Commission/Joint Research Centre, Seville, March 27–28, 2003), table 2, http://www.jrc.es/projects/enlargement/FuturesEnlargementII/ICT Spinoff03–2003/TimmerPaperComputers.pdf (accessed November 2003).

14. Klaus Regling and Declan Costello, "The Economic and Budgetary Implications of Global Ageing: An EU Perspective," presented at conference cosponsored by the Center for Strategic and International Studies and the

European Commission (Brussels, Belgium, March 4–5, 2003), http://www.csis.org/gai/brussels/agenda.pdf (accessed November 2003).

15. Jane Sneddon Little and Robert K. Triest, "The Impact of Demographic Change on U.S. Labor Markets," *New England Economic Review* (First Quarter 2002): 53. The projection assumes no change in workforce participation rates.

16. Paul S. Hewitt, "The End of the Postwar Welfare State," *The Washington Quarterly* (Spring 2002): 8. For a classic statement of the relationship between population and economic growth, see Ester Boserup, *The Conditions of Agricultural Growth: The Economics of Agrarian Change Under Population Pressure* (London and New York: G. Allen & Unwin, 1965; reprinted in London: Earsthscan, 1993).

17. United Nations Population Division, "World Population Prospects: The 2002 Revision" and "World Urbanization Prospects: The 2001 Revision" (September 12, 2003), http://esa.un.org/unpp (accessed November 2003).

18. Joseph Chamie, "As the World Ages," *BusinessWeek Online* (April 4, 2002), http://www.businessweek.com/bwdaily/dnflash/apr2002/nf2002044_6710.htm (accessed November 2003).

Chapter Six

1. Cited in Denshō, The Japanese American Legacy Project, "Prelude to Incarceration" (readings developed by the Stanford Program on International and Cross-Cultural Education), http://www.densho.org (accessed November 2003).

2. "Japanese 'Picture Brides' Become Frights in California," *Literary Digest*, August 9, 1919.

3. Paul S. Hewitt, "The Gray Roots of Japan's Crisis," Asia Program Special Report, Woodrow Wilson International Center for Scholars (January 2003), 5, http://wwics.si.edu/topics/pubs/asiarpt_107.pdf (accessed November 2003).

4. Trish Saywell, "Singapore Plays Matchmaker, Hoping to Boost Its Birth Rate," *Wall Street Journal*, January 30, 2003.

5. Kakuchi Suvendrini, "Japan: Govt Acts to Stem Falling Birth Rates," *Inter Press Service*, September 30, 2002.

6. Hewitt, "The Gray Roots," 5.

7. Ibid.

8. Yamada Masahiro, "Kore o shôshika fukyô to naze iwanu" ("Why Isn't This Called a Low-Birthrate Recession?"), *Shokun* (August 1998).

9. Paul Hewitt, "Japan's Newest Bubble Contains Lessons for Other Aging Countries," Center for Strategic and International Studies, forthcoming.

10. "Exporting the Old," *Financial Times of London*, August 9, 2003.

11. Sebastian Moffett, "For Ailing Japan, Longevity Begins to Take Its Toll," *The Wall Street Journal*, February 11, 2003.

12. Richard Jackson, "Germany and the Challenge of Global Aging," Center for Strategic and International Studies (Washington, D.C., March 2003), 5, http://www.csis.org/gai/germany_report.pdf (accessed November 2003).

13. Makoto Atoh, "Why Are Cohabitation and Extra-marital Births So Few in Japan?" (paper, EURESCO conference, The Second Demographic Transition in Europe, Bad Herrenalb, Germany, June 23–28, 2001), 5, http://www.ier.hit-u.ac.jp/pie/Japanese/discussionpaper/dp2001/dp59/text.pdf (accessed November 2003).

14. "Parasites, Mammoni, and Boomerangers," *Demography* 2 (Fall 2002), http://www.socialtechnologies.com/fc/gl/Sample%20GL–2002–18.pdf (accessed November 2003).

15. David E. Horlacher, "Aging in Japan: Causes and Consequences—Part I: Demographic Issues," Interim Report, IR–01–008, International Institute for Applied Systems Analysis (Laxenburg, Austria, August 2002), 56, www.iiasa.ac.at (accessed November 2003), cited in Chikako Usui, "Japan's Aging Dilemma?" Asia Program Special Report, Woodrow Wilson International Center for Scholars (January 2003), 20, http://wwics.si.edu/topics/pubs/asiarpt_107.pdf (accessed November 2003).

16. "A New Class of Drifters," *Japan Echo* 28, no. 4, http://www.japanecho.co.jp/sum/2001/280515.html (accessed November 2003).

17. United Nations Population Division, "World Population Prospects: The 2002 Revision: Annex Tables," table 3, 38, http://www.un.org/esa/population/publications/wpp2002/wpp2002annextables.pdf (accessed November 2003).

18. Zhongwei Zhao, "Low Fertility in Urban China" (paper, Working Group on Low Fertility, Seminar on International Perspectives on Low Fertility: Trends, Theories and Policies, International Union for the Scientific Study of Population (March 2001), http://demography.anu.edu.au/Publications/ConferencePapers/IUSSP2001/PaperZhao.doc (accessed November 2003).

19. Cited in "The Graying of the Middle Kingdom: Will China Get Rich before It Gets Old?" Center for Strategic and International Studies, forthcoming.

20. "China Faces the Challenge of an Aging Society," *Beijing Review*, July 16, 2001, http://www.china.org.cn (accessed November 2003).

21. Xiaochun Qiao, "Aging Issues and Policy Choices in Rural China," (paper, XXIV General Population Conference, Salvador, Brazil, August 18–24, 2001), http://www.iussp.org/Brazil2001/s00/S02_04_Qiao.pdf (accessed November 2003).

22. Cited in Richard Jackson, "The Global Retirement Crisis," Center for Strategic and International Studies (Washington, D.C., April 2002), 67.

23. National Intelligence Council, "The Next Wave of HIV/AIDS: Nigeria, Ethiopia, Russia, India, and China," no. ICA 2002–04D (September 2002), http://www.cia.gov/nic/pubs/other_products/ICA%20HIV-AIDS%20unclassified%20092302POSTGERBER.htm (accessed November 2003).

24. Valerie M. Hudson and Andrea Den Boer, "A Surplus of Men, a Deficit of Peace," *International Security* 26, no. 4 (Spring 2002), table 3, http://mitpress.mit.edu/journals/pdf/isec_26_04_5_0.pdf (accessed November 2003); Bay Fang, "China's Stolen Wives," *U.S. News & World Report* (October 12, 1998): 35; and Centers for Disease Control and Prevention, "Chlamydia in the United States," National Center for HIV, STD and TB Prevention, Division of Sexually Transmitted Diseases, http://www.cdc.gov/nchstp/dstd/Fact_Sheets/FactsChlamydiaInfo.htm (accessed November 2003).

25. Nicholas Eberstadt, "The Future of AIDS," *Foreign Affairs* (November-December 2002).

26. China Population Information and Research Center, "China Sees a High Gender Ratio of New-borns," *People's Daily*, May 10, 2002. Translation provided by China Internet Information Center, http://www.china.org.cn/english/2002/May/32360.htm (accessed November 2003).

27. Hudson and Den Boer, "A Surplus of Men."

28. Rodney Stark, *The Rise of Christianity: A Sociologist Reconsiders History* (Princeton, N.J.: Princeton University Press, 1996).

29. ANZ, "Country Brief: China" (November 25, 2002), 3, http://www.anz.com/Business/info_centre/economic_commentary/China_Nov_2002.pdf (accessed November 2003).

30. "China to Aid Poor, Jobless," *Associated Press*, March 13, 2003.

31. Kong Jingyuan, "Implicit Pension Debt and Its Repayment," in *Restructuring China's Social Security System*, China Development Research Foundation Series, ed. Wang Megkui (Beijing: Foreign Languages Press, 2002), 183.

32. ANZ, "Country Brief: China."

33. Quoted in Mike Moore, "RMA and Space Weaponization: From Force Enhancement to Global Engagement" (paper, International School on Disarmament and Research on Conflicts, August 2002), http://www.isodarco.it/html/trento02-moore.html (accessed November 2003).

34. Anatoly G. Vishnevsky, "Family, Fertility, and Demographic Dynamics in Russia: Analysis and Forecast," in *Conference Report: Russia's Demographic "Crisis,"* ed. Julie DaVanzo (Santa Monica, Calif.: Rand Corporation, 1996), http://www.rand.org/publications/CF/CF124/ (accessed November 2003). On birthrates, see "Human Mortality Database," University of California at Berkeley; and Max Planck Institute for Demographic Research (Germany), both at www.mortality.org or www.humanmortality.de (accessed November 2003).

35. BBC, "Tikhonov's Speech on the International Year of the Child," BBC Summary of World Broadcasts, part 1: The USSR, no. SU/6090/B/1 (April 11, 1979).

36. Sergei V. Zakharov and Elena I. Ivanova, "Fertility Decline and Recent Changes in Russia: On the Threshold of the Second Demographic Transition," in DaVanzo, *Conference Report: Russia's Demographic "Crisis."*

37. Sergei A. Vassin, "The Determinants and Implications of an Aging Population in Russia," in DaVanzo, *Conference Report: Russia's Demographic "Crisis."*

38. Projections by G. A. Bondarskaya, cited in Herbert E. Meyer, "The Coming Soviet Ethnic Crisis," *Fortune* (August 14, 1979): 156.

39. BBC, "Speech at Kremlin Rally by Kirilenko," BBC Summary of World Broadcasts, part 1: The USSR, no. SU/6266/C/1 (November 8, 1979).

40. Janusz Balicki (paper, XXIV IUSSP General Population Conference, Salvador, Brazil, August 18–24, 2001), http://www.iussp.org/Brazil2001/s30/S33_04_Balicki.pdf (accessed November 2003).

41. Cynthia Buckley, "Obligations and Expectations: Renegotiating Pensions in the Russia Federation" (working paper no. 97-98-03, The Population Research Center, University of Texas at Austin, 1998).

42. Buckley, "Obligations and Expectations," table 1.

43. Vishnevsky, "Family, Fertility, and Demographic Dynamics."

44. Peter Hopkirk, *The Great Game: The Struggle for Empire in Central Asia* (New York: Kondansha International, 1990), 5.

45. Buckley, "Obligations and Expectations"; see also Victoria Velkoff and Kevin Kinsella, *Aging in Eastern Europe and the Former Soviet Union* (Washington, D.C.: U.S. Government Printing Office, 1993).

46. Nicholas Eberstadt, "Russia: Too Sick to Matter?" *Policy Review*, no. 95 (June-July 1999), http://www.policyreview.org/jun99/eberstadt.html (accessed November 2003).

47. Population Reference Bureau, "2002 World Population Data Sheet," http://www.worldpop.org/prbdata.htm (accessed November 2003).

48. United Nations Population Division, "Replacement Migration: Is It a Solution to Declining and Ageing Populations?" (2000), 62, http://www.un.org/esa/population/publications/migration/migration.htm (accessed November 2003).

49. Center for Defense Information, *Russia Weekly* (February 16, 2001), http://www.cdi.org/russia/141.html (accessed November 2003).

50. Alexander Morris Carr-Saunders et al., "Royal Commission on Population: Report," Her Majesty's Stationery Office (1949), 7. For a description of the report see British Official Publications Collaborative Reader Information Service, http://www.bopcris.ac.uk/bop1940/ref850.html (accessed November 2003).

51. United Nations Population Division, "World Population Prospects: The 2002 Revision" and "World Urbanization Prospects: The 2001 Revision," http://esa.un.org/unpp (accessed November 2003).

52. Jean-Claude Chesnais, "Below-Replacement Fertility in the European Union (EU–15): Facts and Policies, 1960–1997," *Review of Population and Social Policy*, no. 7 (1998): 83–101, http://www.ipss.go.jp/English/R_S_P/No.7_P83.pdf (accessed November 2003).

53. Massimo Livi-Bacci, "Demographic Shocks: The View from History," conference proceedings, Seismic Shifts: The Economic Impact of Demographic Change (Federal Reserve Bank of Boston, June 2001), http://www.bos.frb.org/economic/conf/conf46/ (accessed November 2003).

54. United Nations Population Division, "World Population Prospects: The 2002 Revision" and "World Urbanization Prospects: The 2001 Revision."

55. Amelia Gentleman, "Chirac Goes on TV to Quell Heat Wave Anger," *The Guardian* (London), August 22, 2003.

56. United Nations Population Division, "World Population Prospects: The 2002 Revision" and "World Urbanization Prospects: The 2001 Revision."

57. "Europe's Population Implosion," *The Economist* (July 19, 2003).

58. Nicholas Eberstadt, "What If It's a World Population Implosion? Speculations about Global De-population," The Global Reproductive Health Forum (Harvard University, 1998), http://www.hsph.harvard.edu/Organizations/healthnet/HUpapers/implosion/depop.html (accessed November 2003).

59. Werner Haug, Paul Compton, and Youssef Courbage, eds., "The Demographic Characteristics of Immigrant Populations," *Population Studies*, no. 38 (2002), table 6.2, http://www.coe.int/t/e/social_cohesion/population/Pop38%20Demo%20chr%20immig%20pops%20eng.pdf (accessed November 2003).

60. European Industrial Relations Observatory On-line, "Lisbon Council Agrees [on] Employment Targets," http://www.eiro.eurofound.ie/2000/04/feature/EU0004241F.html (accessed November 2003); and Klaus Regling (conference presentation, The Economic and Budgetary Impacts of Global Aging, Brussels, Belgium, March 4, 2003).

61. David Willetts, "Old Europe? Demographic Change and Pension Reform" (address to Centre for European Reform, September 23, 2003).

62. Gunnar Andersson, "Fertility Developments in Norway and Sweden Since the Early 1960s," *Demographic Research* 6, article 4, Max Planck Institute for Demographic Research (February 2002), http://www.demographic-research.org/volumes/vol6/4/6–4.pdf (accessed November 2003); and Council of Europe, "Population, Social Cohesion and Quality of Life," http://www.coe.int/t/e/social_cohesion/population/Demographic_Year_Book/2001_Edition/Sweden%202001.asp (accessed November 2003).

63. Council of Europe, "Population, Social Cohesion and Quality of Life."

64. Lena Edlund, Laila Haider, and Rohini Pande, "Out-of-Wedlock—Like Marriage or Like Divorce? European Evidence from Political Preferences," Columbia University (November 18, 2002), table 1, http://www.essex.ac.uk/economics/seminars/seminarpapers/edlundpaper.pdf (accessed November 2003).

65. Ibid.

66. Richard Jackson (remarks made at conference, "The Economic and Budgetary Implications of Global Ageing: An EU Perspective," cosponsored by the Center for Strategic and International Studies and the European Commission (Brussels, Belgium, March 4–5, 2003).

67. United Nations Population Division, "World Population Prospects: The 2002 Revision: Population Database," http://esa.un.org/unpp/ (accessed November 2003).

68. Robert Graham, "French Pension Bill Passed by Parliament," *Financial Times* (London), July 25, 2003.

69. Council of Europe, "Recent Demographic Developments in Europe 2002," http://www.coe.int/t/e/social_cohesion/population/demographic_year_book/2002_Edition/default.asp#TopOfPage (accessed November 2003).

70. Anthony Browne, "Who's Afraid of Declining Population?" *New Statesman*, November 4, 2002.

71. Wolfgang Lutz, Brian C. O'Neill, and Sergei Scherbov, "Europe's Population at a Turning Point," *Science* 299 (March 28, 2003), http://www.iiasa.ac.at/Research/POP/journal/science03.html (accessed November 2003).

Chapter Seven

1. Marilyn Gardner, "Oh, Baby! Look How Your Ranks Grow," *The Christian Science Monitor*, March 06, 2002, http://www.csmonitor.com/2002/0306/p12s01-lifp.html (accessed November 2003).

2. Quoted in Gardner, "Oh, Baby!"

3. Amara Bachu and Martin O'Connell, "Fertility of American Women: June 2000," Current Population Reports, no. P20–543RV, U.S. Census Bureau (Washington, D.C., 2001), http://www.census.gov/prod/2001pubs/p20–543rv.pdf (accessed November 2003).

4. Jason Fields, "Children's Living Arrangements and Characteristics: March 2002," Current Population Reports, no. P20- 547, U.S. Census Bureau (Washington, D.C., 2003), http://www.census.gov/prod/2003pubs/p20–547.pdf (accessed November 2003).

5. Neil Howe, "Young Married Moms Say It Is Time to Quit," *Millennial Generation Monitor* 1, no. 6 (April 2002): 4.

6. S. Bianchi, "Maternal Employment and Time with Children: Dramatic Change or Surprising Continuity?" *Demography* 37: 401–414.

7. Robert Schoen, Young J. Kim, Constance A. Nathanson, Jason Fields, and Nan A. Astone, "Why Do Americans Want Children?" *Population and Development Review* 23 (June 1997): 333–357.

8. Ibid.

9. Mark Lino, "Expenditures on Children by Families: 2001 Annual Report," miscellaneous publication no. 1528–2001, U.S. Department of Agriculture, Center for Nutrition Policy and Promotion, table ES–1, http://www.usda.gov/cnpp/Crc/crc2001.pdf (accessed November 2003).

10. Michelle Budig and Paula England, "The Wage Penalty for Motherhood" (paper presented at the annual meetings of the American Sociological Association, August 1999), http://www.olin.wustl.edu/macarthur/working%20papers/englandMomPenalty.pdf (accessed November 2003).

11. Karen Schulman, "The High Cost of Child Care Puts Quality Care Out of Reach for Many Families," Children's Defense Fund (2000), 4, http://www.childrensdefense.org/pdf/highcost.pdf (accessed November 2003).

12. Alvin Hansen, "Economic Progress and Declining Population Growth," *American Economic Review* 29, no. 1: 1–15.

13. Cited by Kenneth Hill, e-mail to *Slate Magazine* mailing list, January 27, 1998, http://slate.msn.com/id/3669/entry/24037/ (accessed November 2003).

14. Louise B. Russell, *The Baby Boom Generation and the Economy* (Washington, D.C.: Brookings, 1982), table 4–7.

15. This theory of the baby boom is most closely associated with Richard Easterlin. See his *Birth and Fortune: The Impact of Numbers on Personal Welfare*, 2nd edition (Chicago: University of Chicago Press, 1987; first edition, Basic Books, 1980).

16. Diane Macunovich, *Birth Quake: The Baby Boom and Its After Shocks* (Chicago: University of Chicago Press, 2002), online appendix to chapter 4, http://www.columbia.edu/~dm555/birthquake/chp04app.pdf (accessed November 2003).

17. U.S. Census Bureau Population Division, "School Enrollment of the Civilian Population: October 1946," series P-20, no. 1 (September 5, 1947), table 1, http://www.census.gov/population/www/socdemo/school/p20–001.html (accessed November 2003).

18. U.S. Census Bureau Population Division, "Enrollment Status of the Population 3 Years Old and Over, by Age, Sex, Race, Hispanic Origin, Nativity, and Selected Educational Characteristics: October 2000," table 1.

19. College Board, "Trends in Student Aid, 2002" (New York, 2002), http://www.collegeboard.org (accessed November 2003).

20. Lini S. Kadaba, "Homebound," *The Philadelphia Inquirer*, May 30, 2002, http://www.philly.com/mld/inquirer/2002/05/30/news/magazine/daily/3363999.htm (accessed November 2003).

21. Zhu Xiao Di, Yi Yang, and Xiaodong Liu, "Young American Adults Living in Parental Homes," Joint Center for Housing Studies, Harvard University, no. W02–3 (May 2002), http://www.jchs.harvard.edu/publications/markets/di_W02–3.pdf (accessed November 2003).

22. Jean A. Schoonover, "Devalued Doctors," *Washington Post*, August 11, 2003.

23. Claire Hintz, "The Tax Burden of the Median American Family," report no. 96, The Tax Foundation (March 2000), http://taxfoundation.org/prmedianfamily.html (accessed November 2003).

24. Social Security Online, "2003 OASDI Trustees Report," table VI.F2, http://www.ssa.gov/OACT/TR/TR03/VI_OASDHI_payroll.html#wp92759 (accessed November 2003).

25. John S. Billings, "An 1893 View of the American Fertility Decline," *Population and Development Review* 2, no. 2 (1976 [originally published in 1893]): 279–282, quoted in Robert Van Krieken, "Sociology and the Reproductive Self: Demographic Transitions and Modernity," *Sociology* 31, no. 3: 445–471.

26. Frank Newport, "Desire to Have Children Alive and Well in America," Gallup Poll Tuesday Briefing, August 19, 2003.

27. John Bongaarts, "The End of the Fertility Transition in the Developed World" (working paper no. 152, Population Council, 2001), table 2, http://www.popcouncil.org/pdfs/wp/152.pdf (accessed November 2003).

28. American Infertility Association, "Fertility Survey Finds Astonishing Results: Only One of 12,382 Women Answered Correctly" press release, October 24, 2001, http://www.americaninfertility.org/media/aia_survey_results.html (accessed November 2003).

29. American Society for Reproductive Medicine, "Healthcare Professionals' Perceptions of Reproductive Aging Are Not Always Accurate," press release, October 15, 2002.

30. David B. Dunson et al., "Changes with Age in the Level and Duration of Fertility in the Menstrual Cycle," *Human Reproduction* 17, no. 5 (2002): 1399–1403.

31. Ann Crittenden (conference remarks, Maternal Feminism: Lessons for a 21st Century Motherhood Movement, Motherhood Project for the Institute

for American Values and The Barnard Center for Research on Women, October 29, 2002).

32. Michelle Conlin, "The New Gender Gap," *Business Week* (May 26, 2003): 74. http://www.businessweek.com:/print/magazine/content/03_21/b3834001_mz001.htm?mz (accessed November 2003).

33. National Center for Educational Statistics, "Projections of Educational Statistics to 2012," table 20, http://nces.ed.gov/pubs2002/proj2012/table_20.asp (accessed November 2003).

34. Newport, "Desire to Have Children Alive and Well."

35. William Strauss and Neil Howe, "Generation 2000: America's New Conformists," *Axess Magazine* (April 2003), http://www.axess.se/english/archive/2003/nr3/currentissue /millennial_generation.php (accessed November 2003).

36. See, for example, John J. Marcionis, *Sociology* (Englewood Cliffs, N.J.: Prentice Hall, 1993).

37. The European Commission, "The Life of Men and Women in Europe," press release, Eurostat, October 2002, http://europa.eu.int/comm/eurostat/Public/datashop/print-product/EN?catalogue=Eurostat&product=3–08102002-EN-AP-EN&type=pdf (accessed November 2003).

38. See, for example, Richard A. Bulcroff and Kris A. Bulcroft, "Race Differences in Attitudinal and Motivation Factors in the Decision to Marry," *Journal of Marriage and the Family* 55: 3338–3355.

39. Conlin, "The New Gender Gap."

40. World Resources Institute, "Population, Health, and Human Well-being: Afghanistan," http://earthtrends.wri.org/pdf_library/country_profiles/Pop_cou_004.pdf (accessed November 2003).

41. The phrase "Handmaid's Tale" is taken from Margaret Atwood's science fiction novel in which fertile women are drafted by the state to produce babies (Boston: Houghton Mifflin, 1986).

Chapter Eight

1. Theodore Roszak, *Longevity Revolution: As Boomers Become Elders* (Albany, Calif.: Berkeley Hills Books, 2001), 24.

2. Harry R. Moody, "The History of Prolongevity: A Prologue to the Quest for Life Extension in the 21st Century," HRMoody.com, http://www.hrmoody.com/art1.html (accessed November 2003).

3. Centers for Disease Control, "Achievements in Public Health, 1900–1999: Healthier Mothers and Babies," *Morbidity and Mortality Weekly*

Report 48, no. 38 (October 1, 1999): 849–858, http://www.cdc.gov/nchs/fastats/infmort.htm (accessed November 2003).

4. Social Security Administration, "2003 Old-Age, Survivors, and Disability Insurance Trustee Report" (March 17, 2003), table V.A4, http://www.ssa.gov/OACT/TR/TR03/V_demographic.html#wp159501 (accessed November 2003).

5. "The Futurists: Looking Toward A.D. 2000," *Time* (February 25, 1966), 29.

6. John P. Bunker, Howard S. Frazier, and Frederick Mosteller, "Improving Health: Measuring Effects of Medical Care," *Milbank Quarterly* 72 (1994): 225–258.

7. Centers for Disease Control, "Achievements in Public Health."

8. Bunker, Frazier, and Mosteller, "Improving Health."

9. Willard Gaylin, "Faulty Diagnosis," *New York Times*, June 12, 1994.

10. Hand Hygiene Task Force, "Guideline for Hand Hygiene in Health-Care Settings: Recommendations of the Healthcare Infection Control Practices Advisory Committee and the HICPAC/SHEA/APIC/IDSA Hand Hygiene Task Force," *Morbidity and Mortality Weekly Report* (October 25, 2002), http://www.cdc.gov/mmwr/preview/mmwrhtml/rr5116a1.htm (accessed November 2003).

11. Ibid.

12. Linda T. Kohn, Janet M. Corrigan, and Molla S. Donaldson, eds., *To Err is Human: Building a Safer Health System*, Institute of Medicine, Committee on Quality of Health Care in America (Washington, D.C.: National Academy Press, 2000), 1, http://books.nap.edu/books/0309068371/html/R1.html#pagetop (accessed November 2003).

13. Thomas H. Maugh II, "Breast Cancer Treatment Faulted," *Los Angeles Times*, July 3, 2003; and Shannon Brownlee, "Health, Hope and Hype: Why the Media Oversells Medical 'Breakthroughs,'" *Washington Post*, August 3, 2003.

14. Richard A. Knox, "Doctor's Orders Killed Cancer Patient," *Boston Globe*, March 23, 1995. Note that one of the doctors involved in Lehman's treatment, Lois Ayash, later brought suit against Dana-Farber and the *Boston Globe*, and won judgments against both. The *Globe* article, according to an account in *The New York Times*, "erroneously said she had countersigned a faulty medical order that resulted in the death of the columnist." "*Boston Globe* Must Pay in Defamation Suit," *The New York Times*, February 13, 2002.

15. Elliott S. Fisher and H. Gilbert Welch, "Avoiding the Unintended Consequences of Growth in Medical Care: How Might More Be Worse?" *Journal of the American Medical Association* 281, no. 5 (February 3, 1999): 446–453.

16. Ibid.

17. Agency for Healthcare Research and Quality, "Guide to Clinical Preventive Services, 3rd Edition, Periodic Updates," report of the U.S. Preventive Services Task Force, http://www.ahrq.gov/clinic/gcpspu.htm (accessed November 2003).

18. Gina Kolata, "Annual Physical Checkup May Be an Empty Ritual," *New York Times*, August 12, 2003.

19. Archibald L. Cochrane and Max Blythe, *One Man's Medicine: An Autobiography of Professor Archie Cochrane* (London: British Medical Journal Memoir Club, 1989).

20. Archie Cochrane, "1931–1971: A Critical Review, with Particular Reference to the Medical Profession," in *Medicines for the Year 2000* (London: Office of Health Economics, 1979), 1–11.

21. J. Malines, "The Fence or the Ambulance," *Journal of the Soil Association* 7, no. 4 (1953): 24, quoted in W. W. Yellowlees, "Fares the Land, The James MacKenzie Lecture, 1978," *Journal of the Royal College of General Practitioners* 29 (1979): 7–21.

22. J. Michael McGinnis, Pamela Williams-Russo, and James R. Knickman, "The Case for More Active Policy Attention to Health Promotion," *Health Affairs* (March-April 2002), http://www.healthaffairs.org/freecontent/s12.htm#15 (accessed November 2003).

23. Nathan Rosenberg, "Health: The Devil of a Problem" (conference address at the proceedings of the Center for Science, Policy and Outcomes, Science: The Endless Frontier 1945–1995, June 9, 1995), http://www.cspo.org/products/conferences/bush/ (accessed November 2003).

24. World Health Organization, "WHO Statistical Information System," http://www3.who.int/whosis/country/indicators.cfm?country=usa&language=en (accessed November 2003).

25. Ibid., http://www3.who.int/whosis/country/indicators.cfm?country=cri&language=en (accessed November 2003).

26. Ibid., http://www3.who.int/whosis/health_personnel/health_personnel.cfm?path=whosis,health_personnel&language=english (accessed November 2003).

27. Ibid., http://www3.who.int/whosis/country/compare.cfm?language=en&country=CRI&indicator=strLEX0Both2001,strLEX0Male2001,strLEX0Female2001&order_by=strLEX0Male2001&order=DESC (accessed November 2003).

28. Ibid., http://www3.who.int/whosis/country/indicators.cfm?country=usa&language=en (accessed November 2003).

29. Ibid., http://www3.who.int/whosis/country/indicators.cfm?country=cri&language=en (accessed November 2003).

30. World Health Organization, "Tobacco or Health: A Global Status Report," http://www.cdc.gov/tobacco/who/costa.htm and http://www.cdc.gov/tobacco/who/usa.htm (accessed November 2003).

31. Pan American Whole Health Alliance, http://www.pawha.org/costa_rica_statistics.htm (accessed November 2003).

32. World Health Organization, WHO Statistical Information System, http://www3.who.int/whosis/life_tables/life_tables.xls (accessed November 2003).

33. Denise Eldemire, "Health Care in Jamaica," http://www.islamset.com/healnews/aged/Discussion.html (accessed November 2003).

34. Centers for Disease Control, "Prevalence of Sedentary Leisure-time Behavior Among Adults in the United States," http://www.cdc.gov/nchs/products/pubs/pubd/hestats/3and4/sedentary.htm (accessed November 2003).

35. Institute of Medicine, "Promoting Health Intervention Strategies from Social and Behavioral Research," http://www.nap.edu/catalog/9939.html (accessed November 2003).

36. Willard G. Manning, Joseph P. Newhouse, Naihua Duan, Emmett B. Keeler, Bernadette Benjamin, Arleen A. Leibowitz, Susan Marquis, and Jack Zwanziger, *Health Insurance and the Demand for Medical Care: Evidence from a Randomized Experiment* (Santa Monica, Calif.: RAND Corporation, 1988), http://www.rand.org/publications/R/R3476/R3476.pdf (accessed November 2003).

37. John C. Caldwell, "Pushing Back the Frontiers of Death," Cunningham Lecture, Occasional Paper Series no. 3/1999, Academy of the Social Sciences (Canberra, Australia, 1999), http://www.assa.edu.au/Publications/op/op31999.pdf (accessed November 2003).

38. Michael Marmot, "Inequalities in Health," *New England Journal of Medicine* 345, no. 2 (July 12, 2001), http://www.mindfully.org/Health/Inequalities-In-Health-Marmot.htm (accessed November 2003).

39. G. Kaplan, E. Pamuk, J. W. Lynch, R. D. Cohen, and J. L. Balfour, "Inequality in Income and Mortality in the United States: Analysis of Mortality and Potential Pathways," *British Medical Journal* 312: 999–1003.

40. J. M. McGinnis and W. H. Foege, "Actual Causes of Death in the United States," *Journal of the American Medical Association* 270, no. 18 (1993): 2207–2212, cited in McGinnis et al., "The Case for More Active Policy Attention."

41. Centers for Medicare and Medicaid Services, Office of the Actuary, "National Health Expenditures, by Source of Funds and Type of Expenditure: Calendar Years 1994–1998" (December 5, 2001), www.hcfa.gov/stats/nhe-oact/tables/t3.htm (accessed November 2003); and R. Brown et al.,

"Effectiveness in Disease and Injury Prevention: Estimated National Spending on Prevention—United States, 1988," *Morbidity and Mortality Weekly Report* (July 24, 1992): 529–531, cited in Michael McGinnis et al., "The Case for More Active Policy Attention."

42. Gina Kolata, "Hope in the Lab," *The New York Times*, May 3, 1998, quoted in Brownlee, "Health, Hope and Hype."

43. Dora L. Costa, "Understanding Mid-Life and Older Age Mortality Declines: Evidence from Union Army Veterans," *Journal of Econometrics* 112, no. 1 (January 2003): 175–192, http://web.mit.edu/costa/www/jecon2.pdf (accessed November 2003).

44. Dora L. Costa, "Understanding the Twentieth Century Decline in Chronic Conditions Among Older Men," National Bureau of Economic Research (working paper no. w6859, December 1998), http://www.nber.org/papers/w6859 (accessed November 2003).

45. For a good summary of this literature, see "Editorial," *British Medical Journal* 315, no. 7112, http://bmj.bmjjournals.com/archive/7112/7112e1.htm#1-ref8 (accessed November 2003).

46. David J. P. Barker, *Mothers, Babies, and Disease in Later Life* (London: British Medical Journal Publishing Group, 1994).

47. Natalia S. Gavrilova, Leonid A. Gavrilov, Galina N. Evdokushkina, and Victoria G. Semyonova, "Early-life Predictors of Human Longevity," (paper presented at the annual meeting of the Social Science History Association, November 15–18, 2001), http://longevity-science.org/Gavrilova-SSHA-2001.pdf (accessed November 2003).

48. Federal Interagency Forum on Child and Family Statistics, "America's Children: Key Indicators of Well-Being 2002," 27, http://childstats.gov./ac2002/pdf/health.pdf (accessed November 2003).

49. Shin-Yi Chou, Michael Grossman, and Henry Saffer, "An Economic Analysis of Adult Obesity" (working paper no. w9247, National Bureau of Economic Research, October 2002).

50. Bureau of Transportation Statistics, "National Household Travel Survey" (NHTS version 1.0 CD, preliminary release), January 2003, cited in *Travel and Environmental Implications of School Siting*, U.S. Environmental Protection Agency, no. EPA231-R-03-004 (October 2003).

51. A. M. Dellinger and C. E. Staunton, "Barriers to Children Walking and Bicycling to School—United Sates, 1999," *Morbidity and Mortality Weekly* 51, no. 32 (2002): 701–704.

52. J. S. House, K. R. Landis, and D. Umberson, "Social Relationships and Health," *Science* 241: 540–545.

53. Remarks to local Government Association of Queensland, Townsville, Australia, September 11, 2001.

54. Stephanie A. Bond Huie, Robert A. Hummer, and Richard G. Rogers, "Individual and Contextual Risks of Death among Race and Ethnic Groups in the United States," *Journal of Health and Social Behavior* 43 (2002): 359–381.

55. Linda J. Waite and Maggie Gallagher, *The Case for Marriage* (New York: Doubleday, 2000).

56. Rose M. Kreider and Jason M. Fields, "Number, Timing, and Duration of Marriages and Divorces: Fall 1996," *Current Population Reports*, no. P70–80, U.S. Census Bureau (Washington, D.C., 2001).

57. John C. Gannon, "The Global Infectious Disease Threat and Its Implications for the United States," no. NIE99-17D, National Intelligence Council (January 2000), http://www.fas.org/irp/threat/nie99-17d.htm (accessed November 2003); and "Selected NIAID Research Priorites," National Institute of Allergy and Infectious Diseases, National Institutes of Health, http://www.niaid.nih.gov/publications/discovery/tselected.htm (accessed November 2003).

58. Quoted in Gannon, "The Global Infectious Disease Threat."

59. Brownlee, "Health, Hope and Hype."

60. Brendan I. Koerner, "Disorders Made to Order," *Mother Jones* (August 1, 2002).

61. Michael J. Weiss, "Chasing Youth," *American Demographics* (October 2002), 9.

62. Quoted in Rev. Charles E. Bouchard, "Healthcare Reform's Moral, Spiritual Issues," *Health Progress* (May-June 1996).

Chapter Nine

1. Peter Schwartz and Peter Leyden, "The Long Boon: A History of the Future, 1980–2020," *Wired* 5, no. 7 (July 1997).

2. National Commission on Technology, *Automation and Economic Progress* (Washington, D.C.: U.S. Government Printing Office, February, 1966).

3. Quoted in Rachel Emma Silverman, "The Future Is Now," *Wall Street Journal Online*, January 1, 2000, http://www.wsj.com/millennium/articles/SB944516725378711715.htm (accessed November 2003).

4. John Adolphus Etzler, *The Paradise Within the Reach of All Men, with Labor, by Powers of Nature and Machinery* (Pittsburgh: Etzler and Reimhold, 1833).

5. Robert J. Gordon, "Does the 'New Economy' Measure Up to the Great Inventions of the Past?" (working paper no. 7833, National Bureau of Economic Research, 2000).

6. Robert J. Gordon, "Technology and Economic Performance in the American Economy" (working paper no. 8771, National Bureau of Economic Research, 2002).

7. "The Futurists," 28.

8. David Schrank and Tim Lomax, "The 2003 Annual Urban Mobility Report," Texas Transportation Institute (September 2003).

9. Joe Robinson, "Ahh, Free at La—Oops! Time's Up," *Washington Post*, July 27, 2003.

10. Bureau of Labor Statistics, "Current Population Survey," table 19, ftp://ftp.bls.gov/pub/special.requests/lf/aat19.txt (accessed November 2003).

11. W. Michael Cox and Richard Alm, "Time Well Spent: The Declining Real Cost of Living in America," 1997 Annual Report, Federal Reserve Bank of Dallas, http://www.dallasfed.org/fed/annual/1999p/ar97.pdf (accessed November 2003).

12. U.S. Bureau of Labor Statistics, "Occupational Outlook Handbook, 2002-03 Edition," Office of Occupational Statistics and Employment Projections (Washington, D.C.), http://www.bls.gov/oco/home.htm (accessed November 2003).

13. Cox and Alm, "Time Well Spent."

14. Bureau of Labor Statistics, "Employment Situation," table A-10, http://www.bls.gov (accessed November 2003).

15. Ibid.

16. Fred Hirsch, *Social Limits to Growth* (London: Routledge, 1978).

17. Nichols Fox, *Against the Machine: The Hidden Luddite Tradition in Literature, Art, and Individual Lives* (Washington, D.C.: Island Press, 2002).

18. Global Entrepreneurship Monitor (2002), http://www.gemconsortium.org/about.asp (accessed November 2003).

19. Sylvester Schieber (presentation, Conference on the Economic and Budgetary Implications of Global Aging, co-sponsored by the Center for Strategic and International Studies and the European Commission, Brussels, Belgium, March 4–5, 2003), http://europa.eu.int/comm/economy_finance/events/2003/brussels0303/doc9en.pdf (accessed November 2003).

20. Paul S. Hewitt, "Global Aging: Opportunity or Threat for the U.S. Economy?" (testimony to the Senate Select Committee on Aging, February 27, 2003), http://www.csis.org/hill/ts030227hewitt.pdf (accessed November 2003).

21. Joseph Schumpeter, *Capitalism, Socialism, and Democracy* (New York: Harper & Row, 2000).

22. Yoshiaki Nakamura et al., "Effects of Information Technology and Aing Work Force on Labor Demand and Technological Progress in Japanese Industries, 1980–1998" (discussion paper no. CIRJE-F–145, Faculty of Economics, University of Tokyo, January 2002), http://www.e.u-tokyo.ac.jp/cirje/research/dp/2002/2002cf145.pdf (accessed November 2003).

23. Ibid.

Chapter Ten

1. Paul R. Ehrlich, *The Population Bomb,* rev. ed. (1968; reprinted in New York: Ballantine, 1971), xi.

2. United Nations Food and Agricultural Organization, "Compendium of Food and Agricultural Indicators, 2001," http://www.fao.org/es/ess/comp1_en.asp (accessed November 2003).

3. International Conference on Population and Development, "Review and Appraisal of the Progress Made in Achieving the Goals and Objectives of the Programme of Action of the International Conference on Population and Development, 1999 Report," http://www.un.org/esa/population/publications/reviewappraisal/reviewappraisal.htm (accessed November 2003).

4. Amartya Sen, *Poverty and Famines: An Essay on Entitlement and Deprivation* (Oxford: Clarendon Press, 1981).

5. World Bank Group, "Global Economic Prospects and the Developing Countries, 2003," appendix 2 (Washington, D.C.), http://www.worldbank.org/prospects/gep2003/appendix2.pdf (accessed November 2003).

6. American Iron and Steel Institute, Steelworks, http://www.steel.org/policy/energy/background.asp (accessed November 2003).

7. The average yield per acre in 2002 was 37.8; in 1970 it was 26.7. U.S. Department of Agriculture National Agricultural Statistics Service, "Track Records: United States Crop Production" (April 2003), http://www.usda.gov/nass/pubs/trackrec/track03c.htm#soybeans (accessed November 2003).

8. Kevin M. Murphy and Finis Welsh, "Wage Inequality in the 1990s," in *The Causes and Consequences of Increasing Inequality,* ed. F. Welch (Chicago: University of Chicago Press, 2001), 341–364.

9. Bureau of Labor Statistics, "2001 National Occupational Employment and Wage Estimates," http://www.bls.gov/oes/2001/oes252011.htm (accessed November 2003).

10. Elinor Burkett, *Baby Boon* (New York: The Free Press, 2000), cited in Nancy Folbre, "Family Unfriendly," *The American Prospect* 2 (August 28, 2000).

11. Nancy Folbre, *The Invisible Heart: Economics and Family Values* (New York: The New Press, 2001).

12. Stephanie Mencimer, "The Baby Boycott," *Washington Monthly* (June 2001).

13. Adam Smith, *An Inquiry into the Nature and Causes of the Wealth of Nations,* ed. C. J. Bullock (New York: Collier and Sons, 1903), 74–75, quoted in Allan C. Carlson, *From Cottage to Work Station: The Family's Search for Social Harmony in the Industrial Age* (San Francisco: Ignatius Press, 1993).

14. Shirley P. Burggraf, *The Feminine Economy and Economic Man* (Reading, Mass.: Addison-Wesley, 1997), 6.

15. James McNally and Douglas Wolf, "Family Structure and Institutionalization: Results from Merged Data," Papers in Microsimulation Series, no. 2, Maxwell Center for Demography and Economics of Aging, Syracuse University (January 1996), http://www-cpr.maxwell.syr.edu/microsim/pdf/micro2.pdf (accessed November 2003).

16. Dale Fuchs, "Spain Labors to Bring Home Baby—and the Bacon," *Christian Science Monitor*, June 26, 2003.

17. Richard Lowry, "Nasty, Brutish, and Short: Children in Day Care—and the Mothers Who Put Them There," *National Review* LIII, no. 10 (May 28, 2001).

18. Francis Fukuyama, "The Great Disruption," quoted in Lowry, "Nasty, Brutish, and Short."

19. Cited in Virginia I. Postrel, "The Character Issue," Reasononline, http://reason.com/9406/ed.vp.9406.shtml (accessed November 2003).

Chapter Eleven

1. Quoted in David G. Myers, *The American Paradox: Spiritual Hunger in an Age of Plenty* (New Haven, Conn.: Yale University Press, 2000), 292.

2. Mark Lender and James Martin, *Drinking in America* (New York: The Free Press, 1987), 205–206. Annual per capita consumption of alcohol (gallons/decade) was as follows: 6.6/1800; 7.1/1810; 6.8/1820; 7.1/1830; 3.1/1840; and 2.6/1985.

3. S. Mintz, "Limiting Births in the Early Republic: *Digital History*," http://www.digitalhistory.uh.edu/historyonline/limitingbirths.cfm (accessed November 2003).

4. John Stuart Mill, *The Subjection of Women*, chap. 2, Electronic Text Collection, The University of Adelaide Library (originally published in 1869), http://etext.library.adelaide.edu.au/m/m645s/ (accessed November 2003).

5. Employee Benefit Research Institute, "Health Insurance and the Elderly," Facts from EBRI (August 2003), http://www.ebri.org/facts/0803fact.pdf (accessed November 2003).

6. Agency for Healthcare Research and Quality, cited in Paul Fronstin and Dallas Salisbury, "Retiree Health Benefits: Savings Needed to Fund Health Care in Retirement," Employee Benefit Research Institute (February 2003), http://www.ebri.org/pdfs/0203ib.pdf (accessed November 2003).

7. U.S. Department of Labor, "2002 National Summit on Retirement Savings: Final Report," 4, http://www.dol.gov/ebsa/pdf/summitfinalreport.pdf (accessed November 2003).

8. Pension Benefit Guaranty Corporation, "2002 Annual Report," http://www.pbgc.gov/publications/annrpt/02annrpt.pdf (accessed November 2003).

9. Employee Benefit Research Institute, "Private Pension Plans, Participation, and Assets: Update," Facts from EBRI (January 2003), http://www.ebri.org/facts/0103fact.htm (accessed November 2003).

10. Greg Schneider, "Pension Needs Fueling GM's Sales Push; Rivals Feel Forced to Match Offers," *Washington Post*, June 25, 2003.

11. The Pension Benefit Guaranty Corporation, "2002 Annual Report," 41.

12. Ana M. Aizcorbe, Arthur B. Kennickell, and Kevin B. Moore, "Recent Changes in U.S. Family Finances: Evidence from the 1998 and 2001 Survey of Consumer Finances," *Federal Reserve Bulletin*, January 2003, tables 1 and 5.

13. Fronstin and Salisbury, "Retiree Health Benefits," figure 13. EBRI has an online calculator that allows you to calculate your own future health care costs under different assumptions. See http://www.choosetosave.org/tools/rethlth.htm (accessed November 2003).

14. "What Would Jesus Drive? A Discussion Initiated by the Evangelical Environmental Network & Creation Care Magazine," http://www.whatwouldjesusdrive.org/ (accessed November 2003).

15. F. W. Newman, "Remedies for the Great Social Evil," *Miscellanies* 3: 275, quoted in Walter E. Houghton, *The Victorian Frame of Mind* (New Haven, Conn.: Yale University Press, 1957), 367.

16. Rheta Chile Dorr, *What Eight Million Women Want* (Boston: Small, Maynard & Company, c1910).

17. Michael W. Perry, ed., *The Pivot of Civilization in Historical Perspective* (Seattle, Wash.: Inkling Books, 2001), 89, 91, 94.

18. "Mr. Roosevelt's Views on Race Suicide," *Ladies Home Journal* (February 1906), 21.

19. Michael P. Dowling, *Race Suicide, Birth Control* (New York: America Press, [1916]), quoted in "Exerpts from Michael P. Dowling's *Race Suicide, Birth Control*," Women and Social Movements, http://womhist.binghamton.edu/mwd/doc5.htm (accessed November 2003).

20. Margaret Sanger, *The Pivot of Civilization* (1922; reprinted in Elmsford, N.Y.: Maxwell Reprint Company, 1969), Project Gutenberg Etext, http://www.eugenicsarchive.org/html/eugenics/essay8text.html (accessed November 2003).

21. Margaret Sanger, *Woman and the New Race* (New York: Eugenics Publishing Company, 1923), 229.

22. Margaret Sanger, "The Function of Sterilization," *Birth Control Review* (Oct. 1926), 299, reproduced in Perry, *Pivot of Civilization In Historical Perspective*, 90.

23. Paul Lombardo, "Eugenic Sterilization Laws," Image Archive on the American Eugenics Movement, Cold Springs Harbor Laboratory, http://www.eugenicsarchive.org (accessed November 2003).

24. *Buck v. Bell*, 274 U.S. 200 (U.S. Supreme Court, 1927). For a history of the eugenics movement, see "Image Archive of the Eugenics Movement," http://www.eugenicsarchive.org (accessed November 2003).

25. *Skinner v. State of Oklahoma ex rel. Williamson*, 316 U.S. 535 (U.S. Supreme Court, 1942).

26. Steve Selden, "Eugenics Popularization," Image Archive on the American Eugenics Movement, Cold Springs Harbor Laboratory, http://www.eugenicsarchive.org (accessed November 2003).

27. Margaret Sanger, "Is Race Suicide Possible?" *Collier's* (August 15, 1925), 25.

28. Paterfamilias, "Race Suicide and Common Sense," *North American Review* 176 (June 1903): 892–900, reproduced in Perry, *Pivot of Civilization*, 61.

29. Perry, *Pivot of Civilization*, 62.

30. S. H. Halford, "Dysgenic Tendencies of Birth Control," *Population and Birth Control*, Eden Paul, ed. (New York: Critic and Guide, 1917), 232–233.

Chapter Twelve

1. Social Security Online, "2003 OASDI Trustees Report," appendix, table IV.F2, http://www.ssa.gov/OACT/TR/TR03/VI_OASDHI_payroll.html#wp106850 (accessed November 2003).

2. David Koitz, Geoffrey Kollmann, and Dawn Nuschler, "Social Security: What Happens to Future Benefit Levels Under Various Reform Options," no. RL31086, Congressional Research Service, Domestic Social Policy Division (August 20, 2001), 28, table 9.

3. Ibid.

4. Third Millennium, "Media Elite Join Third Millennium's Call for Social Security Reform," press release, March 13, 1995, http://www.thirdmil.org/media/releases/overh.html (accessed November 2003).

5. Don Q. Davidson, "Woodworking Hobby Becomes Family Business," 2 Young 2 Retire, http://www.2young2retire.com (accessed November 2003).

6. Ashley H. Carter, "Research Scientist Turned Educator," 2 Young 2 Retire, http://www.2young2retire.com (accessed November 2003).

7. Federal Interagency Forum on Aging-Related Statistics, "Older Americans 2000: Key Indicators of Well-Being," appendix A, http://www.agingstats.gov/chartbook2000/tables-economics.html#Indicator%209 (accessed November 2003).

8. V. A. Freedman, L. G. Martin, and R. F. Schoeni, "Recent Trends in Disability and Functioning Among Older Adults in the United States: A Systematic Review," *Journal of the American Medical Association* 288, no. 24 (December 25, 2002): 3137–3146.

9. William H. Lucy and Timothy Beatley, *Making Places: Combating Metropolitan Polarization*, forthcoming; see also University of Virginia, "Danger in Exurbia: University of Virginia Study Reveals Outer Suburbs More Dangerous Than Cities," press release, April 30, 2002, http://www.virginia.edu/topnews/releases2002/lucy-april-30-2002.html (accessed November 2003).

10. Alan Ehrenhalt, "The Deadly Dangers of Daily Life," *Governing* (August 2002).

11. Surface Transportation Policy Project, "Mean Streets 2002," http://www.transact.org/PDFs/ms2002/MeanStreets2002.pdf (accessed November 2003).

12. H. D. Sesso, R. S. Paffenbarger, T. Ha, and I. M. Lee, "Physical Activity and Cardiovascular Disease Risk in Middle-Aged and Older Women," *American Journal of Epidemiology* 150, no. 4 (1999): 408–416, quoted in Howard Frumkin, "Urban Sprawl and Public Health," *Public Health Reports* 117, http://www.publichealthgrandrounds.unc.edu/urban/frumkin.pdf (accessed November 2003).

13. M. Wei, J. B. Kampert, C. E. Barlow, M. Z. Nichaman, L. W. Gibbons, R. S. Paffenbarger, and S. N. Blair, "Relationship Between Low Cardiorespiratory Fitness and Mortality in Normal-Weight, Overweight, and Obese Men," *Journal of the American Medical Association* 282 (1999): 1547–1553, quoted in Frumkin, "Urban Sprawl and Public Health."

14. Ibid.

15. Office of the Surgeon General, "The Surgeon General's Call to Action to Prevent and Decrease Overweight and Obesity," http://www.surgeongeneral.gov/topics/obesity/default.htm (accessed November 2003).

16. Centers for Disease Control, "Lower Direct Medical Costs Associated with Physical Activity," press release, October 2000, http://www.cdc.gov/nccdphp/dnpa/press/archive/lower_cost.htm (accessed November 2003).

17. Frumkin, "Urban Sprawl and Public Health."

18. World Health Organization, Centre for Urban Health, "Social Determinants of Health: The Solid Facts" (Copenhagen, Denmark), 32, http://www.who.dk/document/E59555.pdf (accessed November 2003).

19. J. S. House, K. R. Landis, and D. Umberson, "Social Relationships and Health," *Science* 241 (1988): 540–545.

20. The Robert Wood Johnson Foundation, "National Blueprint: Increasing Physical Activity Among Adults Age 50 and Older" (May 2001), 14, http://www.rwjf.org/publications/publicationsPdfs/Age50_Blueprint_singlepages.pdf (accessed November 2003).

21. James F. Fries, "Exercise and the Health of the Elderly," *American Journal of Geriatric Cardiology* 6, no. 3 (1997): 24–32.

22. Robert Wood Johnson, "National Blueprint."

23. Federal Hospital Insurance and Federal Supplementary Medical Insurance Trust Funds, "2002 Annual Report of the Boards of Trustees of the Federal Hospital Insurance and Federal Supplementary Medical Insurance Trust Funds," http://cms.hhs.gov/publications/trusteesreport/2002/tr.pdf (accessed November 2003).

24. Benjamin M. Craig, David S. Kreling, and David A. Mott, "Do Seniors Get the Medicines Prescribed for Them? Evidence from the 1996–1999 Medicare Current Beneficiary Survey," *Health Affairs* 22, no. 3 (May-June 2003), http://content.healthaffairs.org/content/vol22/issue3/ (accessed November 2003).

25. Jerry H. Gurwitz, Terry S. Field, Leslie R. Harrold, Jeffrey Rothschild, Kristin Debellis, Andrew C. Seger, Cynthia Cadoret, Leslie S. Fish, Lawrence Garber, Michael Kelleher, and David W. Bates, "Incidence and Preventability of Adverse Drug Events among Older Persons in the Ambulatory Setting," *Journal of the American Medical Association* (March 5, 2003), 1107–1116.

26. Stephen E. Snyder and William N. Evans, "The Impact of Income on Mortality: Evidence from the Social Security Notch" (working paper no. w9197, National Bureau of Economic Research September 2002), http://www.bsos.umd.edu/econ/evans/wpapers/snyder_evans_notch.pdf (accessed November 2003).

27. Ibid.

28. National Institutes of Health, "Cancer Progress Report 2001," publication no. 02–5045, 34, http://progressreport.cancer.gov (accessed November 2003).

29. Mark Schlesinger, "A Loss of Faith: The Sources of Reduced Political Legitimacy for the American Medical Profession," *The Milbank Quarterly* 80, no. 2 (2002), http://www.milbank.org/quarterly/8002feat.html (accessed November 2003).

30. Center for Science in the Public Interest, "Poll: Science and Money Don't Mix: Americans Think Doctors Are Influenced by Drug Companies' Gifts," press release, July 11, 2003, http://cspinet.org/new/200307111.html (accessed November 2003).

31. Schlesinger, "Loss of Faith."

32. Sarah Hrdy, *Mother Nature: A History of Mothers, Infants, and Natural Selection* (New York: Pantheon Books, 1999).

Index